Professional Tiling

How to Install, Repair, or Replace Ceramic Tile

by Edwin M. Field and Selma G. Field

An Audel® Book

Macmillan Publishing Company
New York

Maxwell Macmillan Canada
Toronto

Maxwell Macmillan International
New York   Oxford   Singapore   Sydney

8|12

LAD 4|08

TC 22

693.3
FIE

Copyright © 1993 by Macmillan Publishing Company, a division of Macmillan, Inc.

While every precaution has been taken in the preparation of this book, the Publisher assumes no responsibility for errors or omissions. Neither is any liability assumed for damages resulting from the use of the information contained herein.

Macmillan Publishing Company
866 Third Avenue
New York, NY 10022

Maxwell Macmillan Canada, Inc.
1200 Eglinton Avenue East, Suite 200
Don Mills, Ontario M3C 3N1

Macmillan Publishing Company is part of the Maxwell Communication Group of Companies.

Production services by the Walsh Group, Yarmouth, ME.

Library of Congress Cataloging-in-Publication Data

Field, Edwin M.
    Professional tiling : how to install, repair, or replace ceramic tile /
by Edwin and Selma Field.
        p.   cm.
    "An Audel book."
    Includes index.
    ISBN 0-02-537741-8
    1. Tile laying—Amateurs' manuals. 2. Tiles—Amateurs' manuals.
I. Field, Selma G., 1925– . II. Title.
TH8531.F54   1993
698—dc20   92–5343
                                                   CIP

Macmillan books are also available at special discounts for bulk purchases for sales promotions, premiums, fund-raising, or educational use. For details, contact:

Special Sales Director
Macmillan Publishing Company
866 Third Avenue
New York, NY 10022

10 9 8 7 6 5 4 3 2 1
Printed in the United States of America

Contents

Preface

Professional Tiling was written for those involved in the installation of ceramic tile. The jobs to be undertaken can be small or extensive. If you already have experience working with tile, the pages in this book can serve as a refresher and also offer helpful installation suggestions.

If ceramic tile installation is a completely new experience, this book can "walk" you through all of the processes necessary to turn out a professional job. There can be a great deal of satisfaction in handling a tile installation on your own, and having a sound method of guidance as you proceed through each step makes the task easier. The pages and chapters in this book have been arranged to provide you with this information.

If you want to learn more about specific ceramic tile products, a listing of manufacturers is provided at the end of this book. In many instances, in addition to specification sheets and product photographs, manufacturers often provide installation information.

How to Use This Book

As you read through this book, you will notice that certain chapters appear to have pockets of information and instructions that are repetitive and bear a similarity to previous areas of discussion. There are reasons for this.

People use "how-to" books in different ways. Some read through an entire book before beginning a project, while others selectively pick only the chapter or area relating to the particular job and start their work from this vantage point. The reintroduction of important material in sections of this guide, therefore, is designed to satisfy each type of person. For most people, a combination of both the overview and step-by-step processes will be most effective.

Certain information bears repeating. There are installation techniques and work rules that are extremely important and will save you time, trouble, and expense. Selective repetition, therefore, helps in reminding you of the value of a particular set of instructions. This system also offers you easy accessibility and rapid information retrieval even while working on the job.

An all-inclusive index has been prepared to help you locate specific information. If you are reasonably comfortable with the tiling process and only require assistance with certain areas, this index will direct you to the appropriate section.

Do not be afraid to ask questions of the experts. If you run into installation stumbling blocks, ask the technicians at the store or supply house where you made your tiling purchases. They are generally well prepared by training and experience to offer practical advice, and in some instances, demonstrations of installation procedures.

A selection of photographs showing the potential of tile is offered throughout this book. These pictures visually indicate that variety of installation options and the versatility of the product. The majority of the photographs show home installations; however, a few light and heavy commercial tile application photos have also been included.

Steps in the Tiling Project—Planning and Preparation

Of course, tile can be installed by a professional. If, however, you would rather do the job yourself, the process is simple enough, with a bit of guidance, for a home handyperson. The work is often a joint venture with many people contributing.

A completed tile project, like any decorating effort, takes on the personality of the people who do it. There are definitive choices to be made concerning colors, sizes, shapes, and patterns. Tile structural strength, moisture resistance, surface quality, and overall design decisions also affect the result. The first chapter will give you a brief history of tile and its decorative and utilitarian potential. It will also introduce you to the tile products you might use on various projects, and it provides help in making preliminary decisions.

There is a sequence that must take place no matter what the tiling project or how the work assignments are divided. Once the decision to tile is made, many smaller specific decisions follow: Will a wall be tiled from floor to ceiling, or should there be wainscotting? What, for example, will be the height of the tiled wall? After tiling, where will the focal points in the room be? Will the tile installation fit into the household budget? Plus many other questions pertinent to each part of the tiling project.

The first step, then, is to pose the questions and begin considering the answers. As you think about your project, other questions will come to mind. A quick read through this book will serve to raise still other questions—and provide you with the answers. You should also visit as many dealers as you can to see what products are available in your particular area.

The next step is to measure accurately the area to be tiled. This information is vital for computing the proper quantities of tile to buy. Always remember to buy an additional supply of tile to cover the waste and breakage inherent in any installation, as well as to provide for future repairs. See Chapter 4 for more details about this subject.

Tile colors, types, and shapes will have to be selected to suit the decor and style of the installation. Grout colors will also have to be picked out. Review Chapter 2 before making these choices.

Tile application materials, mortar, adhesive, and grout must be selected and the proper types and quantities purchased. See Chapter 6 for detailed information about these products. Tools to handle the installation must be secured and brought to the job site. Many may come from the household tool chest, while others can be rented, borrowed, or purchased. See Chapter 3 for the tools you will need. Pay attention to the safety rules and cautions mentioned in Chapter 1.

The areas to be tiled must be cleared of excess material so that work can proceed in an orderly fashion. Furniture, baseboard, nails, picture frame hooks, and the like will have to be removed.

Subsurface walls, floors, and other areas to be tiled must be prepared to accept tile. See Chapter 5 for information about this important preparation procedure. The surfaces must be able to support the weight of the tile. They must be clean and clear of anything that could get in the way of the tile work. In order for the job to move along satisfactorily, the surfaces, if floors, should be level; if walls, should be perpendicular. Other projects—counters, patios, etc.—require similar preparatory attention. It is important that all of the preliminary work is completed before tiling is started.

If the tile area is to be installed on a wall, check with Chapter 9 for job specifics in this area. Chapter 8 provides insights into floor tile installation. If the tile work involves countertops, see Chapter 11. For patios or outdoor steps, review Chapter 10.

Steps in the Tiling Project—Doing the Work

Once the room surfaces are prepared and ready to accept the tile, the next step is marking the chalk lines which will serve as installation guides.

Test or dry tiles plus the necessary grout or joint spaces are trial set into the marked areas to check fit and position. Any tiles that must be cut to fit the spacing are trimmed to size using the proper cutting tools.

The tiles are now ready for bonding. The adhesive material is spread on the working surfaces, and tiles are set into place.

After a sufficient amount of drying time, the joint lines between the tiles are grouted. Once the grouting material is permitted to dry a bit, the joint lines are struck or worked so that the entire job takes on an even appearance.

The installation is concluded by washing down and polishing with dry toweling.

Most of the supplies used in your tile installation have specification sheets or carry manufacturers' instructions on the outside of containers, bags, or boxes. Read and follow all instructions carefully, and save them, well marked, for future reference.

Caring for Your Tile Installation

Since a great deal of work goes into any tile installation, it makes sense to learn how to care for the tile. Chapter 15 covers this subject.

If, during the lifespan of the tile installation, one or more of the tiles becomes damaged, you will need to know how to repair these tiles. Review Chapter 14 for this information.

12-Point Tiling Program

The program offered below is an instant guide which provides an overview of the steps in readying for and doing a tile installation.

- PLAN out the tile installation. Decide where, what, when, and how.
- PRICE the tile for budget purposes. Know your tile and supply costs.
- PURCHASE the necessary tile. Buy for the job, breakage, and future repairs.
- PREPARE the room or area to receive tile. Make sure of strong subsurface support.
- PENCIL or chalk in working lines. These lines will guide your work.
- PUT DOWN adhesive. This product holds the tile securely in place.
- POSITION the tile in the bonding material. A good fit makes a neat and professional job.
- PICK a section of the tile and start grouting. Do a workable portion at a time.
- PERFECT joint lines make a job look good. A toothbrush handle works well.
- PLUNGE sponge or cheesecloth pad in clean water and wash down. Clear grout residue off tiles.
- POLISH the tiles with toweling. Give the tiles a clean finish.
- PROCEED with the next section to be tiled—floor, wall, countertop, patio, etc.

Acknowledgments

The authors are indebted to the following people for their assistance with portions of this book.

Barbara Abbott, The Wenczel Tile Company, Marketing Department

Rita D. Backhurst, Metropolitan Ceramics, Sales Department

Robert Blanton, Photographic Assistance

William D. Cissna, Mannington Ceramic tile, Public Relations Rep.

Rich Citro, MAPEI, Technical Representative

Richard M. Dodd, Lufen International, Marketing Coordinator

Suzanne Stilson Edgar, EPRO, Inc., President

Richard V. Elliott, Port Authority of NY & NJ, Publications Coordinator

Deborah S. Forsythe, Stiles, Executive Vice President

Tina Freud, Firebird, Inc., Sales Department

William Guinan, Technical Assistance

Peter C. Johnson, Jr., Summitville Tiles, Inc., Director of Sales

Liz King, Summitville Tiles, Inc., Public Relations Representative

Robert J. Kleinhans, TCA, Inc., Executive Director

Rebecca B. Lee, Quarry Tile Company, National Marketing

John W. Mullowney, Superior Tile Cutter, Inc.

Cynthia A. Perry, American Olean, Administrative Assistant

Lynda Roberts, Huntington/Pacific Ceramics, Inc., Advertising Agency
Marjorie Rosenberg, Q.E.P. Co., Inc., Vice President
Dan Roulston, Ro-Tile, Inc., Advertising Manager
Joann M. Rustemeyer, Italian Tile Center, Public Relations
Linda Shea, Dal-Tile, Advertising/Public Relations, Vice President
Susan Van Voorhees, American Olean, Public Relations Manager
James J. Walsh, Walsh Associates, President
Kathy Whittier, Walsh Associates, Production Manager

CHAPTER I

Introduction to Tiling

History of Tile

The history of tile use goes back many thousands of years. There are examples, particularly of wall tiles, dating back to Crete in the 18th century B.C. The floors in ancient Roman homes or villas used tiles to provide a distinctive decorative decor. The ancient Egyptians, honoring the lives of their deceased, beautified the crypts within the pyramids with interior tile formations. Decorative tiles were also used in Babylonian and Persian homes and buildings. Today, in historic Moslem mosques, one may still view decorative tile work that has survived the centuries.

The Aztecs and Incas of early Mexico produced tile designs and styles unique to their culture. In certain early civilizations, mosaics using tiles as a base told the stories of the region's culture in pictures. The Moors in Spain and North Africa used wall and mosaic tiles six or seven hundred years ago. In 14th century Germany, a tile used principally with stoves was developed. Each tile had an architectural or other motif in ornamental relief embellished with a glaze of green, yellow, or brown. The 16th century Italians were well known for their majolica tiles. Some are still in place and may be seen in the doors of convents or on altarpieces in churches. One of the early Renaissance examples of decorative tile work may be seen in the painted floor tiles in the Hall of Justice in The Alhambra in Granada, Spain.

Each civilization and culture appears to have learned to make use of ceramic tile products. Generally, the tiles were and continue to be made using materials native to the specific region. Some cultures have used tiles in a strictly decorative or artistic sense while others have made more constructive use in walls, floors, and even roofs.

As we return to our time period, early tile use appears to have been concentrated in public buildings, particularly hospitals, schools, and factory settings requiring a sanitized interior appearance and utility. Gradually, as the manufacturers increased the tile varieties and colors, and as new installation techniques and materials became available, the use of tile, once considered an option of only the wealthy, gained popular acceptance.

Tile is also often found in most unusual places. The next time you ride through a tunnel, take a look at the interior. The ceiling and wall areas of tunnels are frequently covered with small squares of tile similar to those you will be using in your home installation. A case in point is the Lincoln Tunnel connecting New York and New Jersey. The Port Authority operating the tunnel notes there are 7,852,000 white tiles in the three tubes that make up this tunnel. The individual tubes run from 7,500 to 8,000 feet or about a mile and a quarter each.

The south tube of the tunnel has 1,530,000 wall tiles and 1,660,000 ceiling tiles. The north tube has 1,500,000 wall tiles and 800,000 ceiling tiles and the tunnel's center tube has 1,530,000 wall tiles and 1,660,000 ceiling tiles. Tiles used are $4\frac{1}{4}'' \times 4\frac{1}{4}''$ and $6'' \times 6''$ each. A word of caution: Be careful driving through the tunnel. The traffic may be heavy and it may be difficult to keep track of your tile count.

In different sections of our country, the amount of tile installation varies. In the northeastern United States, where most homes have basements, about 80% of floor tile installations are made over a plywood base. On the other hand, in California and Florida, sites of many basementless homes, the majority of floor tile installations are made on concrete slabs. Florida and California are also three or four times more active in tile installation work than the northeastern section of the United States. One probable reason is that Florida and California are warm weather states where cool tiles are welcome. In the northeast, when the winter is cold, floor tiles may not be as comfortable as a carpet-covered floor.

Why Tile?

Once you consider tile for your installation, you will recognize that this ceramic product has a great potential. It is decorative, durable, long-lasting, wears well, is easy to maintain and relatively inexpensive over the long haul. Although it may cost a bit more for installation than other materials, its longevity, minimal maintenance, repair and service costs more than make up for initial expenditures. A ceramic tile installation generally does not need to be waxed or sealed, nor does it need constant special treatments as do most wall, floor, or ceiling products. There are, however, tile sealants which we will talk about later in this book. Ceramic tile handles most corrosive substances, such as chemicals, well. It adapts to light or heavy foot traffic and is as much at home in a busy residence as it is in a factory or mall. It complements or fits in well with other products like wood, metal or stone so that it may be used with almost any decor.

You Can Tile It Yourself

Working with tile is not complicated or difficult: it only requires an expenditure of time and adherence to simple, easy-to-follow directions. The tile installation you complete can save you a modest amount of money in installation time. It will also provide you with the satisfaction of a job well done.

Modern adhesives and grouts simplify each of the tasks involved in a tile job. New products on the market include easy-to-use premixed organic mastics or adhesives, premixed grouts, plastic joint spacers that are disposable, and latex caulking compounds that are flexible and easy to use.

Special backing boards and other installation materials can increase the installation's normal lifespan as well as the appearance of the job. Tiny ceramic guideposts, for example, fired into and an integral part of many tiles, or special plastic separation markers for other tile models help assure picture-perfect installation with straight, even lines between tiles. We will discuss installation types and special job aids later in this book.

Tile manufacturers are aware of the demand for easy, troublefree tile installations. They also are sensitive to homeowner interest in a variety of tile shapes, sizes, and colors, and as a result, offer an excellent

Fig. 1–1. Italian tile used on a floor in a modern family room. *(Courtesy Italian Ceramic Tile)*

range of options to select from. Figs. 1–1 through 1–6 show some examples of tile use in homes.

Practical, Cost-Effective, Enjoyable

Tile installation in your home can be practical, cost-effective, and enjoyable. The few specialty tools required may be borrowed from the ceramic tile dealer or rented reasonably at local rental shops. New products on the market simplify the installation and help turn out a professional job. They also permit rapid installation and fast turnaround use of the rooms. The colors, shapes, and sizes available today offer a wide range of decorative choices.

If cost is an important factor, tiles can be purchased if they go on

Fig. 1–2. Wall tile used in a pattern and floor tile are combined in this bathroom. *(Courtesy American Olean Tile Co.)*

sale before they are required for your job and saved until you are ready to do the installation. Although manufacturers may introduce new models, colors, shapes, or designs, most tiles never really go out of style. Neither do they have a shelf life so that often earlier styles may be purchased at substantial savings. You should be aware, however, that colors or shades may vary in different lots, so that you can purchase enough tiles to complete the job you have in mind.

Your completed tile installation in one or more rooms of your resi-

Fig. 1–3. Countertop and backsplash using the same type and size tile. Tile on countertop edging tilts inward so that countertop water does not flow onto floor. *(Courtesy American Olean Tile Co.)*

dence can provide a great deal of satisfaction. Most do-it-yourself jobs in the home offer a sense of gratification, but tile installation seems to give special sense of pride.

On With the Job

It's now time to move forward with your own tiling job. Start by reading through the pages of this book. Familiarize yourself with the chapters and learn what each section contains. Scan the index at the back of this book so that if you run into any installation difficulty, you will immediately know where to turn.

Fig. 1–4. Tile can be utilized in almost any area of a home including a sunroom. *(Courtesy The Stiles Tile Co.)*

In preparing to do your tiling project, you may want to contact some of the suppliers listed in the Supplier Section at the conclusion of this book. The manufacturers will usually send you product specification sheets and information on how to best use their products as well as the names of nearby sources.

After you have completed all of your preliminary research and preparation, you may want to buy the tile products for the job and to

Fig. 1–5. Attic space can be made more attractive with a tile floor installation. *(Courtesy The Stiles Tile Co.)*

gather the necessary tools together so that they are accessible as needed. Set aside a time period to work on your tiling project so that you won't feel rushed. Make sure that everyone in your house knows that you are preparing to work on the job so that there is as little inconvenience as possible.

Now, some words of advice, caution, and encouragement. If, during the course of the installation you run up against a problem that appears difficult to resolve, seek counsel at the store or distributor where you purchased your tile supplies. In most instances, a technician at the store can give you a remedy to the problem. You may want to check with a professional installer. Most installers enjoy offering advice and will go out of their way to help, especially since you really are not competition.

The only way to complete a job is to start one. Countless individuals, just like you, have successfully installed tile in their homes. You can do it too!

Fig. 1–6. This kitchen effectively uses tile on floor, workspace and storage area. *(Courtesy Italian Ceramic Tile)*

Safety Precautions

Be cautious. Whenever you cut, chip, or drill tile, wear safety glasses and an air mask. When you work with a saw, drill, or pliers on a piece of tile, tiny chips can be thrown off. Safety glasses protect your eyes from these chips. A great deal of dust can be generated in the tile installation process, and a face mask can keep harmful particles away from your nasal passages and lungs. If possible, seal off the room where you are working from the rest of your residence. This sealing process can help keep non-work areas cleaner.

Glossary of Tile Terms

This book is about do-it-yourself tile installation techniques. In making purchasing and installation decisions you should become familiar with the vocabulary common to the tile trade. The tile glossary has been included in this beginning chapter to provide you with this information.

Many subjects will be covered more extensively in the pages of this book. If you are looking for detailed information about a specific subject, also check the index at the end of the book.

ABRASION RESISTANCE—The ability of a tile's glaze to tolerate the wear and tear of foot traffic.

BACKER BOARD—(also known as *concrete glass reinforced fiber board*)—Used in areas behind or under tile installations that have the potential for water or dampness damage. These sheets are water-resistant and serve as permanent protection. You may also consider using water-resistant gypsum board.

BACKSPLASH AREA—The tiled wall area behind a sink, stove, or countertop. A course or more of tile is installed above the counter tile to protect the wall area.

BEATER BLOCK—A carpet-covered piece of wood or other strong material used to seat tiles firmly in the adhesive. Used after the tiles have been put into place.

BICOTTURE TILES—Ceramic tiles which have been fired twice during the production process.

BISQUE OR BISCUIT TILE—An untreated body of clay from which a ceramic tile is formed.

BULLNOSE TILE—Tiles used specifically for trim. This particular tile has a rounded edge and is used to finish wall jobs and to turn outside corners of installations.

BUTTERING (also called *back buttering*)—A process whereby small quantities of adhesive are placed on individual tiles (like buttering a piece of bread) prior to the installation. Back buttering is used to insure that the thin-set adhesive is bonding to the tile. This is not a practical method to use on an entire installation, however, it may be necessary in certain sections of the job. Generally, the use of this procedure alone may produce an uneven, inconsistent job and slow down the entire process. See *floating method*.

CARBORUNDUM—An abrasive material that is sometimes added to tile glazes to reduce the danger of slipping.

CERAMIC TILE—A thin, sized piece of building material made of clay and fired at a specified temperature to a specified hardness. The face of the tile may be glazed or unglazed.

CHALK LINE—A cord line or twine, coated with chalk, that is used to define the line where tile work is to start. The ends of the twine are secured at both beginning and end points. The cord is then snapped against the floor or wall surface, leaving a straight chalk line, usually blue.

CLAY—A type of fine-grained earth composed mainly of aluminum silicate and mixed with appropriate products to form the basis for ceramic tile.

CLEAVAGE MEMBRANE—A sheet separating the backing surface from the metal which reinforces the tile mortar. It is used primarily when backing surfaces can be harmed by water or if instability exists. A thick bed mortar is used with these sheets or membranes.

CONDUCTIVE TILES (also known as *anti-static tiles*)—Tiles especially designed to absorb electrostatic charges by conducting them into the ground or other grounding source. These tiles are usually used in hospital operating rooms or in computer settings where there is danger of static electricity causing harm or disruption of equipment.

COUNTERTOP EDGING TILES—Trim used to edge countertop tile installations. Tiles are designed with a slight upward slope to reduce spills from the counter.

CRAZING—Fine hair lines that sometimes develop on the face of tiles during the glazing process. Tile body and glaze tensile stress can cause this crazing. The process is sometimes done purposely for decorative reasons.

CRYSTALLINE FINISH—A extra thick layer of glaze, usually on smaller-sized tiles, applied to achieve a decorative effect.

CURING—The period after a tile installation is completed when the tiles should be untouched and allowed to set.

CUTTING ENHANCERS, CARBIDE, DIAMOND, RUBY— Products which are impregnated in saw blades, sandpaper, scoring wheels, and other specialty devices used to cut and trim tile to proper size.

DOOR SADDLE—A marble saddle used in door areas which serves as a bridge between the tile installation in one room or one area and the floor covering (wood, carpet, etc.) in another. The saddle is cut to fit the designated space and set in place with the same adhesive as used for tiles.

DOUBLE TILE FIRING—The standard method for glazing tiles involves first the firing of the shaped raw clay into a hard, solid body or bisque. A glaze or design is then applied to the bisque and the tile is refired.

DUST-PRESSED TILES (also known as *dry-pressed tiles*)— Tiles formed by pressing and drying the raw materials into their required shape before firing or hardening. The alternative formulative procedure is to extrude the raw materials.

ENCAUSTIC TILE—Tile made of two or more clays smoothed and kiln fired.

EPOXY ADHESIVE—An adhesive utilizing epoxy resins and epoxy hardeners in proper proportion for thin-set tile installations. This type of adhesive is strong and easy to apply.

EXTRUDED TILES—Tiles made by forcing raw, unhardened malleable clay through a mold and then cut into shape.

FINISHES—Glazed tile finishes include bright gloss, high gloss, satin, or matte finish. Unglazed tiles may be finished with textured or embossed, ribbed, etched, or polished surfaces.

FLAT-BACK TILE—Tile with a smooth surface on the under or reverse side as opposed to tile designed with small, protruding ceramic buttons or lugs.

FLOOR TILES—Unglazed or glazed tiles produced specifically to stand the pressures, traffic, impact, and abrasion of floor use.

FLOATING METHOD—An acceptable adhesive method for installing ceramic tile. Adhesive is spread on the job floor using the proper trowel. The tile is then placed on the adhesive in its approximate position, next to the other tiles that have already been installed. A slight twisting movement of the newly installed tile sets it firmly into place.

FROST-PROOF TILE—Tile with a low water absorption level not affected by freezing or thawing conditions and used for outdoor installation.

FURAN MORTAR—A mortar mixture made of furan resin and furan hardeners in specific proportions. Used specifically for areas where chemical resistance is of paramount importance in the adhesion process.

GLAZED TILE—Tile treated with a transparent coating fused to the tile body during high-temperature firing in a ceramic kiln. The result is a smooth, impervious surface with decorative potential. The glaze is sometimes known as topping.

GLOVES—Worn when working with tile installation adhesives and grouts as protection from chemicals. Use rubber gloves or gloves which can protect from chemicals.

GROUT—A range of materials such as mastic, mortar, silicone rubber, etc., used as a binder and sealer in the joints between rows of tile. Comes in a range of varieties and colors.

IN CORNER—A type of trim tile used to make a right angle turn where the wall area next to piece is tiled and faces a tile surface that is horizontal.

INSET TILE—Individual tiles or tile pieces used with larger monocolored tiles to form patterns or decorative designs.

KILN—A high-temperature oven generally fired by electric or gas. It is used to bake the formed clay into a hardened tile and/or a glazed, hardened tile product.

LATEX-CEMENT SYSTEMS—Tile grout and mortar systems which use as a base cement mixtures to which latex has been added. This improves the flexibility of the mortar or grout mixture.

LEVEL (also known as a *spirit level*)—A tool, generally used by carpenters, to assure that floor or wall surfaces are level. A small oil bubble inside a glass tube on the tool accurately reacts to the downward or sideward off-level balance of a wall or floor. When the bubble moves into the exact center of the tube, the floor or wall may be considered level.

LUGS (also known as *button-back tiles*)—Tiny ceramic protuberances on the underside of some tile products fired into the tile body. These "buttons" improve tile adhesion and help make an installation more secure.

MASTIC—A pasty, mortar-like material composed of organic adhesives. This mixture cures quickly as a result of the evaporation of the solvents in the mixture. Used mostly with non-load bearing tile installations.

MATTE FINISH—A dull finish used on some tiles as opposed to a glazed, shiny finish found on others.

MECHANICAL STRENGTH—A measurement of the strength of floor tiles or other types of tiles to determine their ability to support loads/weight.

MOSAIC—Small pieces of tile, inlaid or placed together, to make an eye-pleasing pattern. The mosaic tiles may be either glazed or unglazed and run from tiny pieces to about four inches in size. Mosaic tiles have generally been fired at high temperatures and are considered vitrified tile.

MORTAR—One of a range of tile-setting materials used to permanently bond tiles to a backing surface.

NON-CERAMIC TILES—Tiles including precast terrazzo, marble, and slate. Though non-ceramic, these tiles may use the same setting and installation techniques as ceramic tile. Other non-ceramic products that have a similar tile-like appearance include mirror tile, polyester tile (also known as epoxy tile), metal tiles, and plastic tile.

NON-POROUS TILE—A tile body prepared and fired to become moisture resistant and to limit the passage or collection of fluid into or through it. Non-porous tiles are generally used for outdoor installations. Porous tiles, on the other hand, are not extremely moisture resistant.

NONVITREOUS—A clay which has been fired at a low to moderate temperature in a ceramic kiln. This type of firing does not produce a tile as strong as vitreous-fired tiles. Nonvitreous tiles may be glazed or unglazed and are most often used for wall tile installations.

OPEN TIME—The time period in which an applied adhesive can stay on the floor or wall before it dries out and is no longer useful for bonding purposes.

ORANGE PEEL SURFACE—A slip-resistant textured surface with the pitted appearance of an orange skin. The surface texture contributes to its protective capabilities.

ORGANIC ADHESIVE—Used only on interior installations, this adhesive is prepared from organic materials. It's ready for use as is and requires no additional liquid or powder mixtures to make it functional. It cures by evaporation.

OUT CORNER—A ceramic tile trim used in an installation to turn a right angle corner where the adjacent wall is also tiled but faces away from the horizontal tile surface.

PICKET TILE—Tiles shaped like the pickets on a picket fence. This type of tile can be used singly to create patterns or used in combination as a border for installed square tiles.

POLISHED TILE FINISH—A lustrous, smooth finish terracotta or porcelain tile surface. The finish is produced by running rotating discs across the surface of the tiles.

PORCELAIN TILE (also known as *china tile* or *fully vitrified tile*)—This type of tile is made of selected raw materials which when fired result in a non-porous bisque with great mechanical strength.

POROUS TILES—Tiles that are not extremely water-resistant. These tiles should not be used in any installation where danger of water contact exists.

POT LIFE—The time period that a mixed tiling adhesive will stay pliable enough to spread on the floor or wall surface and create a satisfactory bond.

PRIMER (also known as *bonderizer*)—A liquid pre-installation treatment of the surfaces onto which tile is to be installed. It prepares the surface to accept the ceramic tile adhesive and prevents the subsurface from withdrawing moisture from the tile adhesive.

RIBBED SURFACE TILE—Tile which has a ribbed finish on the top surface to make it slip-resistant.

RUBBER FLOAT—A squeegee type of tool with a wide working bottom made of rubber designed to apply grout.

RUBBER MALLET—Hammer-like instrument used to strike a beater block when seating tiles.

RUNNING BOND—A tile patterning system in which each course of tiles is staggered one-half the tile width of the previous course of tiles. The system is repeated during the course of the installation to create the patterned effect.

SAFETY GLASSES—Eye protector devices which should always be worn when cutting, chipping, or sawing tiles.

SATIN FINISH—A soft, smooth-looking glossy tile finish.

SCORING A TILE—The scribing of a line onto the surface of a tile with the proper instrument to create a deep scratch or groove. The tile is then snapped at the grooved line using a tile cutting tool, or cut with a tile saw or tile pliers.

SEALERS—Clear coatings applied to the surface of unglazed tile to protect it from dirt, grease, and stains.

SEMI-VITREOUS—Clay which has been fired in a kiln at a higher temperature than temperatures used for nonvitreous tile and a lower temperature than for vitreous tiles. Semi-vitreous tiles are moderately strong and moderately resistant to abrasion. Tiles may be glazed or unglazed.

SETTING BED—The layer of mortar or specialty adhesive used to attach ceramic tile to the subfloor or subsurface of the installation. The setting bed may be thin-set, mud, or mortar.

SETTING COURSE—The first course or line of tile set in a tile installation. This is the base course upon which other courses depend for their even or level spacing.

SKIRTING TILES—Special tiles used along baseboard areas to finish off an installation.

SPACERS—Wood or plastic spacing devices used when individual ceramic tiles do not have spacers or spacing lugs as an integral part. These lugs help maintain an even joint width between the tile rows. After the tiles are set or cured, the spacers may be removed, or if designed for this purpose, they may be grouted over.

STEP TREAD TILES—Special tiles with abrasive or ridged surfaces made to prevent slipping. These tiles can overhang the step edges.

TERRACOTTA—A clay used by tile manufacturers to make unglazed, red-orange body tiles. Surfaces are usually smooth. Tiles of this type are often produced by Italian and Mexican tile makers.

THICK BED (*mud set*)—A cement-based mortar used as a backing surface on which tiles are laid out and set. A mixture of sand and Portland cement is used for floor installations while a Portland cement, sand, and lime mix is used for wall jobs. The mortar or mud is at least ¾ inch thick and may go up to 1 inch for walls and to 1-¼ inches for floor installations.

THIN-SET—A technique using a thin layer of an epoxy or other special adhesive material to set and secure tiles. This thin-set process needs a sound, level backing surface since the thickness of the adhesive surface is ⅛ inch or less as opposed to the heavier thick bed techniques. From a practical standpoint, the thin-set process permits installation on surfaces that cannot carry heavy loads.

TILE CUTTING TOOL (also known as a *snap cutter*)—A tool that allows the installer to score a marked tile accurately with a carbide, diamond, or ruby wheel and break the scored piece off efficiently and accurately. A gauge assists in measurements. A metal breaking bar, part of the instrument, exerts even pressure across the break while a rubberized mat beneath the scored tile takes up the shock of the pressure. The combination of the pressure bar and rubber mat concentrates the pressure in the correct way for successful results and prevents tile breakage in all directions.

TILE NIPPERS—A plier-like tool used to trim or nip around the edges of ceramic tile. These pliers allow close trimming or nibbling away of portions of pieces of tile to fit specific installation requirements. Tiny bites are taken out of the piece in order not to break off a whole section of the tile. A stone is used to file bites down smooth.

TILE SAW (also known as a *tub saw* or *wet saw*)—A saw designed with a special diamond-impregnated cutting blade and a source of constantly running water. The diamond blade cuts through the tile along marked lines and the water keeps the ceramic cool and lowers dust levels.

TRIM TILES—Special application tiles used to finish off installations. Trim tiles, in a great variety of sizes and shapes, cap off a job, assist in making angle turns, edgings, etc.

UNGLAZED TILES—Highly durable tile bodies which are left plain or untreated after the initial firing process. Tile may be fully vitrified or semi-vitrified, and have natural clay colors added to the clay with chemical colors or oxides.

VITREOUS—Clay which has been fired to a high temperature in a kiln. High-temperature firing turns it into a hard, durable glass-like product which is highly resistant to abrasion. Vitreous tiles may be glazed or unglazed and are most often used for floor installations.

WALL TILES—Glazed tiles used for wall installation. Decorative or plain colored, these tiles do not require any special mechanical strength or impact or abrasive resistance.

WAINSCOT—When applied to a tile installation, refers to a tiled surface reaching to chair-back height.

WHITE BODY EARTHENWARE TILE—Tile which uses as raw material clays that produce a white body. This tile can be coated with a transparent or colored glaze, and is generally used for wall tile installations.

CHAPTER 2

The World of Tile

How Tiles are Made

In the simplest production format, most ceramic tiles in the United States are manufactured by pressing or extruding special clay mixtures into specific shapes and forms (Fig. 2–1). The green, unfired bisque forms are then baked or heated to very high temperatures in a kiln or oven where the tiles become hardened or cured (Fig. 2–2). A variety of hardened and usable tile products is made from the pieces being fired.

For many tile manufacturers, most production processes are controlled by automation. Clays are pressed in hydraulic molds and moved to kilns controlled by computers. This allows mass production in an era when large quantities of reasonably priced products, in the center of the consumer demand spectrum, are an economic necessity. In addition to cost-effectiveness, automated control systems generally produce tiles with minimal variations in size, color, and surface batch.

On the other hand, the movement toward mass-produced products has opened up the market for specialty tile producers. These are small manufacturers or craftspeople who have the ability to produce shorter runs of selected tiles with unusual colors, designs or shapes. The prices may be higher, but increased consumer demand for a wider range of choices make the operations feasible. On a personal level, this gives you additional options when seeking tile for a unique or specially-designed installation. Many of these tiles are produced by rolling out the clay and stamping out the suitable shapes. This process is similar to the method used by a baker to stamp out cookies with a cookie cutter.

Fig. 2–1. The various ingredients that go into the makeup of tile are weighed and mixed prior to shaping and firing in a kiln. *(Courtesy Quarry Tile)*

You should be aware that there are a number of competitive non-ceramic products similar in use and appeal to tile. Marble, slate, and pre-cast terrazzo products, for example, use some of the same installation techniques and setting products as ceramic tile. These products are quite attractive and may also be used in such installation settings such as floors and wall surfaces. They are made in a range of small sizes, one-foot squares, and even much larger pieces. The size options can often provide time and cost savings.

To respond to the competition of these non-ceramic products, the ceramic tile industry has developed systems to put together multiple tiles in sheets. These sheets are each several feet square and can speed up installation and cut costs.

To further their competitive edge, tile manufacturers have also developed special exterior panels. These are insulated, pre-grouted, vitreous or nonvitreous sheets of weatherproof tile. The design allows the

Fig. 2–2. Stacks of molds being prepared for kiln firing. The molds shape the tile while the firing process hardens the clay mixture so that it becomes hard and durable. *(Courtesy Quarry Tile)*

sheets of tile to be placed on surfaces without danger of cracking, even though there are small irregularities or non-level sections in the construction area. Units can be installed rapidly cutting construction costs.

Selecting Tile

Ceramic tile is extremely versatile. It can be used to decorate the living areas of your new home or as a prime material for remodeling an older residence. Once you have made the decision to use tile in your home and to handle the installation yourself, the next step is the selection of the correct tile for the job. You will have to consider where the tiles are to be used and then make appropriate choices as to tile quality, sizes, quantity, shapes, and colors. You will also want to know about the durability of the tile you have selected and its particular strengths and weaknesses relative to your needs.

Tile Quality

One way in which ceramic tiles are rated is the ease with which the tile body absorbs water. The most vitreous tile on the market is porcelain. This glass-like product has a water-resistant body. The common wall tile is the least vitreous. It absorbs water unless its top surface is made water-resistant by glazing.

Among other factors to consider when making tile decisions are thickness and glazing. When you purchase wall tiles, for example, you should be aware that tiles to be used in wall areas do not have to be as thick as floor tiles. On the other hand, a thin, less expensive tile installed on a floor which receives heavy traffic flow may not hold up well and may require early replacement. Thick tiles are designed and manufactured to bear the brunt of weight and activity. Using a thin tile on a countertop may also be unwise. It, too, can be easily damaged by heavy kitchen preparation activities.

The choice of glazed or unglazed tiles, too, rests with their potential use. Unglazed tiles may be damaged by moisture so that obviously they are not particularly suitable for bathroom or kitchen installations. Tiles with glazed surfaces can be slippery. It is not sensible, therefore, to use this type of tile in floor areas such as showers, pools, or any place where one may slip. Treated tiles with non-slip surfaces would be the proper choice for this application.

Mosaic Tile

Mosaic tile is another choice you may want to consider for floor, wall, or countertop installations or for special jobs where, for example, you may have to tile around a circular or irregular support area. Standard mosaic is composed of tile two inches or smaller in size (Fig. 2–3). Its patterns include squares, hexagons, pebbles, octagons, combination squares, and rectangles. Mosaic tile is generally a vitreous tile but may be fired until it has a porcelain body. This type of tile has excellent freeze-thaw stability and may be used in both wet and dry locations. The small mosaics are mounted on a backing sheet. In some instances, the individual tile mosaic pieces are attached by means of a silicone rubber adhesive product. These mosaics sheets are installed with the tile facing up. The netting or backing sheets are cemented to the floor, and when dry, the mosaics are grouted. A great many of the mosaics on the market come already grouted.

Fig. 2–3. Mosaic tile in 1 inch by 1 inch squares. *(Courtesy American Olean Tile Co.)*

Other mosaic sheets depend on a different attachment technique. They use a face-mounted system where paper covers the tile mosaics. When installing the sheets, adhesive is applied to the backside of the mosaic tiles which are then pressed into place. After the adhesive is dry, the face paper is moistened with water and is peeled off the mosaics. After a drying period, the tiles are grouted.

Some sheets even come pre-grouted. Their mounting technique

Installation Tip: Purchasing sheet-mounted tile, whether mosaic or full-size tile (3″ × 3″, 4″ × 4″, etc.), is usually more expensive than buying individual tiles. Consideration must also be given to the bonding quality of the sheet material used as tile backing. On the other hand, sheets of tile are easier and faster to install. The joint lines are already established and either even or can rapidly be straightened out.

allows for complete flexibility. They may be installed flat on a floor, wrapped around a supporting pipe or mounted in almost any position.

Stories That Tile Backs Can Tell

A tile's back can serve the same purpose as an I.D. tag. It has a story to tell. The tile backs are often covered with manufacturer's identifying names, numbers, production and color codes. The information is fired into the ceramic body. When additional tiles are needed for a future repair or renovation, the ordering information is set in stone.

You can also learn a great deal of additional information about tiles from the way they are formed and fired. Some tiles have ridges along the back: others have small button-like protruberances, while still others are plain and flat. Many tiles also have spacer lugs or small abutments fired onto their sides. These lugs automatically determine the proper spacing between each tile in an installation. If the tiles used do not have these pre-fired, pre-attached lugs, molded plastic spacers will have to be used to get the proper spacing between tiles. Styles vary, but many of these plastic spacers can be covered with grout and left in place. In most instances, they are taken out and reused once the adhesive has set.

Tiles with back ridges are an indication that the tiles were probably manufactured by the extrusion process. A clay mixture was put into one end of a mold and the formed clay, in the shape of flat tile, was extruded out of the other mold end. Extruded tiles are usually vitreous. The back ridges serve a purpose: they can hold comparatively large quantities of adhesive and, as a result, bond to surfaces effectively. Such ridged-back vitreous tiles are especially useful for floor installations and are also excellent for countertops where a great deal of heavy use is expected.

Tiles with small buttons on the reverse side indicate that they have probably been pressed in a mold. When they are stacked for firing in the kiln, the buttons serve as separation legs between tiles. Button-back tiles are usually non- or semi-vitreous. Although the buttons serve a useful purpose in the kiln, the same buttons are not as useful in the adhesion process because they do not bond as well as flat-backed or ridged-back tile. As a result of their back design, air can be trapped in the space between button and tile back and potentially allow tile movement. The non- and semi-vitreous tile are most useful on walls and other vertical surfaces and countertops that are not subject to heavy use.

Tiles with flat backs dominate the tile market. Manufactured using

the same pressing process as button back tiles, flat back tiles are usually kiln-fired to the high temperatures required for a vitreous or
semi-vitreous finish. These tiles can be used for almost any type of
ceramic job.

About International Tiles

In European countries, although there are automatic tile producers, some manufacturers do not use automated equipment. These companies are recognized especially for their production of tiles with individualized textures, patterns, and attractive color variations. From a
business standpoint, the European tile production process appears to
be more individualized than its American counterpart. Although the
European system offers a wide range of tile possibilities, it does not
always make for product uniformity. Nevertheless, many tile manufacturers in this country recognize the marketability of these pattern design choices and import the tiles in large numbers. Often, they relabel
the imported tiles, placing their own logos and/or company names on
the imported products.

Italian tile manufacturers, in the main represented by the Italian
Tile Center with headquarters in New York City, are the world's largest
producers and exporters of ceramic tiles. Italy has over four hundred
individual tile factories and produces about 35% of the world's tile supply. The United States, for example, imported approximately 245.5 mil-
lion square feet of Italian tile in 1988.

Because Italian tile is so popular in this country and you may be
purchasing these tiles for your installation, it is important to learn to
recognize Italian tile types and to understand their applications. There
are eight commonly produced Italian tiles. These include four glazed
and four unglazed varieties. According to the *Designer's Guide To Italian Ceramic Tiles,* published by and courtesy of the Italian Trade Center, the unglazed tile varieties include:

Clinker Tile: Used for **exterior floor and wall applications as
well as interior floors.** This tile is similar to the Italian Red Stoneware mentioned below. The tiles are formed using either an extrusion
process or by dust pressing. These tiles are colored with oxides and may
be found glazed or coated with a thin layer of transparent glass.

Porcelain Tile: Known also as china tile or fully vitrified stoneware, this tile contains raw materials similar to those used for manufac-

turing china. The result is a non-porous bisque of high mechanical strength that can be used for **interior or exterior floors.** The tiles are nearly always unglazed; however, different colors are produced by dispersing mineral oxides through the bisque. Special effects are also created by polishing the surface or applying a thin layer of glass to bring out deep color.

Red Stoneware: This tile is typically Italian—red, vitrified tiles that are generally unglazed. Because of its physical properties—resistance to frost, chemicals, abrasion and excellent mechanical strength—Red Stoneware is suitable for use in **heavy traffic areas on interior and exterior floors in both residential and industrial settings.**

Terracotta Tile: This brick-colored material has been used **indoors and out** since ancient times. Most often it is shaped into large tiles of greater than average thickness. Terracotta is never glazed, although once installed, it may be oiled or waxed to bring out its traditional warm luster. Terracotta is also manufactured with several finishes from rustic to smooth to highly polished.

The following four tiles, according to the *Designer's Guide To Italian Ceramic Tiles,* are always glazed:

Cottoforte Tile: This is a typical Italian composition which produces a pink-red bisque of average to good mechanical strength. It is suitable for **most interior applications.** As it takes well to glazing and decorating, cottoforte tile is the bisque used for most decorated, double-fired tiles.

Majolica Tile: This is another typically Italian bisque that is yellow-pink in color. It takes a non-transparent glaze and is commonly used for **interior wall tiles.**

White Body Earthenware Tiles: This composition, common throughout the world, produces a white tile body which takes colors easily and can be coated with a transparent glaze. Mostly used for wall tiles, white body bisques are sometimes used for **interior floor tiles for light traffic areas.**

Monocottura Tile: Many types of Italian tiles can be glazed and processed by the single-firing method (monocottura method) which gives the tiles different and more pronounced characteristics. This production process allows the simultaneous firing of the clay body with the glaze.

Tiles produced by this method demonstrate higher mechanical resistance and better glaze-body adhesion than glazed tiles produced by the double-fired method. Monocottura tiles are commonly found with a red or white body, a matte finish, a flat back, and slightly less than average thickness.

Glazed tile is usually fired twice, once to bisque and once to attain the glazing quality. Other countries, like Mexico, provide tile for sale in the United States through tile distributors. In most instances, the tiles offered are typical of the varieties in common use in the country of origin. They are in demand by homeowners and decorators particularly for this reason.

Types of Tiles

Tiles are composed of a mixture of refined clay, ground shale or gypsum, talc, vermiculite, sand, and water. You can purchase ceramic tiles glazed with a shiny, mirror-like surface or non-glazed with a flat matte surface. In order to produce a glazed surface, the cured, or once-fired tile "biscuit" or bisque has a glazed color applied to its surface. The tile is then baked a second time in the kiln at high temperatures. The applied glaze, in the color selected, melts from the intense heat of the kiln and covers the surface of the tile with a glass-like finish. Glaze hardness is determined by the amount of time the glaze-covered bisque remains in the kiln and the temperature to which it is fired.

Glazed tiles are available in high gloss, semi-matte, matte, and textured finishes. Tiles with a soft glaze are most suitable for wall tile installations while tiles with any of the above glazes can be used for floor, wall, and countertop installations.

Unglazed tiles, on the other hand, may have colors mixed into the clay prior to the initial baking in the kiln.

In addition to a rainbow range of tile color possibilities, you may also select tiles with patterns (Fig. 2–4). These may be designed, sculptured, smooth, or printed beneath a protective glaze surface during manufacture. Some tiles even have ceramic designs and decals fired beneath the glaze (Fig. 2–5). Animals, flowers, birds, whales, fruit, and a wide range of general or pre-selected scenes in color are favorite subjects. They may be used to decorate an entire room or partial sections, or selected areas such as a fireplace mantel. You often see decorated tile in swimming pool areas as pool depth numbers set into the tiled pool sides at various points.

Fig. 2–4. Tile is available in geometric designs, rustic surfaces and even with fossil-like pattern surfaces. *(Courtesy Italian Ceramic Tile)*

Designed and Handcrafted Tiles

There are *handcrafted and handpainted designed tiles* available on the market. One company, Firebird, Inc., specializes in one-of-a-kind murals and design patterns (See Supplier section). This tile manufacturer handcrafts the bisque and then handpaints each tile individually. This handpainting offers the consumer the opportunity to make selections of unusual patterns, designs, and murals. Although the process of actually installing tile is covered later in this book, the special circumstances that must be considered when installing handcrafted tiles should be mentioned here. Handcrafted tiles, as opposed to extruded or other mass-produced tile, are irregular. Each tile may be just a bit different in size than the next. When these design tiles are installed in

Fig. 2–5. Bold new designs in ceramic tile can create a variety of special effects. Stained glass, mosaics and fabrics are some of the looks that can be achieved. *(Courtesy Italian Ceramic Tile)*

mural form, special attention must be paid to positioning and the width of the grout lines because of the tile irregularities.

Tile Types

One of the simplest forms of tiles is the *Spanish patio tile*. It is made of terracotta and is generally created as a thick, large tile. Many of these tiles are manufactured in Mexico where floral patterns are often placed under or in a glaze. *Encaustic tiles* are also made of terracotta clays but differ in that they are made of two or more terracotta clay colors. One color clay forms the bisque while the other color terracotta clay is pressed into depressions on the tile surface to form a design. This pressed clay is then smoothed over and fired to bisque.

If you are selecting tile for your floor, you may want to choose *quarry tile*. Quarry tile is generally unglazed and available in a range of earth tone or brownish colors. It may, however, also be purchased glazed to give a fuller range of colors. Quarry tile is produced by the extrusion method to allow both indoor and outdoor use. It is made in a range of shapes and sizes. Generally, quarry tile is ⅜ inch to ½ inch in thickness and may be made in 4-, 6-, 10- and 12-inch squares, as well as several other sizes. You can also find it in rectangular, hexagonal, octagonal, and a variety of other shapes. This tile is dense, strong, and capable of bearing heavy loads of traffic.

Quarry tile can play a useful role in your add-on greenhouse or home sunroom. These heavy, hardened tiles, similar to the ones you will use for your floors and hallways, can act as solar collectors, absorbing warmth from the sun's rays and slowly releasing the collected heat as the air cools down in the evening or on overcast days. Because darker colors generally absorb heat better, earthtone colors are suggested for greenhouse and sunroom floor areas. Research has also shown that unglazed tile appears to absorb heat better than glazed tile.

The use of tile as a supplemental heat source requires some special consideration. For example, the greenhouse must be facing the proper direction to capture the sun's rays for tiles to be most effective. There must be a certain minimum floor mass beneath the tiles to serve as a heat collection and retention area. Check with your solar energy contractor for specifications.

If you are choosing wall tile for your room, you should be looking at *glazed tiles*. These tiles can be bought in 2″ × 4″, 4-, 6-, 8-inch squares and certain other sizes on special order. A little thinner than quarry tile, glazed tile usually runs from ¼ inch to about ⅜ inch in thickness. Glazed tiles, available in a full range of bright and deep colors, can be used for kitchen and bathroom walls, for kitchen counters and vanities, and for floors if they are of the proper type and thickness. Glazed tile may have a high gloss, or a textured or matte finish. You can also choose a crazed-type finish which gives the tile a slightly cracked-looking surface appearance. These tiles are made by using a heavy topping of glaze which shrinks when fired at selected temperatures. The result is an unusual crystalline finish. A clear overglaze is usually applied to these tiles and fired to assure a smooth product finish. Some of the tiles with crystalline finish are subject to etching through exposure to fruit acids like lemon, grapefruit, grape, and the acid in vinegar. Crystalline finish tiles should not be used for food preparation countertop areas unless the manufacturer warranties that they can handle this type of exposure.

Be sure to check the glazed tiles for special surfaces if you have a specific use for the tiles. For example, if you are going to use glazed tiles for floor areas, be sure that you get tiles with slip-resistant surfaces. If you are going to use the glazed tile for workareas like countertops, choose tiles with a heavy-duty glaze.

If you are looking for a tile to serve really heavy duty purposes in an area not subject to frosts and freezing, consider *paver tile*. This tile is similar to the quarry tile described previously—it is thick, extremely strong, and can stand a great deal of abuse and wear. You may have seen paver tile installed on shopping center floors since its surface usually has a slip-resistant finish. In residences, paver tile works well on floors and even walls if your color scheme runs toward earth tones. The tile comes in 4″ × 8″ and 8-inch squares and may be ordered in other sizes. If frosts and freezing weather conditions are not a problem in your area, this tile may also be used outdoors. Paver tiles are manufactured using the pressed tile process as opposed to the extruded techniques used with quarry tile.

Tile Trims

No matter what size tile you select, trim tiles will probably be required. Trim tiles finish off areas around floors, doors and walls, counters, showers, and bathtubs. The standard tile, also known as a *field tile,* has four edges. None of the edges is finished and field tiles are not designed to turn corners. The field tiles are also not made to finish off a job. As a result, you must select trim pieces which are finished to complement almost every tile installation. The following are some of the choices you may make:

There are *angle tiles* which permit sharp left or right 90° turns. They eliminate the necessity to make a round or partial circle to go from one point to another in the installation.

An *apron tile* may be selected when you want to finish off the front of a countertop. These are half-size tiles used to fill in narrow areas.

Almost every job has a base and there are tiles designed specifically for floor line or base areas. *Base tile,* sometimes referred to as base trim or runner tile, has a finish to the top edge of the tile. It is used in instances where the floor has been tiled but the walls will not be. The finished top edge completes the floor job and gives it a professional finish.

A *quarter round tile trim* is called a bead. These narrow, 90° pieces are used to achieve a professional job on corners and edges.

The *bullnose tile* is designed to complete a portion of the installation without going around a corner. It consists of a standard field tile with one curved edge that is finished. Remember, field tiles normally have four unfinished edges.

Whenever you work on a countertop with field tiles, you have to finish off the job. *Countertop trim,* or *sink caps,* are set on the outside edge of the countertop. A special raised lip built into the tile sink cap prevents water or liquids from dripping off the work area onto the floor.

If the tile job you are working on requires right angle turns, you will need *tile cove pieces.* The cove corners are designed to turn either inward or outward. If you have to make a right angle turn at the base of a job, you will need floor-level tile cove base pieces. You will have to check your requirements when ordering cove pieces. Some have finished edges while others have unfinished edges. It's important to remember that the inside surface of cove pieces are hollow. In many instances, this will allow you to adjust for corners not exactly in plumb.

Should you desire rounded corners on your tile job instead of angular corners, *rounded in and out tile trim corner pieces* can be purchased for the installation. The selection is a matter of aesthetic choice.

There are additional tile trim items important to specialty tile installations. If you are tiling a swimming pool, for example, *tile edging trim* to cover the coping or *tile trim nose pieces* can finish off certain jobs. If the installation you are working on is a window area, *sill tile trim* has a finishing edge on one side and a rounded corner on the other side of the tile. Sill trim can often make an otherwise difficult window sill installation easier and quicker.

Other ceramic tile trims are available to help you finish off a tile installation so that it looks professional. There are *curb trims* which sit on top of or across areas of installed field tile and *tile stretcher trims* to provide the necessary fit across specific areas of the installation. *Miter trim* tile pieces fit together to develop a perfect miter joint in corners of certain jobs. Some of these choices, as well as other tile shapes, are shown in Fig. 2–6.

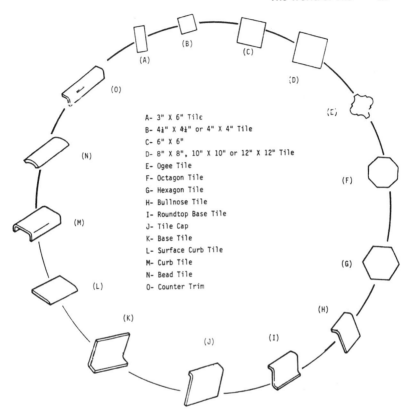

A- 3" X 6" Tile
B- 4½" X 4½" or 4" X 4" Tile
C- 6" X 6"
D- 8" X 8", 10" X 10" or 12" X 12" Tile
E- Ogee Tile
F- Octagon Tile
G- Hexagon Tile
H- Bullnose Tile
I- Roundtop Base Tile
J- Tile Cap
K- Base Tile
L- Surface Curb Tile
M- Curb Tile
N- Bead Tile
O- Counter Trim

Fig. 2–6. Ceramic tile trim is available in many shapes and sizes.

Installation Tip: Although specific tile sizes will be discussed in this book, you should be aware that all manufacturers do not make universally-sized tiles. One company may produce a 4″ × 4″ tile and another a 4-1/4″ × 4-1/4″. A common size, 4″ × 4″, has been selected to clarify calculations and charts. Always check the sizes of the tiles purchased against the room or space requirements so that a sufficient quantity of tile is bought to complete an installation.

* Work Surface: Areas To Be Tile-Covered

Length _____ Width _____ Total Square Feet/Inches _____

Length _____ Width _____ Total Square Feet/Inches _____

Length _____ Width _____ Total Square Feet/Inches _____

* Room(s) To Be Tiled

{ } Bathroom   { } Fireplace   { } Family/Playroom
{ } Kitchen   { } Swimming Pool { } Patio
{ } Other Area _____

* Areas To Be Tile-Covered

{ } Walls   { } Countertops
{ } Floors
{ } Other_____

* Tile Size Requirements

{ } 1-¼"—No. of pieces/sheets_____
{ } 4"— No. of pieces _____ { } 10"—No. of pieces_____
{ } 6"—No. of pieces _____ { } 12"—No. of pieces_____
{ } Other sizes _____ { } No. of pieces_____
{ } Total number of pieces (estimate)_____

* Tile Shape Requirements

{ } Square   { } Octagon
{ } Rectangle   { } Ogee
{ } Hexagon   { } Irregular
{ } Other_____

* Tile Type Requirements

{ } Glazed   { } Unglazed   { } With anti-slip surface

* Tile Colors

{ } Earthtone colors
{ } Other color choices_____

* Specialty Tile Requirements

{ } Designs on tile surface
{ } Sculptured tiles
{ } Other _____

Note: Remember to increase your total purchase of tile pieces to compensate for waste, breakage, etc.

Fig. 2–7.   Checklist for the tile purchaser.

CHAPTER 3

Tools and Equipment

About Tools

The correct tool can not only simplify and speed an installation, but it can also help turn out a more professional job.

Some jobs can be handled with just a few tools while others require a larger number designed specifically for the project. Today, however, one need not buy tools for a job, especially if they may not be needed again. There are rental centers in most areas of the country which rent almost any type of specialty tool for a day or longer.

The tile industry, like any other professional building trade group, has designed tools and equipment to simplify and speed up installations. Most of the tools are relatively inexpensive and easy to use. The following is a list of available tools that you may want to consider for tile installations. Some installation tips follow to make your job easier by providing you with some time- and money-saving hints. All of the tools mentioned are not necessary for every job. Read this chapter, review your job specifications, and gather the tools needed for your installation.

Measuring Tools

Chalk Line—A simple marking system, the chalk line clearly designates where tiles are to be placed on the installation surface. Once the required measurements of the room or wall, etc., are taken, one end of the chalk line is secured to a selected point. The other end if either hand-held or secured to a second point. The line, a piece of strong twine coated with chalk (usually blue), is firmly snapped against the wall or floor surface. This will leave a blue line on the designated surface to be used as a guide in laying out the preparatory work or tiles. The chalk is easily erased if changes are required in the measurement format.

Installation Tip: *Although a chalk line tool may be commercially purchased, you can make a simple chalk marker for the job out of a length of common string, a stick or two of easily obtainable school chalk and a couple of push pins. After surface measurements are taken, place the push pins at the designated points and tie the length of string to these pins. Run the piece of chalk over the length of taut string. Snap the string to make the surface marking. Remove the pins and string after use.*

Layout or Jury Stick—The layout or jury stick is a handy, simple device to estimate the number of tiles required to do a job. It also can be used as a marking ruler to clearly define wall and floor working lines. You can use any straight piece of wood of the correct length to make this tool. A workable size is approximately 3 feet in length with a width of approximately 2 inches. The thickness can be anywhere from ¼ to ½ inch. The exact length of the stick is adjusted for the size of the tiles used on the job plus the selected grout widths.

After securing a piece of wood with the proper dimensions, the next step is to "give the tool a brain" by clearly marking it. This can be accomplished using a ruler or a dividing compass or the actual tiles & spaces. The number of sets of figures inscribed on the layout stick depends, as indicated previously, on the sizes and types of tile in use. A line is penciled on the stick to indicate the size of each individual tile. Another line alongside the first line is used to mark the width of the individual grout line (⅛ inch, ¼ inch, ⅜ inch, ½ inch, etc.). The layout stick will have tile and grout line marking lines along its entire length.

To use the layout stick, set it on the length of the area (floor, wall, etc.) to be tiled just as you would if you were measuring the area with a yardstick. If, for example, your layout stick is 3 feet long and the floor length is 12 feet, you would move the stick four times to measure the length. If you have marked the layout stick to indicate eight 4-inch tiles and ½ inch grout separations on the 3 feet of stick length, then this one stretch of floor would need 32 tiles (4 lengths of the room × 8 tiles and grout lines per 3′ layout stick = 32 tiles).

Repeat the process for the room's width; for example, 15 feet wide. Five lengths of the layout stick would indicate that 40 tiles would be required (5 widths of the room × 8 tiles and grout lines per layout stick = 40 tiles).

To determine how many tiles are required for the entire floor installation, multiply the number of tiles required for the strip of 12-foot floor length (32) times the number of tiles required for the 15 foot floor width (40). In this example, you would need 1280 pieces (32 × 40) of 4″ tile for the job.

> **Installation Tip:** *Always remember to purchase an additional supply of tile beyond your estimates. This will allow for waste and breakage during the installation. It will also assure that you have a supply of the same type and color tile available should you need to repair any tile damage that may occur in the future.*

Level—Carpenters and craftspeople in all trades use levels for construction and renovation work (Fig. 3–1). The level accurately indicates whether a particular area is horizontally or vertically off a known central position. It indicates, for example, whether a standing wall or board is upright or leaning forward, sideways, or away from a given center point. It also tells whether floors are even or running up or down hill. This tool is also known as a *spirit level.*

Levels have sealed tubes imbedded but visible in a wood or metal body. Each tube has a small air bubble. This bubble moves back and forth when the level is tipped in one direction or another. The tubes are clearly marked with a center line. If the air bubble moves to one side of the marked line when in use, it is indicative that the surface level is off in a particular direction. If it moves to the other side of the marked line, it alerts the mechanic that the pitch is off in another direction and requires correction. If the bubble remains in the exact center of the marked line, the area being measured is considered level.

Marking Pencil/Pen—An accurate indication of where tiles and other fixtures are to be placed is important to any installation. A good mark-

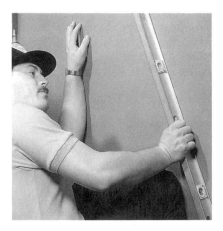

Fig. 3–1. A carpenter's level is used to assure that walls are perpendicular and that rows of set tile are level. Levels are also used on floors. *(Courtesy Summitville Tile)*

ing pencil or felt tipped marking pen makes marking an area easier. The pencil has to be of a variety that can clearly mark wood or similar surfaces. The felt-tipped pen is used for shiny, ceramic surfaces which will not accept a clear or defining pencil mark.

Measuring Tape—You can, of course, measure with a common yardstick. These are inexpensive, easy to locate, and 36 inches in length. A 6 foot or longer measuring tape, however, gives you the option of measuring large areas with one continuous pull of the tape. Most measuring tapes also have clips which can be attached to

---

Installation Tip: Whenever possible, make sure that the walls and subsurfaces to be tiled are level. Individual tiles are not flexible and can crack or will not fit properly if surfaces are too far out of level. If you have to work on an area out of level which cannot be repaired, consider using sheets of mosaic type tile. These are smaller tiles, put together in larger sheets that are often pre-grouted. They allow for greater installation flexibility and also minimize visual distortions.

> **Installation Tip:** Use a pencil that writes as darkly as possible so
> that you can see the marks through the dust and dirt generated dur-
> ing construction. A mechanic's marking pencil, available in most
> lumber supply shops, is much thicker than a standard office pencil.
> The pencil thickness protects against breakage, and the mark it
> makes is highly visible. If you use a felt-tipped pen, the ink should
> be of the washable variety.

your belt. This frees your hands and makes locating the measuring tape
during work easier.

A 6-foot or larger *folding ruler* may also be used on the job. This
tool can be slipped into workclothes pockets so that it is easily located.
Plumb Line—This tear-shaped marking instrument consists of a
heavy metal body with measurement string centrally attached to the
bob. A plumb line or plumb bob looks a great deal like a miniature ice
cream cone with a long piece of string attached to its widest end. The
pointed or narrow end of the cone always faces downward during use.
Used to determine a wall's vertical line, it is important to use a plumb
bob before installing wall tile to assure that the line of tile will be vertically accurate. These may be solid or adjustable (Fig. 3–2).

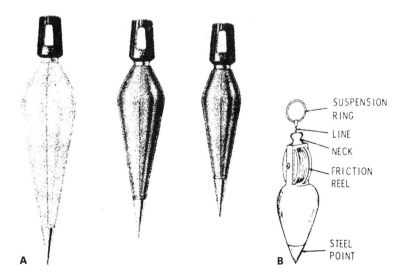

A   B

Fig. 3–2. Plumb bobs. (A) Solid; (B) Adjustable.

Installation Tips: *To use a plumb bob, measure to locate the center of the wall area under construction. On the ceiling, approximately 1" from the measured wall area, fasten a string holder (nail, hook, etc.) and hang the plumb bob line from the fastener so that it drops but does not touch the floor. When the bob has stopped moving, make two pencil marks on the wall in back of this string. One of the marks should be made a very short distance from the top of the wall and the other a very short distance from the bottom. Stand a short distance away from the wall. When you look at the plumb bob string, the pencil marks that have been made should not be visible because they are visually covered by the string. If they are not covered, readjust the marks until they blend properly into the background of the vertical plumb line.*

Once these conditions are met, use a chalk line or cut a piece of heavy string or twine the height of the wall being worked on. Place hooks or nails at the upper and lower wall marks. Attach one end to the top hook or nail and the other to the lower. Make the twine as tight as possible without pulling out the nails or hooks to which the ends have been secured. Remove the plumb bob line. If you are using a homemade chalk line, run a piece of chalk along the line attached to the top and bottom of the wall. Snap the string sharply by pulling the line taut and releasing it. When it strikes the wall, it will leave a chalk mark on the area clearly marking the wall's vertical line. Once this line is marked, the striking line can also be removed and the tile installation started with confidence.

Square (also known as a *Carpenter's Square*)—This measurement tool is used by carpenters to determine whether a particular area under construction is in square. Made of metal, the device looks like two rulers permanently joined at right angles.

If the area measured is in square, the two adjacent edges along which the square is placed will abut the metal of the square. If not, one or both of the edges may be out of square. The amount either edge may be off can be calculated by referring to the ruled angle markings on the square.

Other squares may also be used, depending on the requirements of your installation.

Tile Cutting Tools

Circular Tile Cutting Blade—This circular cutting blade (Fig. 3–3), which fits into a standard electric drill, is made specifically for ceramic work. The cutting surfaces of the blade or bit are carborundum-treated to drill through ceramic surfaces and to cut holes directly through the tile to accommodate pipes or other small round fixtures.

If the measurements of the hole to be cut allow the use of a standard-sized blade, this cutting tool can be utilized. If not, a different cutting device must be used.

Fig. 3–3. Saw blade for wet or tile saw. *(Courtesy Target)*

Circular holes may also be cut out of a piece of tile using several alternative techniques. After the required-sized circle is clearly marked on the face of the tile with a felt-tipped marking pen, a ring of tiny holes can be drilled around the perimeter of the marked circle. A small-diameter, carbide-tipped bit is used for this purpose. After the holes have been drilled through, the section is broken out and removed. A carborundum stone or carborundum paper is used to smooth out any rough edges.

Another technique is again to mark the hole area clearly on the face of the tile with a felt-tipped marking pen. Draw a line through the center of the marked circle extending the line to both upper and lower edges on the face of the tile. Cut the tile in half on the marked line. Using a tile nipper, chip away at the tile hole to the edges of the circle. Use a carborundum stone or carborundum paper to smooth out the chipped areas.

Always follow manufacturer's safety and use recommendations for equipment. The suggestions usually accompany the individual tools.

Installation Tips: *For safety's sake, secure the tile before beginning any hole-cutting process. Place the tile on a piece of wood. Use a number of nails around the perimeter to hold the tile firmly in place. The tile is now ready to be worked on. Do not attempt to use the drill with cutter blade unless the tile is firmly anchored. Remember to use your safety glasses when working on this job.*

If the reverse side of a tile is perfectly flat, mark and drill the hole from the back side of the tile when using a circular saw hole.

Tile Cutter—No matter what the size of a room, almost all installations require that some tiles be cut to fit the job. The quickest and easiest way to do this is with a tile cutter or *tile snapper* (Fig. 3–4). The cutter is a simple piece of equipment, an all-in-one tool that combines an angle-measuring device, carbide, diamond, or ruby cutting wheel, pressure bar, and soft rubberized backstop base to snap the tile. The measured, marked tile, is placed in the cutting tool and positioned at the required angle using the on-board angle gauge. The surface of the tile is scored along the marked line with

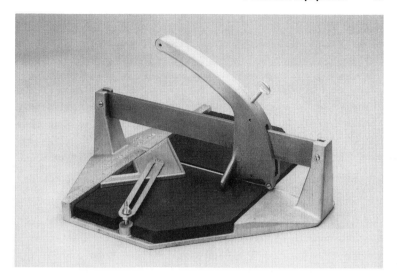

Fig. 3–4. A tile snapper is an all in one cutting tool that allows the installer to score and then cleanly snap the tile into accurately measured sizes. *(Courtesy Superior Tile Cutter, Inc.)*

the glass cutter. A downward pressure on the tile cutter handle will break the piece of tile along the scored line. Tile snappers may be obtained in midget, standard, and large sizes to handle the various size tiles on the market.

If a tile cutter is not available, you can score the tile with a standard glass cutter using a straight edge as a guide across the tile face. Place the scored line over a thin piece of dowel, round pencil, or the like, and use downward pressure against each side of the tile. The tile should snap cleanly at the scored line.

Tile Saw—If your installation requires a large number of tile cuts, if you want to speed up the tile cutting process, or if you just want to make the cutting procedure easier, you may want to consider a tile saw. This piece of equipment is a motorized saw with a water-cooled diamond-impregnated blade (Fig. 3–5). The marked tile to be cut is placed in the saw's protective safety holder. Water automatically runs onto the tile surface to cool it down during the cutting process. The saw

Installation Tips: A tile cutter can often be borrowed or rented from the store where you have purchased your tile. If it is not available from this source, there are usually rental stores where it can be obtained. For best results, be careful and don't rush when you use the cutter. It is expected that some tiles will be damaged no matter how careful you are. This is why a waste percentage was calculated into the original quantity of tile purchased.

If the tiles you are working with have a ridged back, always make your cuts parallel to the ridges.

When measuring pieces of tile requiring straight cuts (by hand or with a tile saw, tile cutter, etc.) to fit along the wall, use the following marking/measurement system: place a tile piece, finished side up, exactly on top of the last full tile that you have installed. Place one additional tile on top of this tile. You now should have a set of tiles stacked three high. Move the top so that it has one of its edges against the wall you are working toward. Now, using the edge of the topmost tile as a guide, mark the cut-off line on the middle with a fine felt tip pen. If the installation is in a corner, repeat the procedure twice, once on each wall's corners. Use the same three stack pile, marking off the same second tile in the batch. Cut the marked tile using the standard procedures.

If an irregular tile cut is necessary to fit a job, first cut a pattern from cardboard. Transfer the contour design to the tile surface using a fine tip pen. Cut the tile using tile nippers or appropriate tool.

blade (Fig. 3–3) is brought across the tile face surface to cut along the marked line.

Rounded trim tile, which cannot be cut by an ordinary snap cutter, can be cut with a wet saw. This saw is probably the only device capable of effectively cutting through these designed pieces of tile.

Installation Tip: This piece of equipment may be rented at a rental supply store. If the installation is a large one, for cost-effectiveness you may want to lay out the tiles ahead of time and schedule your installation work so that you need the rental equipment for the shortest possible time.

Fig. 3–5. Tile or wet saw is a motorized saw with a water-cooled diamond impregnated blade for easily cutting tile. *(Courtesy Target)*

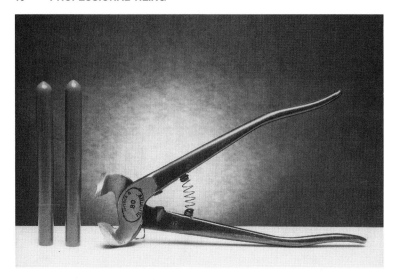

Fig. 3–6. Tile nippers, also known as tile pliers, are used when tiles must be cut in irregular shapes and patterns. *(Courtesy Superior Tile Cutter, Inc.)*

Even though a wet saw has the capability of easily slicing through hard ceramic tile, it is reasonably safe to use. Standard safety precautions should, of course, be observed at all times when using this equipment.

Tile Pliers—Tile pliers, also known as *tile nippers,* are used when tiles must be cut to irregular shapes and patterns (e.g., around toilet bowls, sink bases, etc.). These nippers usually have carbide tips designed specifically to cut tile easily and smoothly (Fig. 3–6). The plier grip allows for a great deal of pressure and ceramic tile tends to break easily when leveraged pressure is applied. Always take small bites or nips out of the piece of tile in the marked areas so as not to damage the piece. Take it slow and easy.

Whetstone/Carborundum-Laced Paper—These abrasive items are used to file down and smooth rough pieces of tile. Rough areas on tiles

---

Installation Tip: If possible, score the marked line with a glass cutter before applying the tile pliers. This makes the job easier and helps avert larger breaks when applying the plier pressure.

usually occur after they are cut or nipped with a tile pliers. Often, only a tiny piece must be removed from a trimmed tile to make it fit. In these instances, the stone or abrasive paper is drawn back and forth across the tile until the offending piece is worn away.

Tile Installation Tools

Beater Block—When tiles have been positioned individually in the adhesive and you want to make sure that they are equally and well seated, use a beater block before the adhesive has had an opportunity to dry thoroughly. The beater block is placed across a series of the tiles and lightly tapped with a hammer or rubber mallet to assure proper seating. Mosaic installations, too, may benefit from the beater block process for firm seating of the sheets of squares.

> **Installation Tip:** Beater blocks are easily and inexpensively constructed by wrapping a conveniently-sized piece of board (a 2 × 4 will do) with scrap carpeting or with layers of other dense fabric. Always place all of the nails securing the carpeting or wrapping material on the top side of the beater block. This will assure that when the beater block is used, the tiles will not be damaged by the nails. Use the 4″, wide side of the board as the flat tile contact side.

Cheesecloth—Suggested by tile technicians as a substitute for sponges in grout cleanup, cheesecloth, according to the experts, does a more effective, cleaner job, packing tighter and creating more even joints. Only cotton cheesecloth works.

Grout Liner (also known as a *Joint Striking Tool*)—After tile has been grouted and allowed to partially harden, the next step is a finishing process. The procedure, tamping down the grout between each row, is designed to make sure that the grout is securely in place. It also assures that each row is similar. One of the easiest way to do this job is to run the narrow edge of a toothbrush handle or popsicle stick between the row of tiles. The edge of the handle or stick makes a very slight indentation and smooths down any rough areas on the still flexible grout.

Mixing Containers—If you are buying small quantities of adhesive, mortar, or grout, chances are the product will come in prepackaged, ready-to-use containers. You can then work directly from the containers.

On the other hand, if the installation is large, it will probably be more economical to purchase the mortar, adhesive, or grout in bulk and mix it according to manufacturer's instructions. At this point, mixing containers are useful.

Installation Tip: Be cautious on the job! If the installation is to be extensive, requiring that large quantities of grout, mortar, or adhesive be mixed, use mixing containers that can easily be moved around and divide the mixture into manageable lots. Don't take a chance of injuring yourself by lifting excessive weight.

Pointed Trowel—The pointed, metal trowel is a good general purpose tool and performs several functions (Fig. 3–7). If there are small areas requiring mortar fill prior to tile installation applications, the pointed trowel is an ideal piece of equipment to handle the project. It can also be used to mix small quantities of mortar and to fill and point up areas that need repair. The trowel, with its pointed front, can often reach sections inaccessible to the notched trowel generally used to apply tile adhesives.

V-Notched Trowel—The V-notched trowel (Fig. 3–8) is used to apply the material that cements tiles into place. The trowel portion of the tool allows you to pick up the adhesive from the container and efficiently bring it to floor or wall areas for use. The V or notched portion of the metal instrument, usually found on two edges of the tool, is used to spread the adhesive on the working surfaces. The tool spreads the adhesive evenly in rows with a specific depth depending on the size and distance apart of the notches.

Polishing Cloths—Scrap cloth, usually soft, flexible toweling that has seen better days, is useful for a number of purposes during the tile in-

Fig. 3–7. Pointed trowel.

Installation Tip: The size of the V, or notches on the trowel, can control the distance between adhesive rows and the height of each row of adhesive. Trowels with small notches are used for installations where smaller tiles must be placed (e.g., 4-inch and smaller tiles). A trowel with larger notches would be used for large tile installations where wide, deep rows of adhesive are required. (e.g., 10-inch tile or 12-inch installations).

stallation process. Dampened, the cloths are used to clean off any adhesive on the surface of the tile squares after installation. After the grouting has been completed, the dry cloth is used to wipe off excess grout and to polish the tile surfaces.

Rubber-Faced Float—This tool is used to apply grout between rows of tiles (Fig. 3–9). After the tile adhesive has thoroughly dried, the liquid grout mixture is poured onto sections of tile. The float draws the grout across the face of the tiles and packs it down into areas between them. As it moves across the tile section, the float also cleans excess grout off the tile face.

Installation Tips: When moving the rubber float across the face of the tiles, tilt the float at about a 45° angle and use a downward pressure on the tool. If you are familiar with the use of snow shovels, the angle and forward motion of the float is similar to that. The work, however, is not as difficult. While it is not as effective, a rubber squeegee can be used to move the grout if a rubber-faced float is not available.

Sponges—Upon completion, every job requires cleanup. Sponges can absorb great quantities of water and are handy for cleanup jobs. After the tile adhesive or grout has been applied, any extra residue can easily be wiped up using a damp sponge.

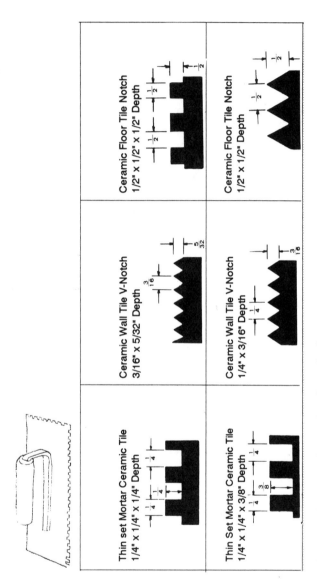

Fig. 3–8. V-notched trowel and notch sizes.

Thin set Mortar Ceramic Tile
1/4" x 1/4" x 1/4" Depth

Thin Set Mortar Ceramic Tile
1/4" x 1/4" x 3/8" Depth

Ceramic Wall Tile V-Notch
3/16" x 5/32" Depth

Ceramic Wall Tile V-Notch
1/4" x 3/16" Depth

Ceramic Floor Tile Notch
1/2" x 1/2" x 1/2" Depth

Ceramic Floor Tile Notch
1/2" x 1/2" Depth

2189947

Fig. 3–9. Rubber-faced float for applying grout.

Safety Tools for Tile Work

Rubber Gloves—All adhesives and grouts used in tile work contain many chemical additives. During the course of any tile installation, you will be in contact with these products. It is possible to be sensitive to any one of the these chemicals: the sensitivity may evidence itself as a simple rash, or it can be more extensive, affecting various parts of your body. The safest way to work with adhesives, grouts, sealers, etc., is to handle these products using rubber gloves made to withstand the appropriate chemicals.

> **Installation Tip:** Always follow the manufacturer's instructions on the product label. If you do get adhesives, grouts, sealers, etc., on your skin during a tile installation, rinse the affected area off as soon as possible with a good supply of water. If a rash, headache, or other condition occurs and persists, consult your physician.

Safety Eye Glasses—A glazed piece of tile has many of the same properties as glass and stone. When you work on tile, cutting, chipping, drilling, or sanding in order to fit the pieces into a portion of an installation, pieces of tile can chip off and hit your eyes, causing a great deal of pain and damage. The best preventive measure is a set of safety glasses worn whenever the work calls for any of these tasks.

Safety Mask—An inexpensive, useful item available to individuals working with tile installations is a safety mask. A great deal of dust is generated mixing mortars and grouts, sanding tile pieces with carbo-

---

Installation Tip: Purchase a good set of safety glasses. They last a long time and can be used for many other jobs. A cheap set of glasses may not always be effective enough to ward off sharp blows from fast moving objects. Make sure that the method or holder for placing and holding the glasses over your eyes is comfortable, secure, and strong.

---

rundum paper, or cutting pieces of tile with a carbide-bladed tile saw. The light, easy-to-use safety mask fits over the nose and mouth and helps filter out generated dust. It is especially valuable to those who develop dust and chemical sensitivities.

Other Useful Tools

Hammer—The common hammer is probably one of the most useful tools on a job. On tile jobs, for example, it is used to nail down everything from subflooring to wood framing. The hammer's claw end can be used to remove nails and obstructions. If a rubber mallet is not available when the beater block is used on the installed tiles, the hammer can lightly tap the block against the tiles.

Pry Bar—When installing tile near an existing floor, it is often necessary, prior to the tile work, to remove the wood baseboard molding. You may want to save the wood molding so that it can be replaced when the tile work is completed. You can, of course, remove the molding with a claw hammer or other makeshift tools, but the easiest the best way to do it is with a pry bar, a tool specially designed for the purpose.

Some pry bars are called by trade names such as Wonder Bar®. About 12 inches in length, the metal pry bar has a strong, thin, bevelled edge on one end and a curved nail-pulling edge on the opposite end. When it is necessary to remove wood molding, the thin edge of the pry bar is worked down behind a section of the molding. The pry bar can be tapped gently with a hammer to move it effectively into place. The design of the pry bar allows the installer to use leverage to loosen the securing nails gradually and gently and move the molding away from the wall. The pry bar is drawn slowly along the molding, gently prying it away from the wall until the section is removed. The reverse side of the pry bar is then used to remove the nails that once held the molding in place. The pieces can then be reused after the job is completed. The reuse of molding is sometimes necessary when an unusual design or make of molding cannot be replaced.

Installation Tip: *Be gentle when using the pry bar on the wood molding. Many times the wood is old and very dry. The length of the pry bar and your own weight against the bar give it a great deal of leverage or prying strength.*

Working Board—A long piece of ordinary wide lumber or plywood, the working board is used to allow you to walk over an area of tiles recently laid. Before the adhesive dries thoroughly, you may have to reach an area halfway into a room to make some adjustments. Laying the board across the tile surface permits you to cross over the tiles without damaging the installation.

Other Tools—There are additional tools that can prove useful in your tiling work. These might include a caulking gun for areas around tubs and showers; a floor scraper to remove any rough surfaces from the base floor; putty knives for close trimming work; utility knives to chip off a piece of board that is obstructing an area of the installation; can opener, contour gauge for complicated areas, cold chisel for tile repairs, spreaders for mastic, a thinset mixer for your $\frac{3}{8}$-inch drill, pliers, screwdrivers, or sandpaper.

A Final Word

Before starting on any project, gather the tools that you will need. Keep them all in one place so that they are readily accessible. Make sure that all of the tools are clean and in good shape. If, for example, you will be using a carbide bit to cut holes in a piece of tile, be sure before you start on the job that the bit is not dull. If a wood saw will be needed, make sure the teeth are sharp enough to do the job. Once you start the job, you will be busy with a great many other details, so an orderly system for readying your tools for the job will make the entire process easier and quicker.

Remember that there is no longer a need to buy costly equipment that you will probably not require again. Some of the tools you will be using can be rented at a nominal charge. It is better to rent first rate products for your installation.

CHAPTER 4

Purchasing Tile

Purchasing Guidelines

This chapter covers buying tiles, tile trim, and accessories. It will also offer some layout options as well as tile styles and decorative choices.

Tile works well with almost any decor. It is colorfast and, unlike many other wall, floor, and countertop coverings, will not fade. Where carpeting, wood, and linoleum floor coverings may have an eight- to ten-year useful life span, ceramic tile can easily last the life of a structure. The decorative possibilities of tile are endless. If you decide to outline a window, create a border, or develop a unique pattern for part of a room, tile lends itself to these applications (Figs. 4–1 and 4–2). There are also feature strips of tile in over a dozen colors. Strips in 6″ × 1″ or ½-inch sizes permit a great variety of installation designs. They can be interspersed with standard tiles, used as attractive borders, or to highlight or outline an area in many creative ways, for example, to frame a special area rug or border an inlaid wood floor.

Tile manufacturers offer an extensive color palette. Some present over seventy different color selections, many with grouts to match. Tile buyers generally opt for the more neutral colors. Still, some of the available options are striking and have the capacity to excite the visual senses. While you may want to create a bold and daring visual impact, you should keep in mind the enduring qualities of tile. The color and

Fig. 4–1. Design tile set around the framework of a set of doors.

design you choose should be livable over time unless you can easily afford the time and expense of frequent replacement. Do not allow the name of a particular tile color affect your selection or rejection of a tile. Tile colors and the names attached are simply marketing tools used by the manufacturers.

Color should be seen in both natural and artificial light, under the conditions of the room or space in which the tiles will be used. Colors look different under fluorescent lights than under incandescent lights. Fluorescents have a tendency to change hues while incandescent light can add a pinkish tone to the tile color. Areas that are generally bathed in sunshine may require different color treatments than those that are shaded from natural light. Tiles may look slightly darker on floor sur-

Fig. 4–2. Tile wall murals can be used in a number of different areas of a home including kitchen cooking nooks. Designed border tiles will help complement the mural. *(Courtesy Firebird, Inc.)*

faces than on wall surfaces. If possible, take two, three, or more different tiles in the colors of interest to your home. Rather than in-store viewing, look at the tile colors under your home lighting and living conditions.

Use reds, oranges, and bold yellows to brighten and warm an area; pastels to lighten; blues and greens to calm and cool; greys and beiges to create neutral backgrounds for accessories; black, white, dark blues, maroons, deep greens, rich browns, or metallics to make a sophisticated statement.

A great deal of time and effort will go into your installation so that the tiles, accessories, and fixtures selected for the job should be exactly what you want. While tile may be initially expensive in relation to other floor and wall coverings, considering its lifespan and the ease with which it can be maintained, in the long run, tile installation can be cost-effective.

Purchasing Tips: If economy is a paramount factor in the installation, it is wise to take time and patience to shop several suppliers. Prices differ even on the same product. You may want to wait to make purchases during sales or closeouts. Some suppliers deal in manufacturers' seconds. These are quality tiles that may have slight flaws or blemishes which may not affect use. These are usually kept in an area known as the "bone pile." Select carefully when purchasing seconds. Run your fingers over the entire surface to feel for glaze blisters, crazes, unglazed spots, or cracks. Consider the projected amount of your time and work that will go into the installation.

Buying Tile Accessories

If the tile installation is in a bathroom or shower stall, there are useful tile accessories that can complement the job. These items, which should be considered because of their convenience and adaptability, are designed to be part of the actual tile installation. They are produced of ceramic material, can be installed in the conventional manner, and are available in color options to match or contrast with the tile. Arrangements to locate exact accessory tile color matches should be made in time for the actual installation. Bathroom accessory items might include ceramic soap holders for bathtub installations, toilet paper roll holders, towel racks, robe hooks, and toothbrush and tumbler holders (Fig. 4–3).

Tile Availability

There are a number of places to purchase a supply of tile. Telephone books, yellow pages, and newspapers, radio and television ads can provide the names of local tile dealers. A list of the leading tile manufacturers is provided in the supplier section of this book. These

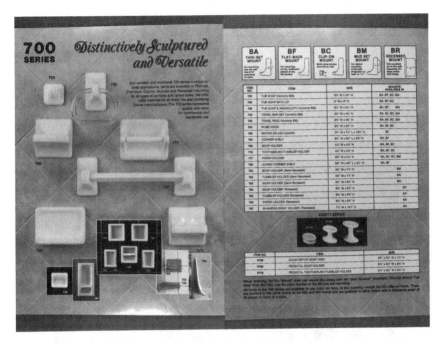

Fig. 4–3. (A) Tile accessory units are available in a variety of colors. Most companies carry a range of stock colors and offer the option of ordering special colors. (B) In addition to color selections, tile accessory units come in a variety of mounting choices including clip-on mount, recessed mount, flat back mount, thin-set and mud-set mount. *(Courtesy AC Products)*

manufacturers can give you the names of nearby suppliers who handle their products.

Tiles also may be ordered from catalogs. There are companies selling a variety of tile types and styles by direct mail. You can secure a color catalog containing a manufacturer's offerings, and review it in the comfort of your home. Selections may be made and orders for required quantities placed, and the order will be shipped directly to you. When calculating costs be sure to add shipping and handling charges and any taxes to the cost of the tile. Make sure the provisions for returning any damaged tile are clearly understood.

Tile showrooms operate throughout the country. Some are individually-owned dealerships and others are franchise operations. Both types of stores offer in-store opportunities to make a wide variety of tile selections.

Some tile stores have combined special computer software and videotape equipment which allow them to offer potential customers an opportunity to preview styles, colors, and shapes of tile under different room settings. A specific room can be called up on the television screen and with the flip of a switch, different tile choices are visually positioned in the room. Colors, tile sizes, and patterns can be moved around until satisfactory combinations are determined.

During certain periods, many of the stores may offer closeouts on particular tile styles. These are items which may be discontinued because the manufacturer has ceased to produce a particular style, or color, or because the individual store may be overstocked with a line of tile. In order to turn over or reduce inventory, a group or groups of tile may be put on sale.

Custom tile houses are likely places to purchase specialty tile. These are suppliers or manufacturers who can provide special orders of almost anything you want in the tile trade. They can prepare shapes and sizes to fit a particular demand as well as specially-colored tiles. If a specific design is desired, the artwork can be prepared using ceramic-friendly material and the picture or design fired directly onto unglazed tile. An additional firing coats the designed tile with a clear glaze to make it permanent. There are full color booklets available which show the variety of design possibilities. Adornments of tile can cover most everything: flowers, birds, land and seascapes, and famous people to name a few (Figs. 4–4, 4–5, and 4–6). Tiles may also be purchased with patterns, under glaze, designed and cut into their face. These tiles can provide unusual decorative effects.

It makes good sense when considering a tile purchase to obtain copies of various manufacturers' brochures. These colorful specification sheets and illustrations provide a great deal of product information and offer some interesting installation concepts.

Layout Patterns and Design Options

Preliminary Considerations

Tile patterns can be used to create special effects in almost any room. If you select tiles with a fairly busy pattern, the room area will appear smaller. The same effect can be gained by mixing the colors of

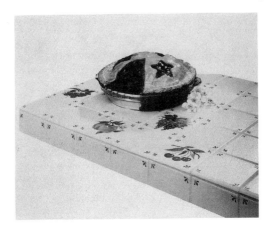

Fig. 4–4. Decorative tile inserts featuring such motifs as fruits, herbs, spices, flowers, vegetables and even a village scene are offered by tile manufacturers. These tiles also have coordinated corner designs. *(Courtesy Summitville Tiles)*

the tiles. If the tile colors chosen for the room are dark, expect the space to appear smaller than it really is. Light tile colors visually open up a room and impart spacious feelings. A rule of thumb in tile sizing is that small tiles make a given surface appear larger and large tiles do just the reverse.

Using alternating color tiles will develop one type of design, while mixing and/or alternating different size tiles will create different design patterns (Figs. 4–7 and 4–8). A lengthwise repeated pattern of tiles will add a feeling of depth to a room while tiles run crosswise in a room will give the space a shorter and wider appearance. Borders or separations using complementary color and rows of smaller tiles can develop still an additional series of design patterns.

Keep in mind that you will have to furnish or accessorize the area you are tiling. It is wise to work out the enitre color scheme before you start.

Floor Layout Patterns

Layout and design can play a role in determining tile quantity requirements. The following patterns (Fig. 4–9), courtesy of Metropolitan Ceramics, suggest the wide range of floor design options available. Included in the selector chart are choices that range from linear and

Fig. 4–5. Decorative tiles are available in many different designs. This set of tiles depicting colonial-era characters is a collection licensed by the Colonial Williamsburg Foundation to ensure authenticity. *(Courtesy Summitville Tile)*

cobblestone patterns to circular patterns. An imprint of a 12-inch footprint (Figs. 4–9A and 4–9B) demonstrates the scale of each pattern. Creative pattern layouts can provide some unusual design effects for border areas or complete floors. Fig. 4–10, courtesy of Winburn Tile Manufacturing Company, indicates just some pattern and design possibilities.

Before Buying Tile

There are preliminary steps which should be taken prior to the actual tile selection process. The number and type of tiles required for a particular installation impact the ultimate purchasing decision. Tile re-

Fig. 4–6. A country scene handpainted on ceramic tile by tile manufacturer artists is a charming, yet practical idea for a kitchen backsplash. *(Courtesy Summitville Tile)*

quirements may be developed using room measurements or through charts which offer pre-calculated short cuts.

It is a good procedure to lay out the projected tile application on graph paper indicating exact room sizes and related measurements. Using this technique, tile calculation requirements, which you may have already completed, can be double-checked at the store selling the tile, as can color and shade variations.

How to Compute Your Tile Needs

As we have noted, tiles are available in a range of sizes from tiny mosaic pieces up to 10″ and 12″ squares. It is possible to special order

Fig. 4–7. 6″ × 6″ squares combined with 2″ × 2″ squares to form a design. *(Courtesy American Olean Tile Co.)*

other sizes, but you must remember that tile is not a flexible product. If an individual tile spans too great an area, the opportunity for stress breakage of the glass-like, non-flexible tile surface increases. The standard sizes of tile that you will be working with are usually squares. The squares generally measure 1-⅛-inch, 4, 6, 8, 10 and 12 inches, but there are also other size variations available. There are rectangular shapes (3″ × 6″), cloverleaves, curves, ogee tile shapes (which may be best described as having two rounded sides and two flat sides), hexagons, and octagons.

For specific jobs, consider purchasing tile in sheets. Some are pre-grouted while others come without grout. A sheet of 1″ mosaics or smaller or 4″ squares is held together with an adhesive and backing. Handling tile in this manner can speed up the job if the wall or floor layout is suitable for sheet-type installations.

You should be aware that in the pre-grouted sheets a fungus inhibitor may be mixed into the grout. This is perfectly suitable for bathroom installations where the sheets may be used in showers or tub areas, but the inhibitor-laced sheets should not be used in kitchen areas. This is especially important if the tile is to be used for countertops or other food work areas.

Ceramic tile is usually purchased in boxes of 80 pieces. It may be possible to purchase smaller additional quantities from a dealer if lesser

Fig. 4–8. Tile patterns are easy to create to add wonderful design interest to floors, counters, tables, backsplashes, showers, and tub walls. In some instances, tile shapes are combined to create a series of geometric patterns reminiscent of quilts or Navajo rugs. *(Courtesy Summitville Tile)*

Metropolitan Ceramics TILE PATTERN SELECTOR

These are but a few pattern options employing one, or mixed sizes of our all purpose unglazed ceramic tile. The approximate number of pieces per square foot of each size and the approximate percentage of each size tile in the pattern is shown in each case.
The size 12 footprint demonstrates the scale of the pattern.
Patterns can also be achieved simply by blending several colors of tile into the pattern to alter the appearance and scale of the pattern.
Scale can also be adjusted to room size by employing larger size tile in larger rooms and vice versa. Matching grout color produces a monolithic appearance, contrasting grout color heightens the pattern effect. Highly contrasting grout colors require more careful installation clean-up, and the use of "grout release" coating on the tile prior to grouting is suggested.

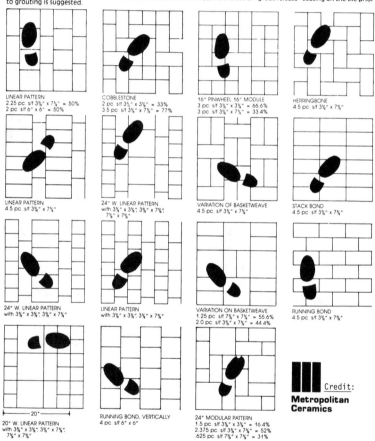

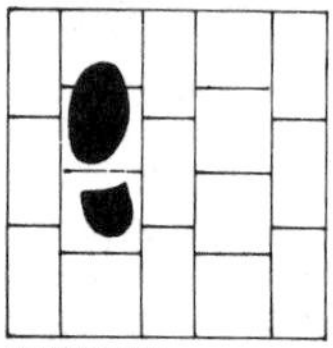
LINEAR PATTERN
2.25 pc. s/f 3⅝" x 7⅝" = 50%
2 pc. s/f 6" x 6" = 50%

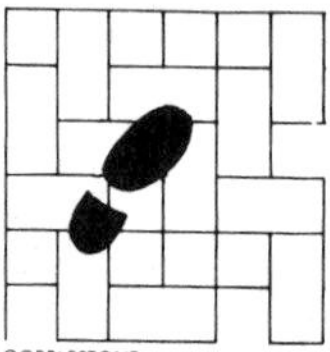
COBBLESTONE
2 pc. s/f 3⅝" x 3⅝" = 33%
3.5 pc. s/f 3⅝" x 7⅝" = 77%

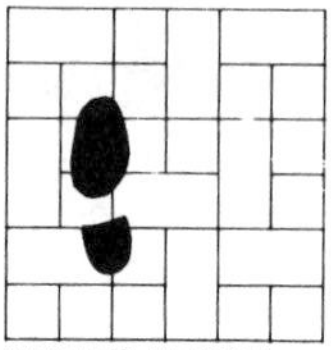
16" PINWHEEL 16" MODULE
3 pc. s/f 3⅝" x 3⅝" = 66.6%
3 pc. s/f 3⅝" x 7⅝" = 33.4%

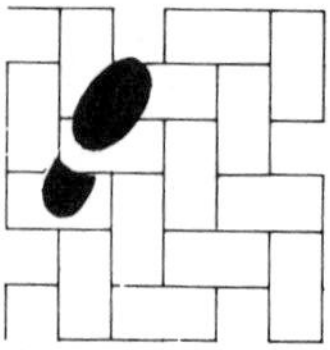
HERRINGBONE
4.5 pc. s/f 3⅝" x 7⅝"

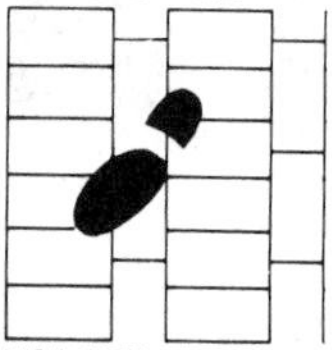
LINEAR PATTERN
4.5 pc. s/f 3⅝" x 7⅝"

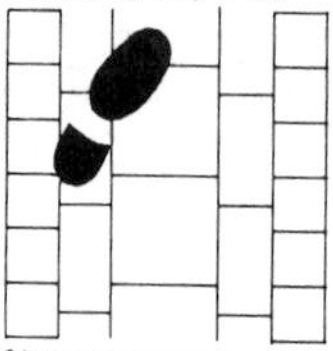
24" W. LINEAR PATTERN
with 3⅝" x 3⅝", 3⅝" x 7⅝", 7⅝" x 7⅝"

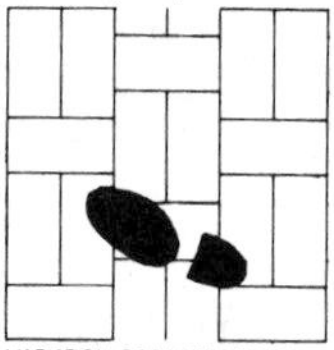
VARIATION OF BASKETWEAVE
4.5 pc. s/f 3⅝" x 7⅝"

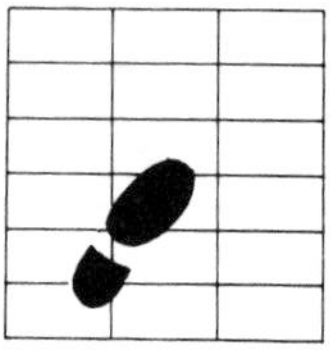
STACK BOND
4.5 pc. s/f 3⅝" x 7⅝"

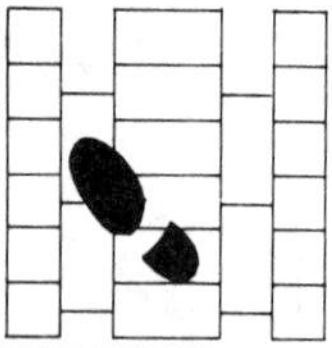
24" W. LINEAR PATTERN
with 3⅝" x 3⅝", 3⅝" x 7⅝"

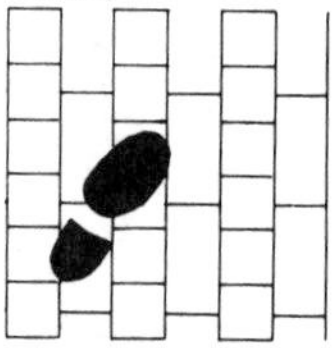
LINEAR PATTERN
with 3⅝" x 3⅝", 3⅝" x 7⅝"

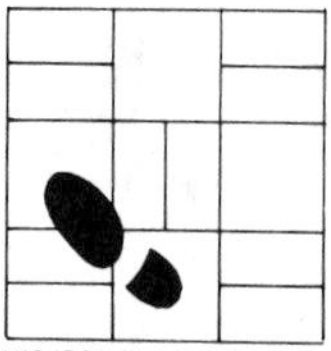
VARIATION ON BASKETWEAVE
1.25 pc. s/f 7⅝" x 7⅝" = 55.6%
2.0 pc. s/f 3⅝" x 7⅝" = 44.4%

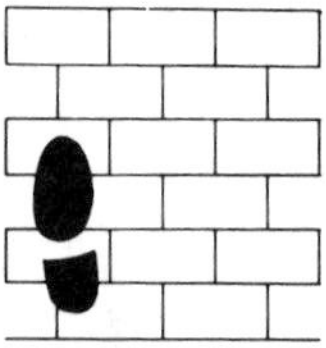
RUNNING BOND
4.5 pc. s/f 3⅝" x 7⅝"

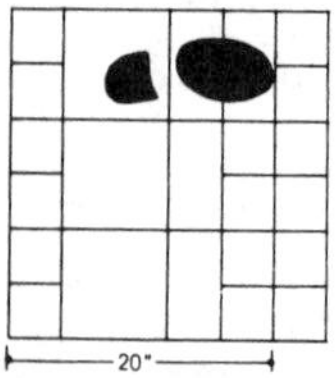

20" W. LINEAR PATTERN
with 3⅝" x 3⅝", 3⅝" x 7⅝", 7⅝" x 7⅝"

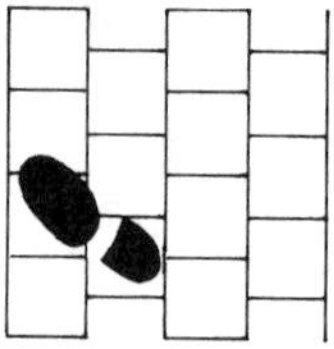
RUNNING BOND, VERTICALLY
4 pc. s/f 6" x 6"

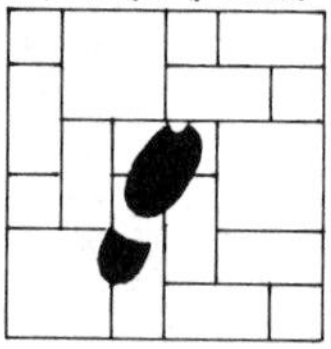
24" MODULAR PATTERN
1.5 pc. s/f 3⅝" x 3⅝" = 16.4%
2.375 pc. s/f 3⅝" x 7⅝" = 52%
.625 pc. s/f 7⅝" x 7⅝" = 31%

Credit:
Metropolitan Ceramics

Scale: 3/4" = 1'0" (assuming a 3/8" joint)

Fig. 4–9A.

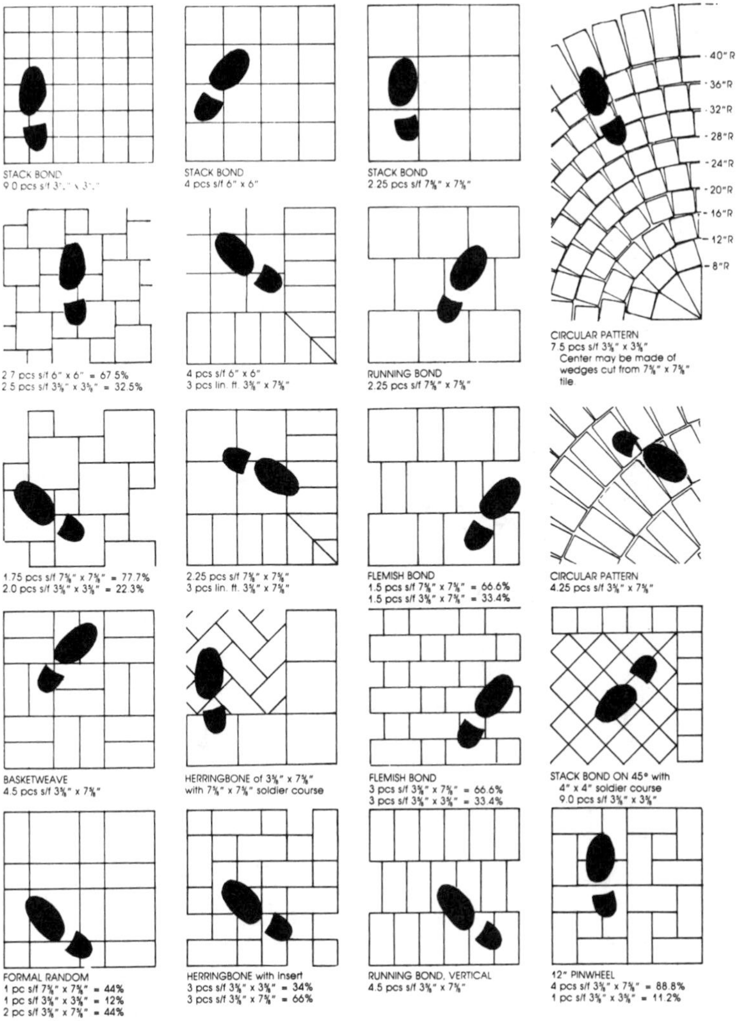

STACK BOND
9.0 pcs s/f 3⅝" x 3⅝"
STACK BOND
4 pcs s/f 6" x 6"
STACK BOND
2.25 pcs s/f 7⅝" x 7⅝"
40"R
36"R
32"R
28"R
24"R
20"R
16"R
12"R
8"R
CIRCULAR PATTERN
7.5 pcs s/f 3⅝" x 3⅝"
Center may be made of wedges cut from 7⅝" x 7⅝" tile.
2.7 pcs s/f 6" x 6" = 67.5%
2.5 pcs s/f 3⅝" x 3⅝" = 32.5%
4 pcs s/f 6" x 6"
3 pcs lin. ft. 3⅝" x 7⅝"
RUNNING BOND
2.25 pcs s/f 7⅝" x 7⅝"
1.75 pcs s/f 7⅝" x 7⅝" = 77.7%
2.0 pcs s/f 3⅝" x 3⅝" = 22.3%
2.25 pcs s/f 7⅝" x 7⅝"
3 pcs lin. ft. 3⅝" x 7⅝"
FLEMISH BOND
1.5 pcs s/f 7⅝" x 7⅝" = 66.6%
1.5 pcs s/f 3⅝" x 7⅝" = 33.4%
CIRCULAR PATTERN
4.25 pcs s/f 3⅝" x 7⅝"
BASKETWEAVE
4.5 pcs s/f 3⅝" x 7⅝"
HERRINGBONE of 3⅝" x 7⅝" with 7⅝" x 7⅝" soldier course
FLEMISH BOND
3 pcs s/f 3⅝" x 7⅝" = 66.6%
3 pcs s/f 3⅝" x 3⅝" = 33.4%
STACK BOND ON 45° with 4" x 4" soldier course
9.0 pcs s/f 3⅝" x 3⅝"
FORMAL RANDOM
1 pc s/f 7⅝" x 7⅝" = 44%
1 pc s/f 3⅝" x 3⅝" = 12%
2 pc s/f 3⅝" x 7⅝" = 44%
HERRINGBONE with insert
3 pcs s/f 3⅝" x 3⅝" = 34%
3 pcs s/f 3⅝" x 7⅝" = 66%
RUNNING BOND, VERTICAL
4.5 pcs s/f 3⅝" x 7⅝"
12" PINWHEEL
4 pcs s/f 3⅝" x 7⅝" = 88.8%
1 pc s/f 3⅝" x 3⅝" = 11.2%

Scale: ¾" = 1' 0" (assuming a ⅜" joint)

METROPOLITAN CERAMICS, P.O. BOX 9240, CANTON, OHIO 44711

Fig. 4–9B.

SIGNET™

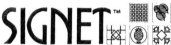

Metropolitan Ceramics
P.O. Box 9240 CANTON, OHIO 44711

Here are a variety of tile patterns showing mixed sizes of modularly dimensioned tile with suggested placement of our SIGNET tiles. Areas shown are approximately 32" x 32".

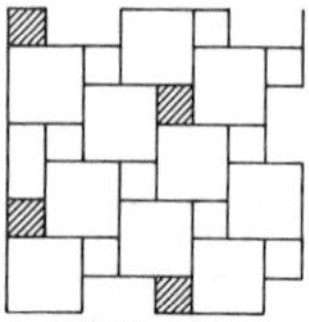

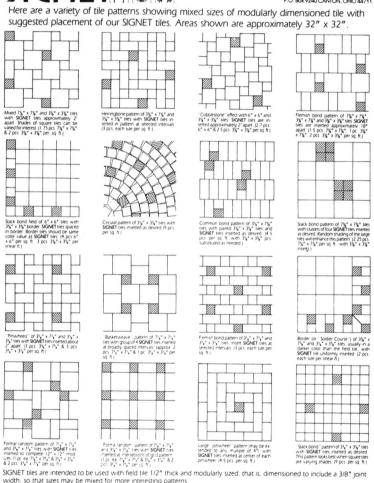

Mixed 7⅝" x 7⅝" and 3⅝" x 3⅝" tiles with **SIGNET** tiles approximately 2' apart. Shades of square tiles can be varied for interest. (1.75 pcs. 7⅝" x 7⅝" & 2 pcs. 3⅝" x 3⅝" per sq. ft.)

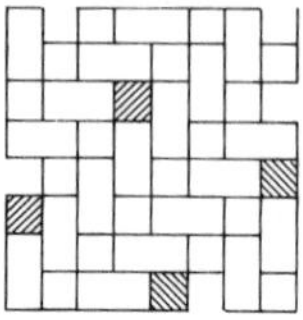

Herringbone pattern of 3⅝" x 7⅝" and 3⅝" x 3⅝" tiles with **SIGNET** tiles inserted in pattern at selected intervals. (3 pcs. each size per sq. ft.)

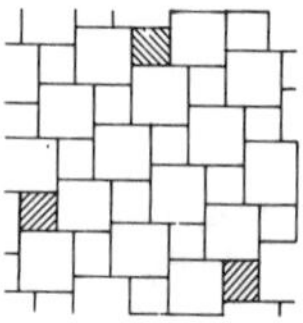

"Cobblestone" effect with 6" x 6" and 3⅝" x 3⅝" tiles. **SIGNET** tiles are inserted approximately 2' apart. (2.7 pcs. 6" x 6" & 2.5 pcs. 3⅝" x 3⅝" per sq. ft.)

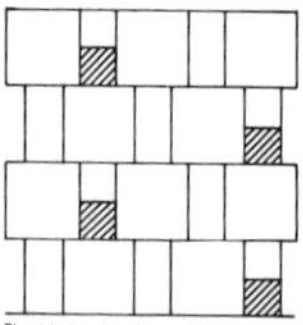

Flemish bond pattern of 7⅝" x 7⅝", 3⅝" x 7⅝" and 3⅝" x 3⅝" tiles. **SIGNET** tiles are inserted approximately 18" apart. (1.5 pcs. 7⅝" x 7⅝", 1 pc. 3⅝" x 7⅝", 2 pcs. 3⅝" x 3⅝" per sq. ft.)

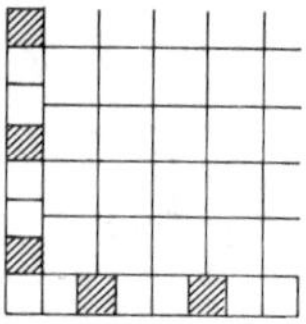

Stack bond field of 6" x 6" tiles with 3⅝" x 3⅝" border. **SIGNET** tiles spaced in border. Border tiles should be same color value as **SIGNET** tiles. (4 pcs. 6" x 6" per sq. ft. 3 pcs. 3⅝" x 3⅝" per linear ft.)

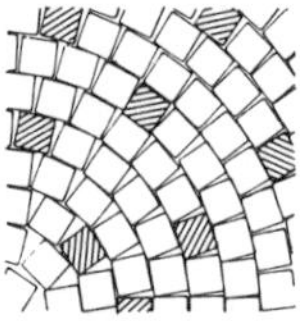

Circular pattern of 3⅝" x 3⅝" tiles with **SIGNET** tiles inserted as desired. (9 pcs. per sq. ft.)

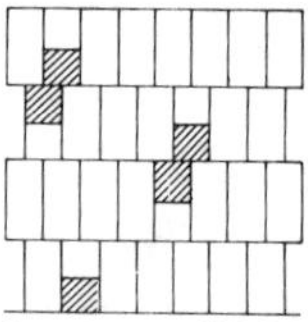

Common bond pattern of 3⅝" x 7⅝" tiles with paired 3⅝" x 3⅝" tiles and **SIGNET** tiles inserted as desired. (4.5 pcs. per sq. ft. with 3⅝" x 3⅝" pcs. substituted as needed.)

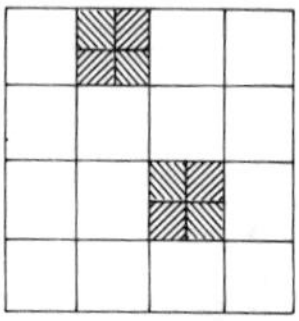

Stack bond pattern of 7⅝" x 7⅝" tiles with clusters of four **SIGNET** tiles inserted as desired. Random shading of the large tiles will enhance this pattern. (2.25 pcs. 7⅝" x 7⅝" per sq. ft., with 3⅝" x 3⅝" inserts.)

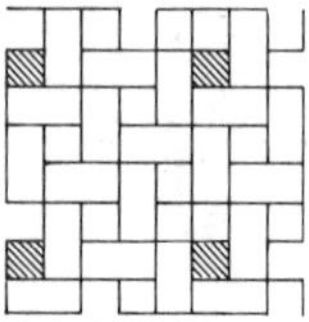

"Pinwheels" of 3⅝" x 7⅝" and 3⅝" x 3⅝" tiles with **SIGNET** tiles inserted about 2' apart. (3 pcs. 3⅝" x 7⅝" & 3 pcs. 3⅝" x 3⅝" per sq. ft.)

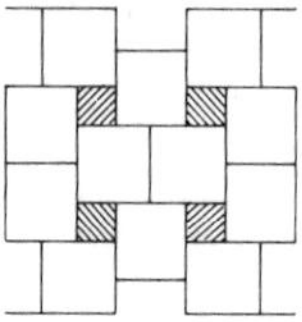

"Basketweave" pattern of 7⅝" x 7⅝" tiles with group of 4 **SIGNET** tiles inserted at broadly spaced intervals. (approx. 2 pcs. 7⅝" x 7⅝" & 1 pc. 3⅝" x 3⅝" per sq. ft.)

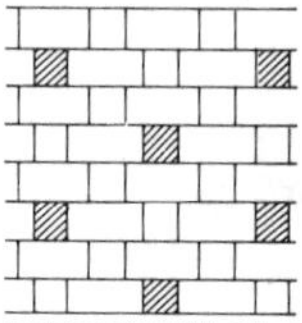

Flemish bond pattern of 3⅝" x 7⅝" and 3⅝" x 3⅝" tiles. Insert **SIGNET** tiles at selected intervals. (3 pcs. each size per sq. ft.)

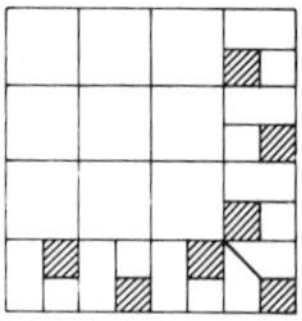

Border (or "Soldier Course") of 3⅝" x 7⅝" and 3⅝" x 3⅝" tiles, usually in a darker color than the field tile, with **SIGNET** tile uniformly inserted. (2 pcs. each size per linear ft.)

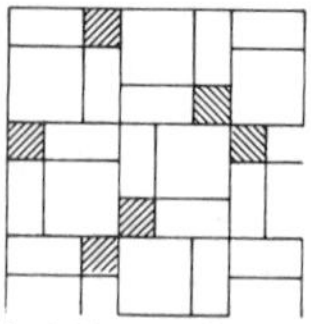

Formal random pattern of 7⅝" x 7⅝" and 3⅝" x 7⅝" tiles with **SIGNET** tiles inserted to complete 12" x 12" modules. (1 pc. ea. 7⅝" x 7⅝" & 3⅝" x 3⅝" & 2 pcs. 3⅝" x 7⅝" per sq. ft.)

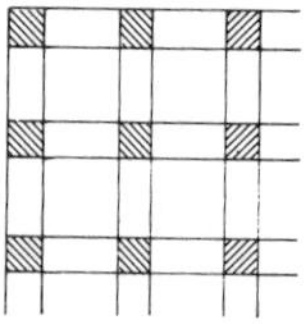

"Formal random" pattern of 7⅝" x 7⅝" and 3⅝" x 7⅝" tiles with **SIGNET** tiles inserted at intersections of grid pattern. (1 pc. ea. 7⅝" x 7⅝" & 3⅝" x 3⅝" & 2 pcs. 3⅝" x 7⅝" per sq. ft.)

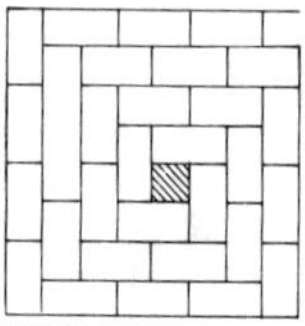

Large "pinwheel" pattern (may be extended to any multiple of 4") with **SIGNET** tiles inserted at center of each pinwheel. (4.5 pcs. per sq. ft.)

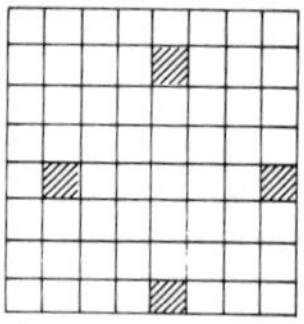

"Stack bond" pattern of 3⅝" x 3⅝" tiles with **SIGNET** tiles inserted as desired. This pattern looks best when square tiles are varying shades. (9 pcs. per sq. ft.)

SIGNET tiles are intended to be used with field tile 1/2" thick and modularly sized, that is, dimensioned to include a 3/8" joint width, so that sizes may be mixed for more interesting patterns.

Fig. 4–9C.

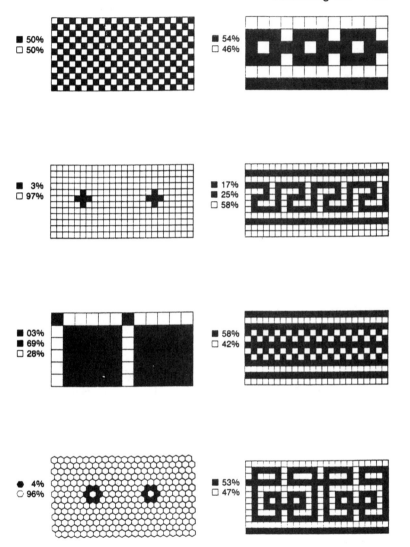

Fig. 4–10. *(Courtesy Winburn Tile Mfg. Co.)*

Table 4–1. Calculating Waste Allowances

Job Size in Square Feet	Additional Purchases
Installations up to 50 sq. ft.	14% more tile
Installations up to 100 sq. ft.	10%–12% more tile
Installations up to 200 sq. ft.	8%–9% more tile
Installations up to 300 sq. ft.	7%–8% more tile
Installations up to 1000 sq. ft.	5%–6% more tile
Installations from 1000 sq. ft. and up	3%–4% more tile

amounts are required to complete an installation. When purchasing tiles for your job, be sure to make allowances for waste, breakage, and future repair requirements (Table 4–1).

When actually laying out the installation, select tiles from a variety of different boxes so that subtle variations in color will not be apparent. Lay out the tiles from assorted boxes alongside each other. In this way, any variations will be distributed throughout your installation.

Tables 4–2 and 4–3 will provide some general guidelines for tile quantity requirements. Estimates are given to the nearest even number. Tile may be purchased in a broad range of sizes from tiny chips imbedded into sheets of varying sizes to 12″ × 12″ squares. Special order sizes and shapes are also available on request.

To find the square footage of an area to be tiled, measure the length times the width of the area. Convert the square footage to square inches by multiplying by 144. To find the approximate number

Table 4–2. Calculating Number of Tiles Needed

Square Feet to be Covered	Number of Tiles Needed			
	4″× 4″	6″× 6″	9″× 9″	12″× 12″
50	450	200	90	50
100	900	400	180	100
200	1800	800	355	200
250	2250	1000	445	250
300	2700	1200	535	300
400	3600	1600	715	400
500	4500	2000	890	500
750	6750	3000	1335	750
1000	9000	4000	1780	1000
2000	18,000	8000	3560	2000

Table 4–3   Number of Tiles Needed with Allowance for Joint Size

Number of Tile Required per 100 Square Feet	Size and Number of Tiles			
	2-1/4″ × 2-1/4″ Tile	4″ × 4″ Tile	6″ × 6″ Tile	9″ × 9″ Tile
1/8" installation joint	1740	845	385	175
1/4" installation joint	1600	795	370	170
3/8" installation joint	1475	750	355	165

of tiles to be used, multiply the length times the width of the tile size in inches and divide this number into the total square inches.

For example, a 10-foot by 12-foot floor equals 120 square feet (10′ × 12′=120 sq. ft.); times 144 equals 17,280 square inches (120 × 144: 17,280 sq. in.). If you are using 4″ × 4″ tiles (16 sq. in.), divide 17,280 by 16 and the result would be 1080 tiles.

If you are using 6″ × 6″ tiles (36 square inches), divide 17,280 by 36 and the result would be 480 tiles.

If you are using 9″ × 9″ tiles (81 square inches), divide 17,280 by 81 and the result would be 214 tiles.

Of course, if you are using 12″ × 12″ tiles, you would use 120 tiles.

All measurements should be reduced to inches so that when doing the tile calculations, all areas used are in the same units.

When 1/8, 1/4 or 3/8-inch joint separations are added into the calculations used to determine tile requirements, the number of tiles needed will be slightly less. You can use the following chart as a general guide. Always remember to purchase additional tile to allow for wastage.

Tables 4–4 and 4–5 can assist you in converting figures for your calculations.

Use the following charts if your work requires conversion from one measurement system to the other.

Tile Buying Questions

After reading this book, you will become increasingly familiar with tile, familiar enough to ask questions about a product that you will be living with for years. Some of the questions that might be of concern are:

Table 4–4. Metric Chart

To Change Metric to Inches	Use the Multiplier	The Result Will Be In	Brief Symbol
Length Conversion Information			
Millimeters	.04	Inches	in
Centimeters	0.4	Inches	in
Meters	3.3	Feet	ft
Meters	1.1	Yards	yd
Kilometers	0.6	Miles	mi
Area Conversion Information			
Square centimeters	0.16	Square Inches	in^2
Square meters	1.2	Square Yards	yd^2
Square kilometers	0.4	Square Miles	mi
Hectares (10,000/m^2)	2.5	Acres	—
Weight Conversion Information			
Grams	.0335	Ounces	oz
Kilograms	2.2	Pounds	lb
Tonnes	1.1 (1,000 kg)	Short Tons	
Volume Conversion Information			
Milliliters	0.03	Fluid ounces	fl oz
Liters	2.1	Pints	pt
Liters	1.06	Quarts	qt
Liters	0.26	Gallons	gal
Cubic Meters	35	Cubic feet	ft^3
Cubic Meters	1.3	Cubic Yards	yd^3

(cont.)

1. Is the tile you are considering for a floor definitely slip-resistant?
2. Will the tile you are planning to install resist soiling adequately?
3. Will the floor tile you are considering hold up adequately if there is a great deal of heavy activity?
4. Are sealers, waxes, or polishes necessary to protect the surfaces of the tile you are purchasing or can it be used exactly as installed?
5. Is the type of tile you are purchasing considered a low maintenance tile or is it going to require continuous care?

Table 4–4.   Metric Chart (cont.)

To Change Inches to Metric	Use the Multiplier	The Result Will Be In	Brief Symbol
Length Conversion Information			
Inches	2.5 (2.54 cm exactly)	Centimeters	cm
Feet	30	Centimeters	cm
Yards	0.9	Meters	m
Miles	1.6	Kilometers	km
Area Conversion Information			
Square inches	6.5	Square Centimeters	cm^2
Square feet	.09	Square Meters	m^2
Square yards	0.8	Square Meters	m^2
Square miles	2.6	Square Kilometers	km^2
Acres	0.4	Hectares	ha
Weight Conversion Information			
Ounces	28	Grams	g
Pounds	.45	Pounds	kg
Short tons (2000 lbs.)	0.9	Tonnes	t
Volume Conversion Information			
Teaspoons	5	Milliliters	mL
Tablespoons	15	Milliliters	mL
Fluid ounces	30	Milliliters	mL
Cups	.24	Liters	L
Pints	.47	Liters	L
Quarts	.95	Liters	L
Gallons	3.8	Liters	L
Cubic feet	.03	Cubic Meters	m^3
Cubic yards	.76	Cubic Meters	m^3

6. Is the tile you are planning to use capable of functioning adequately in a relatively damp area? Does the tile have a low moisture absorption level?

7. Is the tile color just a top glaze or does the color run throughout the tile's body?

8. If the tile is glazed, how does the manufacturer rate it on the hardness scale? See Tables 4–4 and 4–5.

9. If the tile is unglazed, what absorption rating is it given by the manufacturer? See Table 4–6.

Use the chart below if decimal equivalents are required with your work.

Table 4–5. Decimal Equivalent Chart

8ths	16ths	32nds	64ths	Equivalents
			1	0.015625
		1	2	0.03125
			3	0.046875
	1	2	4	0.0625
			5	0.078125
		3	6	0.09375
			7	0.109375
1	2	4	8	0.125
			9	0.140625
		5	10	0.15625
			11	0.171875
	3	6	12	0.1876
			13	0.203125
		7	14	0.21875
			15	0.234375
2	4	8	16	0.25
			17	0.265625
		9	18	0.28125
			19	0.296875
	5	10	20	0.3125
			21	0.328125
		11	22	0.34375
			23	0.349375
3	6	12	24	0.375
			25	0.390625
		13	26	0.40625
			27	0.421875
	7	14	28	0.4375
			29	0.453125
		15	30	0.43875
			31	0.484375
4	8	16	32	0.5
			33	0.515625
		17	34	0.53125
			35	0.546875
	9	18	36	0.5625
			37	0.578125
		19	38	0.59375

(cont.)

Table 4–5. Decimal Equivalent Chart (cont.)

8ths	16ths	32nds	64ths	Equivalents
			39	0.609375
5	10	20	40	0.625
			41	0.640625
		21	42	0.65625
			43	0.671875
	11	22	44	0.6875
			45	0.703125
		23	46	0.71875
			47	0.734375
6	12	24	48	0.75
			49	0.765625
		25	50	0.78125
			51	0.796875
	13	26	52	0.8125
			53	0.828125
		27	54	0.84375
			55	0.859375
7	14	28	56	0.875
			57	0.890625
		29	58	0.90625
			59	0.921875
	15	30	60	0.9375
			61	0.953125
		31	62	0.96875
			63	0.984375
8	16	32	64	1.00000

10. Will the tile you are planning to purchase for outdoor use hold up if used in a cold weather area where frosts are common?
11. Does the manufacturer of the tile you are considering have many years experience in the tile business?
12. Once having made a color choice, have you gone through the boxes of tile to make sure that the color variations are not too broad?
13. Are tile fixtures (soap dishes, towel racks, etc.) available in the same or matching colors as the tile you are planning to purchase?
14. Is there a good variety of trim tile available in colors matching the tile you are planning to purchase?
15. Some types of tiles will react to different kinds of foods. If the tile is to be installed on a food preparation countertop area, have you

checked that the tile will hold up to the natural acids produced by certain foods? Crystal-type tiles, for example, are particularly at risk to acid etching damage from the acids found in the liquid of lemons, oranges, grapes, vinegar, etc. Unless the manufacturer warrantees that the tiles will hold up under this exposure, they would be an impractical choice. A number of manufacturers do produce crystal-type tile that is unaffected by exposure to the liquid food acids.

You can also design your own layout using different color pens or crayons on graph paper to mark the position and color of the tiles that will form the design. Patterns may serve to highlight areas of a room, to make a long room optically shorter, a narrow room look wider, or to achieve special effects.

On your sketch, begin the design project by drawing, to scale, the exact design concept you have in mind. You are probably familiar with measurement scales from reading auto road maps. For example, one inch on a map might equal ten road miles. One inch on the drawing might equal one foot of space on the floor. This scale design will be your working model. Color the design so that it provides a fairly accurate picture of the way you would like the final project to appear. Figs. 4–11 and 4–12 show designs using different patterns.

If a curve or bend is to be part of the overall design, you may have to be satisfied with grout lines between tiles that are not equal at all points. Grout lines of varying sizes can make up for any curve space losses or gains between tiles to achieve the desired curve.

At this point in the design project, you should be able to visually count the number of tiles including the number for each color, required from the plotted graph paper. Always remember to order additional tiles both for any breakage during installation and for future repair use.

As a final check, before you permanently install the design tiles, lay them out dry in the floor space allotted to the design pattern. Leave space for grout lines between all tiles. Make absolutely sure that you are satisfied with the design before laying down the adhesive for permanent installation. If there is any doubt in your mind, move the design back to the drawing board.

If the design is satisfactory and you decide to move ahead with the permanent installation, number the tiles in the design plan, then num-

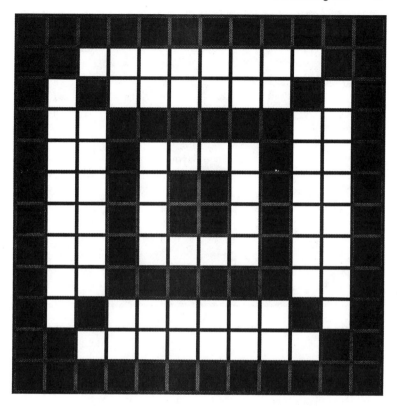

Fig. 4–11. Pattern layout showing design made with whole tiles.

ber the back of each tile with a marking pen so that it corresponds to the design on the graph paper. This makes installing the permanent design easier and quicker and insure accuracy.

The design and layout system can be utilized effectively for all kinds of floor installations including outdoor tile patios. The job begins with a scale drawing of the design and concludes with numerical identification on the reverse side of the tiles prior to permanent tile placement.

Wall Design Layouts

If a special tile wall design is being considered, sketch the artistic work on graph paper. It is important to establish visually whether the

Fig. 4–12. Design layout combining whole tiles of contrasting colors and border tiles.

design is acceptable for the particular installation as well as to fix its potential wall position.

If you are working with an individualized artistic layout to cover a large area, a large rough sketch of your particular design will be especially helpful. The sketch may be done in sections up to the actual size of the completed wall pattern. Use different color pens or crayons to indicate the color to be used in various areas. Actually place the sketch on the wall to show you the way the design will look on completion. This also allows you to make desired changes in design before you start working with the actual tiles. It will also become the basis for the next step, which is accurately drawing the design on large graph paper. Once the pattern is completed on the graph paper, an accurate count of the number of tiles of various colors can be made. Figs. 4–13 and 4–14 show various examples of wall tile layout, with and without designs and special borders.

As with all other installation schemes, when purchasing the tile, always order a sufficient quantity for potential breakage and future repairs.

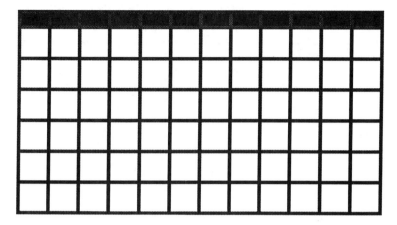

Fig. 4–13. Layout showing half tile contrasting border.

Before you permanently install the artistic tiles, lay them out dry, without adhesive, in a clear working space. Leave space for grout lines between all tiles. Make absolutely sure that you are satisfied with the pattern selected before setting the tiles in the adhesive for permanent installation. If you are not sure about the design, bring it back to the drawing board.

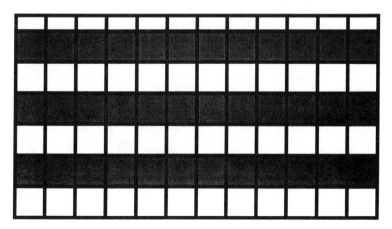

Fig. 4–14. Alternate wall layout with contrasting color and darker grout.

If the pattern is satisfactory, number the back of each tile in the design with a marking pen so that it corresponds to its place on the graph paper. This will make installing the permanent design pattern more accurate, easier, and quicker.

Original Artwork   An original piece of artwork can be developed by a person with artistic capabilities to accent a wall area. With china paint and kiln firing, this can be reproduced and fired onto glazed ceramic tiles. China paints are easily available and come in a wide variety of colors. Once the artwork is painted on the tiles, they can be taken to a local ceramic shop and fired at suitable temperatures.

There are companies specializing in this type of individualized and small run production. They not only handle the firing of the artistic tiles, but will also prepare, on order, special size and thickness tile bodies to match tile already in place.

Large Tile Murals   It is possible to purchase ready-made full wall tile murals in a variety of designs, colors, and sizes. Catalogs or specification sheets depicting patterns, colors, sizes, and other options are available from tile supply stores or from tile manufacturers.

Since mural compositions may include 150 or more tiles, the pieces in layouts should be numbered or coded to correspond to specification work sheets. This facilitates accurate placement of each tile.

Small Decorated Tiles   Specially decorated and designed tiles may be purchased for use in any room or area. These tiles, in a variety of sizes, can fit in as part of a planned wall tile installation or be used as independent decorations to surround fireplace mantels, trim kitchen backsplashes, and the like.

The multicolored designs include flowers, animals, trees, famous people, sea scenes, etc. One tile manufacturer produces a set of characters from Charles Dickens' novels, while another has a set of tiles depicting the months of the year. Decorated tiles are produced in a variety of sizes. Individual manufacturers should be queried for the availability of special designs as well as for measurements of mural and decorated tiles.

Tile Tests and Rating Charts

You should be aware of industry methods to determine the structural strength, durability, and other factors about ceramic tile. These factors can be critical as they relate to such installation techniques as the use of a beater block after tiles are placed. The breaking strength of a piece of ceramic tile is determined by the "pounds of force" necessary to break it. To perform this test, an individual tile is supported at three points. The number of pounds of force that can be applied to the tile before it breaks determines its durability. These tests are, of course, laboratory tests. A glazed wall tile should be able to tolerate a minimum of 90 pounds of force while a floor tile should be able to handle a force of 250 pounds.

In addition to being aware of the strength of a piece of tile, there are other factors that are of interest to a homeowner. Some tiles have the capacity to absorb and then radiate heat. In these times of high fuel prices, this information can be useful and economical. If the tile is to be installed in any area exposed to the rays of the sun, its capacity to absorb solar heat can be important just as is its ability to reverse the process and emit heat. The measurement of the speed at which heat can enter, pass through and be stored in a piece of tile is a measure of its conductivity. All of this information is evaluated and calculated by the tile manufacturer and should be available to the purchaser. The higher the number given to a tile's ability to absorb solar rays, the better. In a reversal of the process, when the sun's rays go down, many tiles can radiate the stored up or absorbed heat outward into a room. Some tiles can only absorb and store heat but their ability to emit or radiate it may be limited. If, when planning a tile installation, these factors are relevant to your job, check with tile manufacturer's specification sheets to make sure that the solar absorbing, conductivity, and heat emission capabilities, are available in the tile you are purchasing. Incidentally, the subsurface area upon which the tile is installed can play a role in the solar absorption and storage process. The use of dark-colored tiles as opposed to those of lighter colors can also enhance heat absorption.

The charts which follow give you methods for measuring certain of the capabilities and capacities of the tiles you are considering for your installation. They are meant to alert you to industry norms and to give you a basis for comparison.

Rating the Hardness of Glazed Tile—the Mohs Scale

In order to measure the surface hardness of glazed tile, the ceramic industry uses a scale called the Mohs Scale. The rating runs from one to ten, with the hardest surface designated by a ten and the least hard surface by a one.

The face of a glazed tile resists scratching in varying degrees. In one instance it takes a diamond to scratch the surface of a glazed tile, while in other instances the metal wheels of a heavy delivery cart may cause surface abrasions. The resistance level to abrasion is what the Mohs scale actually measures.

Before making tile purchases, you should ask for the manufacturer's standards for the abrasion resistance (hardness) of its tile. This is especially important if the tile installation area is subject to abrasion. The following ratings indicate whether a tile is suitable for use in an area subject to rough treatment.

Table 4–6. The Mohs Scale: Hardness of Glazed Tile

Use	Mohs Scale Rating
Heavy Commerical Use	8–10
Moderately Heavy Commercial Use	6–7
Light Commercial or Household Traffic	4–5

Rating the Hardness of Glazed Tile through Use

Another method for determining the visible abrasion resistance of glazed ceramics tile is offered by Mannington Ceramic Tile by Mid-State Tile Co. Although all of the usage classifications do not apply to a home tile installation, the buyer should be aware of the measurement system. The tiles are classified by their usage.

Rating Unglazed Tile for Water Absorption

When making tile purchases, the manufacturer's absorption rating for its tiles should also be requested. This is especially important if the tile installation area is subject to dampness. The following ratings indicate whether a tile is suitable for use in a particular area.

Other Tests and Standards

In addition to the standards and tests mentioned above, there are other tests performed by manufacturers of tile. Industry standards, as provided by Mannington Ceramic Tile, also include measurements of the coefficient of friction to determine slip resistance, and frost resistance.

Table 4–7. Hardness of Glazed Tile by Use

Class	Type of Traffic	Applications
1	Light traffic	Residential bathrooms and bedrooms where light footwear (slippers) are used in areas not subject to outside traffic.
2	Medium traffic	Residential floors such as dining rooms, living rooms, bedrooms and baths where normal footwear is used in areas not subject to outside traffic.
3	Medium-heavy traffic	All residential applications; commerical applications such as residential offices, passages, and lobbies that receive traffic similar to residential use excluding heavy pedestrian use.
4	Heavy traffic	All residential applications; commercial applications such as restaurants, hotels, supermarkets, schools, churches, and other public buildings excluding certain types of traffic areas.
4+	Extra-heavy traffic	All residential and commercial applications. Tile in this classification should be used where optimum durability is required for a maximum traffic load.

The coefficient of a friction test uses a horizontal dynamometer pull meter to drag a weighted shoe heel over the tile surface. An electronic scale measures *slip resistance* of the surface for either wet or dry conditions. A static coefficient of friction of 0.5 is normally used as a basis for slip resistance. Caution should always be used on any wet, hard-surface floor.

The standard test for evaluating *frost resistance* of ceramic tile is to cycle the tile first through freezing conditions, then thawing. The tile's resistance to damage and deterioration caused by extreme climate conditions is then evaluated.

All of the tests and standards are maintained by industry associations, and any additional information can be obtained through these groups.

Table 4–8. Rating Unglazed Tile for Water Absorption

Tile Category	Absorption Rating	Care and Applications
Impervious	0.5% or less	Water cannot damage this tile. It is almost completely absorption proof, and can be used indoors and outdoors.
Vitreous	0.5% to 3%	The tile has limited absorption and can be used indoors and outdoors. It is fairly easy to keep clean and does not require a sealant.
Semi-vitreous	3% to 7%	The tile absorbs water and has a tendency to stain. It must be sealed regularly as a protection. Do not install outside.
Non-vitreous	7% to 15%	The tile is extremely absorbent, and stains easily and permanently. Do not use outside.

Tile Selector

The following information was designed to guide you in the proper choice of tile for your installation. Always check the manufacturer's directions or specification sheets for specific recommendations. In order to select the proper backing and adhesive material to use with a particular type of tile, consult Chapter 6, *Adhesives, Mortars, and Grouts.*

IF YOUR ARE TILING

SUGGESTED TYPE OF TILE

Backsplash Area

Use glazed tile for kitchen and bathroom sink backsplash areas. The tile should be thin and light enough to enable it to hold securely to wall surfaces.

Bathtubs (wall surfaces)

Used glazed tile. The tile should be thin and light enough to enable it to hold securely to wall surfaces. For user safety, consider tiles with a textured surface.

Bathroom Floors

Use a glazed vitreous or semi-vitreous tile. For user safety, select tiles with a textured or slip-proof surface.

Countertops (kitchens)   Use a glazed vitreous or semi-vitreous tile. Make sure tile can tolerate food acids. Use only a natural sealer on surfaces where food is to be prepared.

Doors (frame areas)   Use glazed or unglazed tile. The should be thin and light enough to enable it to hold securely to frame surfaces.

Family Room (floors)   Use a glazed vitreous or semi-vitreous tile. Consider tile with a textured or slip-proof surface for safety's sake. Consider the stain resistance of the tile as food will be used in area.

Entranceway   Use a glazed or unglazed vitreous or semi-vitreous tile. Consider a tile with a textured or slip-proof surface for safety's sake.

Fireplace (mantel-frame)   Use a glazed or unglazed vitreous or semi-vitreous tile. Tile should be thin and light enough to hold securely to framing surface. Check local fire codes to be sure the installation is in compliance.

Kitchen Floors   Use glazed vitreous or semi-vitreous tile. Consider a tile with a textured or slip-proof surface. If kitchen area is to receive a great amount of active use, purchase extra strong tiles.

Living Areas   Use glazed or unglazed tile. Tile should be thin for interior walls and light enough to hold securely to wall surfaces.

Patios (frost areas)   Use unglazed vitreous tiles. Consider a tile with a textured or slip-proof surface. Provide good water

Patios (warm areas)

Shower Stalls (floor area)

Shower stalls (wall area)

Stairs (horizontal surfaces)

Stairs (vertical surfaces)

Windows (frame areas)

drainage around patio so melting ice and snow does not have an opportunity to work on tile areas. Use glazed or unglazed tile. Consider a tile with a slip-proof surface. Use glazed, vitreous tile or unglazed mosaic tiles. Consider tiles with textured or slip-proof surfaces for safety's sake. Use glazed vitreous or semi-vitreous tile. Unglazed mosaic tiles may also be installed in this area. Use glazed or unglazed vitreous or semi-vitreous tile; see floor tile. For safety's sake use a tile with a textured or slip-proof surface. Install these tiles after the vertical or riser tiles have been placed. Use glazed or unglazed tile. Tiles should be thin and light enough to hold securely to riser surfaces. Use glazed or unglazed tile. Tile should be thin and light enough to hold securely to window framing.

Use caution when tiling areas subject to frost and serious water flooding or extreme dampness. Special precautions should be taken before tiling is initiated and the proper tiles should be purchased for these installations.

CHAPTER 5

Preparing for the Tile Job

Installation Components

A tile installation generally has four components: surface preparation, adhesive application, tile setting, and tile grouting. In some instances, a fifth step, sealing, is used to complete the job.

The surface of the installation, the floor, wall or other areas on which tile will be placed, has to be prepared to accept the ceramic product. In addition to simply accepting the squares, rectangles, pieces, or sheets of tile, the surfaces must also be capable of retaining the tile in place on a long term basis. Surface areas may require filling, leveling, smoothing, priming, waterproofing, and often sound deadening. This chapter covers surface preparation.

Floor and Wall Installation

Nothing can move forward in a tile installation until the surfaces that will support the tiles are properly prepared. Adhesives and other substances with varying chemical components will be placed in contact with these surfaces. The walls and floors that will be the tile's undersurfaces may respond in a variety of negative ways unless properly treated. In addition, to carry the weight load of leveling fill, adhesives, and the tiles, it is important to be sure that the structure can bear up, long-term, under the additional weight.

Another consideration is the condition of the surface. A wall or floor that is uneven or not level makes tiling difficult and detracts from the appearance of the finished job. Fig. 5–1 shows the pouring of a special leveling underlayment as one method of correcting this problem.

Some installations require construction of complete framework and retaining subsurface to hold the tile. If, for example, the job calls for a tile-covered cabinet enclosure around a hanging bathroom sink, the undersink area would have to be framed in and covered with a strong material to which tiles could be secured.

> **Installation Tip:** *Attention must be given to the undersurfaces, the installation areas on to which the tile will be set. These areas can be every bit as important as the finished tile work. Give them your attention and you will have a neater, stronger job with long lasting qualities.*

When a full room, wall and floor tile installation is planned, always complete the wall tile work before you start the floor tiling. It is easier to have a clear floor space to do the heavy work as you put up the wall tiles. Moreover, the unfinished floor takes the punishment of tile frag-

Fig. 5–1. Pouring self-leveling underlayment material to level a problem section of a floor. *(Courtesy Summitville Tile)*

ments, grout, and adhesive spills that might pose problems on a completed surface.

Setting the wall tiles in place before the floor tiles offers an additional installation advantage. It makes it easier to set in the cove base tiles, the tiles that will join the wall and floor, if wall tiles are put up first.

Tables 5–1 and 5–2 summarize the recommended preparation work for floors and walls. They also give information on surface condition and some special treatments.

Preparing Floors to Receive Tile

Base Molding Removal

While wall tiling should be completed first, floor and wall preparation may take any order which seems convenient. If the floor is the only area in a room scheduled to be tiled, the wooden toe or base molding—the decorative framing that is installed around the lower perimeter of the room—may have to be removed. Use a pry bar for this process so that the molding can be removed undamaged. It can then be reused after the tiles are installed.

Installation Tip: *The standard method for pry bar removal is to start about 12 to 18 inches from a room corner. The pry bar is slowly forced behind the toe molding and the wood is gently pried. As sections are moved from the wall, a small piece of wood or shim is placed behind the molding. The pry bar is worked down the wall until all of the molding is released.*

Floor Height Considerations

Whether the new floor covering to be installed is wood, a resilient linoleum tile, carpeting, or ceramic tile, consideration must be given to floor height measurements as they relate to other items in the room such as existing doors. The level of the floor may change considerably as a result of the thickness of the planned new floor covering. It is important to be aware of this added thickness factor so that clearances can be checked and corrected before the floor installation work has begun.

Each floor covering has a normal body thickness factor. A piece of

Table 5–1. Suggested Floor Preparation

Undersurface Material	Location	Current Surface Condition	Suggested Preparation Before Tiling	Special Pre-Installation Treatment
Concrete	Outside	Uneven, not smooth, irregular surface.	Level surface; build up with mortar mixture or manufacturer's special leveling mix.	Waterproof area where necessary; patch problem areas before leveling.
	Inside	Uneven, not smooth, irregular surface.	Level surface; build up with mortar mixture or manufacturer's special leveling mix.	
Plywood exterior grade	Inside	Subject to water exposure.	Waterproof undersurface before proceeding.	Test undersurface area for water accumulation problems.
		Area not subject to water exposure.	Make any necessary repairs to board surfaces (e.g., patch all holes).	
			Level all uneven floor surfaces with special manufacturer's product or a mortar mixture.	
Older ceramic tile already in place	Inside	Make sure tiles are securely in place. Surfaces should be clean.	If leveling is required on any low spots, use mortar or special manufacturer's leveling mix.	
Painted floor surfaces			Rid area of paint completely. Sand by hand or machine.	Use putty knife to rid floor area of large, loose pieces of paint.
Metallic floor surfaces			Break out rusty areas; level areas with special manufacturer's leveling mix.	Apply anti-corrosion material to protect undersurface areas.

Table 5–2. Suggested Wall Preparation

Undersurface Material	Location	Current Surface Condition	Suggested Preparation Before Tiling	Special Pre-Installation Treatment
Gypsum board surfaced wall areas	Inside	Uneven, not smooth, irregular surface.	Level surface; build up with proper fill material. Check for pre-mixed manufacturer's filler material.	If using dry set mortar for the installation, prime the gypsum board. If using an adhesive for the installation, priming useful but not necessary.
Painted wall surfaces	Inside	Flaked or chipped paint areas.	Hand or machine sand all paint off of wall surface. Chip off large or flaking pieces with putty knife to speed up process.	
Concrete surfaced wall areas	Inside	Uneven, not smooth, irregular surface.	Level surface; build up with proper fill material.	
	Outside	Uneven, not smooth irregular surface.	Level surface; build up with proper fill material; check for pre-mixed manufacturer's filler material.	
Backerboard surfaces	Inside and Outside	Space between pieces of backerboard as a result of installation.	Use joint paper and material between all board joints. Sand after application and drying for smooth surface.	

91

ceramic tile, for example, may run from ⅜ to ¾ inch thick. A 4″ × 4″ tile is generally ½ inch thick. To the tile thickness must be added the thickness of any underlayment. This might include the mortar repair bed required on a job plus the bed of adhesive used to bind the tile to the floor base. Each material, because of its design, generates a certain height buildup that may materially affect other segments of a room, such as entrance doors, cabinet and closet doors, or radiation.

Installation Tips: *Fortunately, in most instances, wood doors can be trimmed to fit the new requirements. Measure the door, allowing for the required measurement clearance. Remove the door from its hinges. Saw or shave the extra wood off the door. Replace it on its hinges.*

In order to obtain the proper clearances, a tile that will be used for the installation is placed on the floor near the door. A second tile is placed on top of this tile and measurement marks are made on the door's bottom section. Use a level or straightedge to assure that a level cut line is marked on the door.

The door is then taken out of its frame by removing the hinges. Some doors have hinge pins that can be easily tapped out while other doors have hinges requiring removal of hinge screws.

After the door has been cut to the correct measurement, it is rehung in its frame by replacing hinge pins or hinge screws. It may be necessary to place a piece of wood under the door to support and hold it firmly while hinges are being replaced.

If the door is constructed of a plastic material, check with a building supply house to determine the most effective way to trim to size.

Heating Units

Home heating radiator units represent another measurement challenge and may present particular problems. Some space must be maintained between the floor and the radiation for air and heat flow. To cut off all space would be to curtail air movement. It may be necessary to have a plumber raise the baseboard radiation or cast-iron radiator to maintain satisfactory heat flow tolerances between the new flooring and the radiation. Warm air and air conditioning duct grates will also have to be raised when floor measurements change as a result of tile installation. If there are any doubts about these heating unit measurements or installation requirements, check with a plumber or heating technician.

Installation Tips: Before an installation is started, any old flooring material, such as loose tile or linoleum, must be removed. The floor must be thoroughly cleaned and absolutely dry.

If the floor on which the tile is to be installed is concrete, it should be free of holes and other irregularities. If there are small holes or uneven spots in the concrete floor, use concrete patching compound to correct the problem areas. If the concrete floor is painted, the painted surface must be sanded down to assure a workable bond with the tile.

A thin, skin coat of concrete patching compound can be applied to damaged plywood and other wood surfaces. If concrete is to be placed over a wood floor, be sure that the wood is grease- and dirt-free. Use a grease cleaner to assure a good bond between wood and cement.

If a concrete or plywood floor requires a modest degree of leveling before tiling, a self-leveling underlayment material can be used.

If a degree of sound deadening is required in the room where the tile is to be installed, special sound deadening underlayment material is available at the tile supply store. This product is put down before the tile is installed.

Checking Floor Installation Supports for Tile

A standard floor installation consists of two distinct layers. The lower layer is referred to as the subfloor. Based on the age of the home, the subfloor may consist of rough tongue and grove lumber nailed to the floor joists. Sometimes these boards are nailed diagonally to the joists, while at other times they may be put in at right angles. Today, 4′ × 8′ sheets of compressed, treated, special wood-like materials may be used for subflooring. Once the subfloor is installed, a layer of black building paper is placed on top, and the finished flooring is installed at right angles to the subfloor. Do not use compressed board for the finished floor surfaces. In many instances, the adhesive will not take properly.

Always check the floors on which tiles are to be installed. If the surface area is wood, it should consist of at least a ⅝″ smooth, exterior grade plywood. A lighter surface can result in warping and other problems. Make absolutely sure that the old wood floor is securely nailed down. Tile is not designed to survive well over a springy surface. If the floor is warped or damaged in any other way, either cut out the bad section or tear up the entire floor and replace it with a new wood floor. Make sure all nails are hammered down or removed and are not sticking up where they may cause tiles to crack.

Installation Tips: If the current floor requires repair, use ⅝″ indoor-outdoor plywood to cover it. In addition to providing a new surface, the new plywood will increase floor stability. Ordinary or thinner plywood and particle board lack the stability required for ceramic tile backing surfaces.

Glue the sheets of plywood down using construction adhesive between the old and new floor boards. Use ring shank nails or drywall screws to further secure the boards. The nails or screws should be placed about every 6 inches. Leave about ¼″ of space between each of the new pieces of plywood. Make sure that the joints of the newly-placed playboards are not in line with the joints of the boards below.

Some Floor Support Problems

Check the joist areas under the floor. These are the wood beams (usually 2″ × 8″, 10″ or 12″) that actually carry or support the floor. Bridging supports may have to be installed to provide the floor area with additional strength in sections where the tile is to be installed (Fig. 5–2). The bridging supports may be simple 1″ × 4″ pieces of wood or metal supports designed specifically for this task.

If you have a sagging floor area and the section is over a basement, a screw jack or lolly column can be installed to combat the problem. Using the jack and a board crossing a number of the beams, the jack

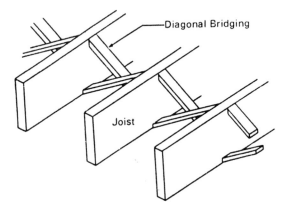

Diagonal Bridging

Joist

Fig. 5–2. Diagonal bridging can provide the floor with extra strength.

head is slowly tightened by screwing against the beam board. The tightening may raise the sagging area sufficiently to correct the problem. This is a job usually handled by a professional.

If you have a floor area that creaks when walked over, try to repair this section before installing the tile. Once the tile is put in place, there is no way to reach the problem area. Try to locate a floor joist near the creaking section either by sound tapping around the area or using a magnetic nail-searching tool. Once the beam is located, hammer large finishing nails through the flooring into the joists.

If the floor to be tiled is the bathroom, fixtures will have to be disconnected before the installation can begin. The toilet bowl and any sink fixture supports will have to be removed so that the floor is clear for work. Tile can be placed around fixtures, but it makes a much neater and professional-looking job if the fixtures are removed, tile installed in areas where fixtures sit and then the fixtures replaced over the newly completed tile floor.

Floor Base Options

There are floor base options for almost every ceramic tile installation. The subsurfaces can be wood, concrete, installed ceramic tile or metal. The selection is dependent on such factors as availability, cost,

> **Installation Tip:** Be gentle when removing toilets and other bathroom fixtures so that you have a clear and empty bathroom floor to tile. These porcelain fixtures break easily. Remember to shut off and/or disconnect all water supply valves. Drain the toilet tank and the toilet bowl thoroughly by flushing and wiping out any remaining water. Use the proper tools on the nuts and bolts securing the fixtures so that no undue pressure is applied that may crack fittings. Put the nuts, bolts, and procelain fixtures in a safe place for reuse. After the tiling job has been completed and allowed to dry, replace all fixtures and reconnect all piping. Check with your plumber concerning any seals that may need to be replaced.

ability of undersurface areas to bear the weight, existing floors, outside conditions that may affect the surface, bonding and tile, among others.

A *concrete cement base over a waterproof plywood subfloor* is one installation possibility. In this instance, the floor area over the subfloor is properly framed in and a concrete setting bed of at least 1-1⁄4″ is poured over wire mesh reinforcement secured to the wood floor. The tile is installed on top of the concrete. As advised elsewhere in this book, always soak the tiles before installation on concrete surfaces. Care must be taken to insure that the joists and the plywood floor are sufficiently reinforced to handle the weight of this type of job.

Epoxy mortar, cement mortar, or an organic adhesive can also be used to install tiles *over wooden floor surfaces.* Use primer over floor surfaces requiring this treatment whenever indicated. Primer is generally recommended because of its ability to seal out moisture and to develop a strong bonding coat between tile and backing surfaces.

If the *floor upon which tile is to be installed is concrete, a dry-set or latex Portland cement mortar* can serve as the bedding coat in which tile is set. An *organic or epoxy adhesive, dry-set mortar, or cement mortar* may also be used to adhere tile to a concrete floor or slab.

> **Installation Tip:** Follow manufacturer's recommendations when selecting the correct bonding material for a particular surface.

Cleaning Concrete Surfaces

At one time, the recommended method for removing old bonding and adhesive material from concrete floors so that a tile installation could be effective, was to "acid etch", or wash the floor with an acid preparation. The idea was for the acid to consume or loosen any offending material from the floor so that it could be cleared and not hamper tile adhesion. This process is no longer recommended since some of the adhesive compounds, according to experts in the field, can prevent the acid wash from ever reaching the concrete.

Today, the suggested remedy when the possibility of a bonding problem exists is to "scarify," or scratch, the concrete surface by mechanical means. There are a number of scarifying methods that may be called into use which require equipment and professional attention. One method may be sandblasting, which is not practical if only a small floor area is involved. If the area is small, a coarse stone on a terrazzo grinder may be used to reclaim the concrete floor surface.

A system using equipment called a Blastrac is the latest recommendation for cleaning a concrete floor of curing compounds and other hard to handle waste. The Blastrac is a complete, self-contained cleaning system which first blasts and then reclaims its abrasive material. Using a rapidly rotating blasting wheel, a metallic abrasive is blasted against the concrete floor surface. A part of the device recovers the abrasives and contaminants and passes this material through an airwash separator. The abrasive is further separated and returned for reuse. The contaminants move in another direction and are collected for disposal.

Preparing Walls to Receive Tile

Before any wall tiling can be started, the walls must literally be stripped bare. Wall surfaces may have a great many items that can interfere with a tile job, including picture frame hooks, electric outlet and switch plate covers, wood stripping, nails, shelves, small hanging cabinets. Based on the style of tile installation planned, the room baseboard may also have to be removed. See section on pry bar and toe molding removal. The objective of removing all items is to have a clean wall so that measuring and working can be accomplished easily and efficiently.

Installation Tips: Use a carpenter's level whenever you do any work on a floor. If the floor is not level, plan on making the necessary corrections before you start the tile job. A tile floor installation over a floor that is not level and not corrected will usually end up visually unacceptable and possibly impractical.

If the present floor is out of level, it may be brought back to a level position with a number of techniques. A thin leveling frame can be built around the necessary areas of the wood floor and a bed of cement poured and leveled using the frame as a guide. The wood floor should be dirt-and-grease free.

A special plastic underlayment can be spread over the floor in a number of layers until the surface is level. Each coat, usually ⅛" thick, must be permitted to dry between courses. When the leveling material has dried thoroughly, the tile floor can be installed.

Before using any method that is liable to add weight to the floor, check the underside of the subfloor to be sure that it can carry the load weight.

If you are planning to add any electrical fixtures to the room, the time to do the job is before you tile. Call in a licensed electrician well ahead of starting the project to learn about any special electrical plans and approval requirements.

Checking a Wall for Plumb

For a good tile installation, a wall should be perfectly plumb, not leaning inward or outward. How far off perfection is too much? This is a difficult question to respond to. If tile is installed on a wall that is seriously out of plumb, the tile job will reflect the variation. On the other hand, a major wall repair for a minor plumb variation may not be practical. The best answer is to approach the job from a visual perspective. If a wall has serious leaning problems, consider making corrections before starting. If a change in wall position or plumb appears to be too large an investment, it may be more practical to use another wall covering until the wall change can be made.

In an earlier chapter dealing with locating the vertical line of a wall, we discussed attaching a plumb line to the ceiling next to the section of the wall to be worked on. The same plumb line can be used to tell whether a wall is leaning inward or outward from floor to ceiling. To get a plumb line on a particular wall, attach the string to a ceiling point approximately ½ to 1 inch from the wall. Let the body of the metal cone fall free and clear the wall. Gently drop the metal cone to the floor but do not let it touch the floor. If the wall appears to be extremely out of plumb, the plumb bob may have to be attached at a point further out on the ceiling than 1 inch.

When the metal cone stops swinging, you will notice its position relative to the wall. If the wall is in plumb, the distance from the wall to the string will be the same from top to bottom. If the wall is leaning, the wall to line measurement at the top and the bottom will vary. The degree of variation will indicate the distance or inches the wall is out of plumb.

Do not confuse the discussion of the wall's plumb with the wall's vertical line. Although both calculations depend on the plumb line device, the plumb of a wall is a measurement of its perpendicular condition, while the vertical line is a chalk drawn line made by a cord to assure a straight line for tiling from left to right.

Repair Options

If there are serious plumb problems with a particular wall, there are a number of options to repairing the offending section.

The entire piece of wall can be replaced. To do this, the plaster, or gypsum board must be removed down to the supporting studs, and wood or metal lath. A level is placed on the bare studs or background structure. Any section of the support that is not perfectly level is shimmed so that the wall background support is completely level. Shims are pieces of wood or other material attached to the supporting studs that are cut to insure leveling of any surface attached to the supporting pieces. After the entire wall area has been properly shimmed and leveled, new wallboard is attached. The edges of the newly-installed wallboard must be properly taped and plastered to make smooth, even joints. The wallboard must be coated with a primer or sealer before tile installation.

Another effective wall repair option is to install thin vertical lumber strips, called furring strips, from top to bottom every 16″ along the problem wall, shimming the strips to compensate for the tilt (Fig. 5–3).

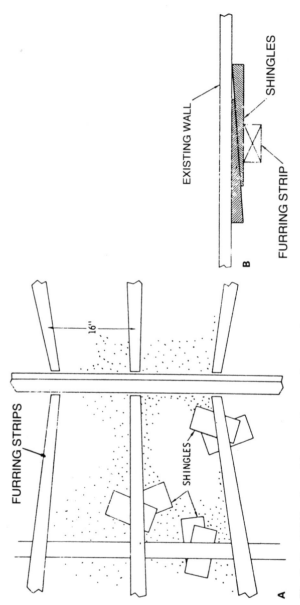

Fig. 5–3. (A) Furring strips can be used to repair walls out of plumb. (B) Top view of use of shingles to adjust for differences in plumb.

New wallboard, gypsum, or wall finish, must now be installed on top of the furring pieces. The edges of the newly-installed wallboard must be properly taped and plastered to make smooth, even joints. The board must be treated with a primer or sealer coating before tile installation.

Installation Tip: If you do not have a plumb line in your tool kit, you can make a substitute. A lead fishing or other formed weight and length of line can be turned into a plumb line that will do the job.

More on Wall Repairs

Just a floor areas that are to accept the tile installations should be level, firm, and secure, wall structures must also be able to support the tiles that are to be applied. Not only should the wall studs and lath backing be in good shape, but the wallboard also must be capable of supporting the adhesive material and the weight of the tiles. If the walls require repair, the work must be handled before the tile installation begins.

Small Holes and Cracks

All small nail holes and other holes and cracks in the wall should be repaired. This can be done with pre-mixed spackle compound purchased in any building supply or hardware store. The process requires some work but a professional job can be turned out with little experience.

For small holes, all loose areas around the hole are cleaned out, then the compound is worked or putty-knifed into the hole or crack. The work area is then smoothed with a putty knife. In an hour or so, after the compound has dried thoroughly, the area is sanded to even it with the wall.

Medium-Sized Holes

If the hole is medium-sized, all loose areas around the hole must be broken away. Wool insulation or other filler material is hand packed into the hole and the hole completely filled with the spackling compound (Fig. 5–4). The installation level of the compound should be just a bit above the old wall surface to allow for any shrinkage. The repaired area is left to dry completely and then sanded to make it flush with wall. The drying process for larger holes will take much longer than for small holes.

> **Installation Tip:** Be prepared for the extra work and drying time requirement on your work schedule.

Large Holes or Significant Damage

If wall damage is substantial, a new piece of gypsum or wallboard may have to be inserted into position before tiling can be started. Using a measuring square, draw in a square or rectangle around the damaged wall section a little larger than the broken area. Now use a sharp utility

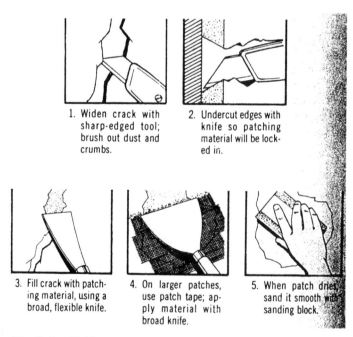

1. Widen crack with sharp-edged tool; brush out dust and crumbs.

2. Undercut edges with knife so patching material will be locked in.

3. Fill crack with patching material, using a broad, flexible knife.

4. On larger patches, use patch tape; apply material with broad knife.

5. When patch dries sand it smooth with sanding block.

Fig. 5–4. Making neat, long-lasting wall repairs

knife to cut into the penciled lines of the square or rectangle. The cutting process is continued until all the damaged pieces within the pencil-marked areas are removed. After the pieces have been removed, all cuts should be squared off, then smoothly beveled toward the inside of the surrounding wall.

A patch piece of new gypsum, a few inches larger on all sides than the hole that has been cut out, is now measured and cut. The additional size of the patch is to give a firm gluing surface when it is attached to the inside of the old wall. Drill two small holes, several inches apart, in the approximate center of the patch piece. Pass a piece of wire through these holes and temporarily secure the wire ends around a dowel stick or other handy piece of wood. The dowel should be 3 or 4 inches larger than the hole in the wall. Spread a good bonding glue around all edges of the patch piece, on the top of the piece. Using the dowel and wire as a handle, ease the patch piece into the hole area, glue side toward the outside wall. The patch may have to be slid into the cut out wall section on an angle. After the patch piece has been passed into the hole, draw it up firmly against the sides of the wall, using the wire and dowel handle for leverage. Slide the dowel stick across the opening that has been cut in the wall and secure the insert by winding and twisting the wire tightly around the dowel handle. Do not use too much pressure or the patch piece may snap. Let the glue harden for at least 24 hours before proceeding further with this project.

After the glue has been allowed to dry, detach and remove the wire and dowel handle from the holding position. Make sure the patch is secure by testing for any loose areas. If everything holds well, place patching compound around all of the four inside edges of the patch. Allow this compound to dry thoroughly.

Once the compounded edging dries, you can now either fill the entire patch area with patching compound until the area is level with the old wall, or you can cut another gypsum board patch sized to fit into the damaged section. If the hole is exceptionally large, the latter option may be the best.

To do this effectively, re-measure the area and cut a piece of wallboard to fit the hole comfortably. This top patch will be glued into place on top of the inner patch. First start by removing the backing paper from one side of this top patch by moistening the paper with water and gently scraping it off with a knife. The objective of this exercise is to give you a rough surface for the finishing spackle when the patch is put into place. Now, on the reverse side where you still have paper, cover the paper with glue and fit it into the repair area. The fitting sequence will be paper side on patch one to paper and glue side on patch two. After the patches have been allowed to dry thoroughly, apply the spackling compound, let it dry completely again and sand until it is flush with the old wall surface. When using patching compound, always remember the compound has a tendency to shrink a little.

Installation Tips: Allow a sufficient amount of time for the patching compound and the glue to dry between each operation. If drying time is not long enough, the glue can come loose and the patching compound break down. This can destroy the entire job and the repair effort will have to be repeated.

If the wall area to be used for the tile installation has sustained a great deal of damage, entire sections of the wall may have to be replaced. It is even possible that all of the walls in the entire room may need to be changed because of deterioration.

You will have to allot time to do this additional carpentry work or you may want to call in a professional to handle this portion of the job.

Tiling Walls with Special Undersurfaces

Most wall surfaces, unless they are brand new, usually have some covering already in place. The walls may have been painted, wallpapered, covered with a plastic laminate of some type, or even a layer of old ceramic tile. Each of these wall coverings requires a degree of attention before the new tile is installed if the new tiles are to adhere properly.

Installed Ceramic Tiles

New ceramic tiles can be installed over existing ceramic tiles provided that the original tiles are solidly in place and the bond to their backing surface is secure. If there are loose tiles they should be removed, cleaned, and cemented before new tiles are placed over them.

Once all the loose tiles are in firmly in place, clean the entire old tile area completely with a tile cleaner. Sand all of the old tile faces lightly so that they have a rough surface area. Clean the tiles again and apply a primer coat. If a mastic adhesive is to be used on the job, a very thin coat of the adhesive can be used as the primer over the old tiles. After the primer dries completely, the area is ready for the adhesive of the new tile installation. Primer helps seal a backing surface and also enhances the bonding capabilities between tile, adhesive, and wall or floor surfaces.

If there is any sign of dampness or water damage behind the old tiles, the cause must be determined and remedied before new tile is installed. Sometimes the remedy is simple, but more often it requires a great deal of work.

Unless corrected, the initial cause of the dampness may reappear. If the portion of the wall on which the new tile to be installed is in such an area, the practical and cautious approach is to remove the old tile as well as the wall material supporting the tiles. Let the area air dry completely, making sure that the supporting wood studs or laths are thoroughly dry before proceeding. Replace the common wallboard or plain gypsum board with sheets of *backer board.* This type of board is also called green board, concrete glass-reinforced fiber board or water-resistant gypsum board. The construction of the water-resistant backer board protects the backwall areas from water damage. In addition, backer board is easy to obtain, simple to measure, cut, and install and tile adheres well to its surface.

Installation Tips: Once the cause of dampness has been located and resolved, do not rush to close off the area. Allow the air to thoroughly dry the section before proceeding.

Ceramic tiles themselves do not deteriorate with moisture exposure, but some backing materials do. This can result in tiles pulling loose and other problems.

Painted Walls

Walls in most homes today are painted. Painted surfaces do not in any way preclude a tile installation. Before a tile installation is begun, however, the painted wall area must be properly prepared. This is done by first scraping away any loose paint. If the paint has a glossy or semi-glossy appearance, hand sand or use a sanding machine on all areas to provide a rough wall surface to help tile adhere. Flat painted surfaces do not usually require sanding unless there are uneven areas.

Installation Tip: *Always use a dirt and grease remover to wash down the walls that are to be tiled. Dirt and grease can prevent good adhesion and bonding.*

Wallpapered Walls

Wallpapered walls can be very finicky. At one time, wallpaper will powerfully adhere to a surface, while under other circumstances it can sag and loosen. The wrong type of tile adhesive, for example, can cause a wallpaper reaction and subsequent loosening.

The best thing to do is to remove the paper completely. The fastest way to do this is with a wallpaper steamer. It takes a bit of elbow grease but the paper can be removed from large areas fairly easily.

Installation Tip: *A small amount of wall surface sandpapering can be helpful to clear the walls of any tiny pieces of wallpaper that may remain after the steaming process. These are very tiny pieces of rolled up paper that may have separated from the back of the wallpaper. After all the wallpaper has been removed, allow the steam-treated wall areas to dry completely before applying adhesive.*

Laminated Plastic Products

Some walls have a plastic laminate firmly attached to the base wallboard. These are strong, colorful sheets, usually running from floor to ceiling, that were in vogue at one time. Ceramic tile can be placed over this type of wall covering if the plastic surfaces are sanded and roughed up. After the sanding is completed, the plastic surfaces should be cleaned thoroughly to remove any residue before the adhesive is applied.

> *Installation Tip:* *The wall area to which plastic laminates are attached should be checked for dampness, stability, or other conditions affecting the adhesion of the tile before adhesive is applied. Make sure that the condition of the wall can securely sustain the addition of the tile.*

Paneled Surfaces

Paneled surfaces may require some preliminary work before a tile installation can be initiated. Most panel boards are ordinarily waxed, polished, or otherwise treated. The wax or polish built up through many applications must be removed. There are a number of wax and polish removers on the market to do this.

After the wax is removed, the wallboard, whether made of ordinary plywood or an expensive panel board, has to be sanded down to improve its bonding surface for the adhesive. The panels can either be hand or machine sanded using a moderately heavy grade of paper designed to work on wood. After the panels are sanded, they should be cleaned thoroughly to remove all dirt and sanded grit. A surface primer should then be applied.

> *Installation Tip:* *Before you begin working on the wall panels, remove all protruding nails, screws, and other items attached to panel surfaces. Fill all holes, breaks, and cracks on the panels with a wood mastic. When the mastic dries, sand the patched areas and clean all the surfaces.*

Priming Surfaces

Priming of walls is done for several reasons. A primer coat can seal out moisture. Dampness creeping through a board to its back bonding surface can play havoc with a tile installation. A good primer coat also helps to improve the bond or the holding quality between the tiles, adhesive, and the backing surface.

There are many forms that a primer coat may take. The primer may simply be a thinned coat of ordinary flat paint or a thinned layer of the same adhesive that will be used to adhere the tile. Some manufacturers will require a special primer coat mixture to match a particular job.

The rather thin makeup of a primer coat allows it to be rapidly applied to the wall area with a paint roller or wide brush.

Installation Tip: *Quick and easy to apply, a protective primer coat can result in a secure, long-lasting tile installation. Be sure to apply a primer coat whenever one is called for. If in doubt as to whether to use a primer on a job, check manufacturers' recommendations or apply as a precaution.*

CHAPTER 6

Adhesives, Mortars, and Grouts

When the surface areas are as smooth, as even, and as level as possible, appropriate adhesive should be applied to accept the tile. Detailed coverage of surface preparation is found in Chapter 5. The function of the adhesive in all installations is to bond the tile securely and permanently to the undersurface. In addition, appropriate adhesives must be used for tiles installed outdoors; for floors or walls; or in specialty areas such as fireplace mantels, sunrooms, steps, or swimming pools.

Apply the adhesive a workable section at a time, then set the tiles in place according to a predetermined pattern. It takes some time for the adhesive holding the tiles in place to set or dry thoroughly, but once it does, grouting is the next order of business. The grout, a flexible product, fills the small spaces between the rows of tiles that were created when the tiles were placed. Fig. 6–1 shows the steps in adhering the tile.

Some jobs require sealing. The sealer is a type of finish applied to protect the tile surface and complete the installation. In some instances, the sealer is a penetrating type which is actually absorbed by the body of the tile as well as providing surface coverage. In other circumstances, the finish merely provides surface protection and a gloss.

Fig. 6–1. Cutaway view showing tiling steps including adhesive on base or foundation, tile on adhesive, grout on tile. *(Courtesy Summitville Tile)*

Adhering the Tile

Thick Set—Portland Cement

Mortar is a building material composed of lime and cement mixed with sand and water (Fig. 6–2). Cement is a mixture of lime and clay mixed with water. Portland cement apparently earned its name from the way the hardened product resembles a tough stone quarried in Portland, England.

For many years, the standard method for setting tiles was to place the tiles in a prepared bed of Portland cement or mortar. The process is still in use today for specific installations. Thick-set or mortar installations are particularly in favor in areas of the country where homes are constructed on slabs rather than over foundations.

The cement or mortar, often called *thick bed, thick set* or *full mortar-bed* is mixed to a workable consistency and placed on the metal lath or other retaining surface on which the tiles are to be installed. The thickness of the mortar-setting beds generally runs from ¾″ to 1″ for wall tile jobs and approximately 1-½″ on floor installations. To install

Fig. 6–2. Mixing mortar for a tile installation. *(Courtesy Summitville Tile)*

tile over the mortar base, a thin bond coat of plain cement is mixed and evenly applied across the surface of the mortar bed. This must be accomplished while the mortar is still plastic or pliable. The coating cement mixture should be approximately $\frac{1}{32}''$ to $\frac{1}{16}''$ in thickness. Once this process has been completed, the tiles are pressed into place in the cement coating layer. A beater block is next used to level all of the tiles that have been installed.

Thick set also has a number of positive and negative considerations. It is particularly useful when working on heavy duty surfaces. If, for example, a floor surface is uneven, a heavier application can be used as a leveling agent. A scratch or light coat of mortar can first be used to fill and smooth out subsurface problem areas.

On the other hand, it takes experience and skill to use this product satisfactorily. Mortar is a heavy product and cannot be used in all installations or on every surface if the underlying structure is not strong enough to hold it.

Additionally, when tiles are used over mortar, the general rule calls for them to be soaked before installation is begun. The newer thin set tile installation methods do not require this additional procedure.

Application Tips: *If the mortar is to be placed over large floor or wall areas, properly designed expansion joints should be used on the job prior to the installation. An alternative technique is to make knife slices every two or three feet through the still-pliable setting bed. This helps to handle any shrinkage that may occur in the mortar body as it dries. If resistance to water penetration is a factor on the job, a protective membrane of polyethylene film or other moisture barrier should be used before putting the mortar in place. Be sure that whatever you use is tightly sealed at all joints so that moisture or water cannot penetrate.*

Remember that nonvitreous tiles, tiles which have not been fired to very high temperatures and still retain some porous qualities, must be soaked in water before they are installed in a thick-set bed. This process is used to make sure that the tiles do not draw water out of the cement bonding coat, causing it to set up improperly.

Thin Set—the Quick and Simple Method

Thin-set mastic adhesives have opened up a range of tile installation possibilities for the do-it-yourself homeowner. In taking all factors into consideration, the new thin-set, thin-bed method for installing tile shortens job time, permits tile applications on a wide variety of backing surfaces, and makes it easier for individuals with minimum experience to turn out a professional tile installation job. The mastics are easy to use and eliminate the need for thick-set mortar on a tile installation. This, in turn, permits using tile on jobs that normally could not bear the weight of the heavier mortar and the tile. Tile soaking before use is not necessary. This saves job time and also does away with the nuisance of soaking.

The thin-set tile setting process is especially useful where rapid installations are called for, where a minimum floor or wall finish thickness is important, or when the installation may be exposed to heat, steam, chemicals, or a constant flow of water. Almost any level surface will accept thin-set adhesives. This mastic product requires only a spread of about ⅛″ thick as opposed to the relatively thick layer required with a thick-set adhesive. Mastics can be quickly and easily applied with a notched trowel. A gallon of quick-set adhesive covers approximately 50 square feet of floor or wall areas.

Application Tip: There are times when the thin-set and the thick-set or full mortar methods can be combined. A layer of thin-set may be floated or placed over the thick-set mortar after it has been cured or dried. This combination allows the installer to level a difficult surface when required and also to obtain the performance of a thin-set mastic adhesive.

Types of Adhesives

Thin-Set Adhesives

A choice of three thin-set adhesive options are available for tile installations. These include organic, epoxy, and dry set or cement-based products. As with almost any product on the market, each of the options offers advantages and disadvantages and has its proponents and detractors.

Organic adhesives, also called mastics, are probably the most widely-used tile installation adhesives. Mastics cure or set rapidly by the evaporation or air drying process. They are ready for use directly from the container in which they are purchased and do not require the addition of any liquid or powder for activation. They are low cost and lightweight and are applied to floor, wall, and other surfaces in one thin layer.

Used to secure tiles to floors (Fig. 6–3), walls, and counters, organic adhesives are compatible with gypsum board, backer board, plaster, sheetrock, concrete wood, plywood, existing older ceramic tile, and other surfaces.

Mastic adhesive also offers a degree of flexibility to the installed tiles. This is important if you are working with a sheetrock surface that may have a tendency to bend a bit if pushed or leaned on. The response to pressure depends on the frame construction behind the sheetrock. The mastic is not as rigid as other adhesives and permits a little flexibility so that tiles are not as likely to break or loosen.

Fig. 6–3. Laying tile in on mastic. *(Courtesy Summitville Tile)*

On the negative side, the mastic product is not effective for leveling an uneven surface. If leveling is required, an additional board surface must be installed over the problem area before application of the adhesive. In addition, mastic adhesives do not have a great resistance to chemicals and solvents. If the tile installation will be exposed to chemical agents, select another adhesive. Epoxy-based adhesives have a higher resistance to chemical damage than mastic adhesives, while latex-Portland cement mortar has an even better tolerance.

Application Tips: *If the weather is extremely humid during the tile installation process, be sure to allow additional time for drying before doing any further work with the tile. Although mastics are known to cure fairly rapidly, let the job cure for a span of 24 hours if possible. Check local building codes for any restrictions on the use of mastic products in your area.*

Mastic adhesives come with two different bases: solvent and latex. Each has a specific installation use.

The *solvent-based mastics* are particularly useful where the adhesive and the tile will be exposed to water on a frequent basis as in a bathroom, tile shower, or sink countertop installation.

Application Tip: *Solvent-based mastic adhesive may be flammable. When you use a solvent-based mastic, make sure that there are no open flames in the work area. Ventilate the room well. The fumes from this mastic can be irritating to some people.*

The *latex-based mastics* are generally used when water around the installation area is not a problem. This adhesive can be used for floors, walls, and even bathroom areas away from water exposure. Latex-based mastic adhesive is not generally flammable nor particularly irritating; however, caution should be exercised anyway when using this product.

Application Tip: *Latex-based mastics are sensitive to heat before they are cured. If you are installing tile around a fireplace or in areas with inlaid, underfloor heating pipes, turn off all heat sources before starting the mastic and tile installation. Give the mastic at least 24 hours to dry before turning on the heat source.*

Adhesives with an *epoxy base* offer another set of options. Epoxies, however, are far more sensitive than other adhesive mixtures. They must be mixed accurately in order to reach the correct setting time or pot life, and they should also be applied at exactly the right temperature in order for the installation to be effective.

Application Tips: *If an epoxy-based adhesive is used, be sure to use an epoxy-based grout with the installation. If you are working on a budget, compare the price of epoxy-based adhesive to other types of adhesive that may be used as effectively. Do not install an epoxy adhesive when the temperatures fall below 40°F or above 90°F.*

The *epoxy mortar system* is one of two epoxy-based adhesives. This system uses an epoxy resin and epoxy hardener that are mixed just before application. This system is applied in a single thin layer, and has a number of strong points to consider. The epoxy mortar system is a good choice when a particularly strong bonding surface is required, when exposure to chemical agents is a possibility, and when surface wear will be considerable. This epoxy mortar system has more flexibility than other epoxy adhesives discussed in this chapter.

Epoxy adhesive is another option made for thin-setting tile installations. It is economical and has excellent bonding strength. It is easy to

Application Tip: *The epoxy mortar system is generally used for commercial tile jobs. It also can be used on particularly demanding home tile installations. Always follow manufacturer's instructions for mixing, as each company may produce an adhesive with different mixture requirements.*

apply on floors, countertops, and the like. The chemical and solvent resistance of epoxy adhesive is better than products such as organic adhesives but not of the highest level. Epoxy adhesives work well on concrete floors, wood, plywood, and existing older ceramic tiles.

Do not smoke around or while using thin-set adhesives. Air conditioners and dehumidifiers should be turned off when using thin set to install tile. These units absorb moisture and may take too much moisture out of the room where the installation is taking place, which in turn may allow the adhesive to dry too rapidly and become a problem.

Application Tip: *Epoxy adhesive may be difficult to apply to walls because it has a tendency to sag. Check the manufacturers' use recommendations and instructions.*

Cement-Based Mortars/Adhesives

Dry-set mortars are generally used for such specialty tile installations as swimming pools, deep set bathtubs, whirlpool baths, or fireplaces. Although the word mortar is in the name, the product has no filling or leveling qualities. However, it is particularly effective on surfaces that are not entirely smooth.

Unlike tiles applied with Portland cement mortar as an adhesive, dry-set mortar tiles need not be soaked prior to installation. This adhesive has a strong resistance to water and impact.

Dry-set mortar is applied in a thin layer and can be used on such surfaces as concrete, backer board, brick, existing ceramic tiles, insulation, styrofoam board, and other surfaces. It is not recommended over such surfaces as plywood, metals, hardboard, or plaster walls. Dry-set mortar does not adhere to the smooth surfaces of these products.

Application Tip: *Dry-set mortar is a non-flammable adhesive which is purchased in dry powder form. It is mixed with water based on the manufacturer's instructions. This type of adhesive is particularly suited to outdoor tile installations. However, although this mortar is not affected by water contact, it is not capable of forming a true water barrier.*

Latex Portland cement mortar, a member of the cement family, is a blend of sand, Portland cement, and a latex additive. A quantity of the dry cement powder is mixed with liquid latex to a heavy creamy consistency. This mixture is allowed to set for about fifteen minutes and then remixed completely. The manufacturer's instructions should indicate the proper thickness. The mix should not be runny or form troughs and ridges when troweled onto a surface for use. If the mix is too thick, it will be difficult to trowel and the mixture should be reworked.

Less rigid than dry-set mortar, the product serves many of the same adhesive purposes. Latex Portland cement mortar may be used particularly in tile installations that may not ever be thoroughly dry, such as swimming pools. For example, manufacturers recommend that a completely-installed Portland cement mortar tile installation in showers or swimming pools be allowed to dry for periods of from two weeks to two months before exposure to water.

Application Tip: *Latex Portland cement mortar sets up rapidly. As soon as the adhesive begins to film over, scrape the mortar away and use a fresh batch of adhesive. Do not use this latex or any other water-mixed adhesive next to wood floors or other wooden products. If the adhesive comes in contact with wood, moisture absorption can develop that may eventually destroy it. If the wood in any way provides a support to the tile installation, this can be a serious problem.*

Finishing the Installation

Once the adhesive has set or cured and the rows of tiles are evenly and firmly in place, the finishing touches must be applied. The spaces between each tile must be filled with a substance which is strong, long-lasting, and decorative—grout. The grout filling between the tile spaces binds the tiles to each other. Alien substances like water, dirt, and grease must be prevented from causing damage between and under the tiles. Grout has this protective capacity. Where tiles are placed in a pattern, grout also has the potential to highlight the designs.

The choice of grout depends heavily on the kind of tiles, the area in which the tiles are located, the adhesive used with the job, and the width of the joint between the tiles.

Application Tips: If irregularities in the alignment or placing of the tile develop as a result of the structure of a wall or floor, these irregularities can be visually toned down by filling the spaces between tiles with a darker-colored grout. The situation can also be partially rectified if a grout color closely matching the tile is used.

Be careful when using dark grouts with light-colored tiles. The grouts may stain the tile surfaces, especially the surfaces of unglazed tiles.

Grout joints run from about a narrow ⅛ inch to a wide ½ inch (Fig. 6–4). If a joint is wider than ⅛ inch, always use a mortar-based grout for the installation. A wide grout joint tends to be weaker than a narrow joint and has a tendency to crack more easily when too much stress is placed on it.

Grout joints can visually affect the tile installation in a number of ways. For example, if the goal is to deemphasize the grid-type structure of the tile job, the grout color selected should be the same as the tile color. In this way, the lines in the layout appear to disappear.

Fig. 6–4. Unsanded wall grout, designed for narrow joints, has been used on this installation. This type of grout is usually used with glazed tile. *(Courtesy Summitville Tile)*

Most grouts are offered in a wide selection of colors; in fact, some of the color possibilities surpass automobile color options. One manufacturer offers nearly one hundred different shades. Grouts, like tile adhesives, also come in a number of material or installation options. They are produced using a variety of ingredients to match installation specifications and some adhesives. The three types of grout available include epoxy-based grout, silicone rubber grout and cement-based grout.

Applying Grout

The technique for applying grout is simple. Make sure the tile and spaces between them are clean and water free. Use a rubber-faced trowel to pick up a quantity of the grout from the container. Spread the grout diagonally across the face of the tiles. Move any excess grout onto other tile areas in the installation and wipe away any remaining grout with a clean, damp sponge or cotton cheesecloth. Once the grout is dry enough, it will form a haze on the surface of the tiles. Polish this surface with a dry cloth.

Industry technicians strongly recommend the use of 100% cotton cheesecloth pads to wash grout residue off tiles. Research, according to the experts, indicates that a cheesecloth pad can provide the minimum quantity of water, pack the grout tighter into the joints, and allow the grout to be finished at a more uniform level in the joints. A cheesecloth cleanup pad has a more abrasive quality than a sponge and needs less water to remove excess grout.

Types of Grout

Epoxy Grout

This type of grout, highly resistant to chemical action, uses epoxy resins and a hardener in its formulation. It has extremely high bonding strength and its resistance to impact is excellent. When epoxy adhesive and epoxy grout are used together on a tile installation, the structural strength of a floor installation, for example, is measurably increased.

This makes it an excellent choice for tile installations in work areas. Epoxy grout is not easy to apply as it has the consistency of heavy syrup.

Application Tip: *When planning to use epoxy grout, a sufficient space between tiles and tile rows must be allowed so that the grout mixture can fill in the open spaces. Space between normal thickness tiles should usually be at least 1/4".*

Silicone Rubber Grout

This is a truly flexible grout product. The main reason for its elasticity is that its single component is nonslumping silicone rubber. Once the silicone grout is applied and cured, which it does rather rapidly, it is resistant to moisture, cracking, crazing, mildew, and shrinking. Most important, silicone grout is stain resistant.

While this type of grout is for interior use only, it will tolerate prolonged subfreezing, hot, or humid conditions. On the down side, silicone grouts are slightly more expensive than cement grouts, and are not available in colors. Silicone grout may be purchased only in white and clear. Silicone grout should not be used in kitchen applications such as countertops and food preparation areas. The chemicals in the grout may be dangerous if they come into contact with food.

Application Tip: *Silicone grout is especially useful in installations where there is the possibility of slight tile movement or shifting as may occur when a sheetrock backing has been used. Because of its structure and design, silicone grout is particularly useful around bathtub and shower edges.*

Cement-Based Grouts

There are three types of cement-based grouts. They include sand-Portland cement grout, dry-set grout, and commercial Portland cement grout. The base of all of these grouts is Portland cement.

*Application Tips: Always use a rubber-bodied trowel when apply-
ing this type of grout to the face of glazed tile. If you do not, you may
scratch the tile faces by forcing the metal trowel blade and the abrasive grout mixture together against the tile surface. The rubber
trowel blade eliminates this possibility because of its flexibility.*

*You can color cement-based grouts yourself. Coloring agents
may be purchased at the tile supply house and mixed with the individual cement grouts. Be cautious when using these coloring agents as
they may stain tile surfaces. Place a sample of the colored mixed grout
on a piece of scrap tile and check for any color changes or damage
before spreading across a complete work surface.*

*If possible, store grout in a moisture-proof area. Cement grout
tends to pick up humidity, harden, lump up and lose its value. If hard
pieces have formed in the storage bag, throw away the lumps before adding water and other material.*

The *sand-Portland cement grout* is field-mixed, that is, it can be
mixed right on the job as needed. This type of grout is particularly
useful with ceramic mosaic tiles, quarry, paver tiles used in floor or
wall installations. There are proportion formulas to follow for mixing
the cement and the fine grade sand. These mixtures depend on the
width of the spaces or joints between the tiles into which the grout
is to be floated. For example, the mixture for joints with widths up
to and including ⅛ inch would be one part Portland cement to one
part sand. If the joint is up to and including ½ inch wide, the mixture used would be one part cement and two parts sand. If the joint
is over ½ inch wide, one part Portland cement to three parts sand
would be the selected mixture. A portion of approximately ⅓ part
lime can be added to any of the above mixtures to provide strength
and some elasticity.

If water retention is important, *dry-set grout* is a good grout
choice. Dry set grout is a mixture of Portland cement and additives that
have similar characteristics to dry-set mortar. In fact, the two dry-set
products complement each other on a tile installation.

Dry-set is not particularly suitable for floor tile installations. It is,
however, used for ordinary wall grouting. Normally, there is no need to
pre-soak the wall tile area before applying dry-set grout. If the resi-

dence is in an area where the weather is hot and dry, it is a good installation technique to soak the wall before application. In this way, the grout will properly set, not dry out and shrink rapidly when applied. You should be aware that the additives in dry-set grout assist the grout in its ability to resist stains and reduce powdering.

Application Technique: *When using dry-set grout, the grout may be given a greater degree of strength if the tile area is wet down during the installation process. This wet-down process is also known as damp curing.*

Commercial Portland cement grout may be the grout of choice when a water-resistant grout mixture of uniform coloring is required. The product, a mixture of Portland cement and a variety of other ingredients, is particularly adaptable as a grouting complement to thick-bed Portland cement mortar tile installations.

Application Tip: *Always damp cure tile wall and floor areas when applying commercial Portland cement grout. After the grout has been worked into the spaces between tiles, clean the tile surfaces and polish them with a dry cloth. The grout curing process takes about three days.*

Latex-Portland cement grout is actually a potpourri grout mixture. It consists of the ingredients of dry-set grout, sand-Portland cement grout, commercial Portland cement grout and a latex additive especially designed for the mixture. The Portland cement and the sand are mixed together in quantities suggested by the manufacturer. Liquid latex, also in manufacturer-recommended amounts, is added to the mixture. This grout can be used for most residential and commercial tile grouting applications. The mixture is not as rigid as other cement-based grouts and requires no damp curing to bring out its best qualities.

Special Use Mortars and Grouts

Furan Mortar and Grout

Although you may not need this type of mortar or grout for your current tile installation, you should be aware that *furan mortar and grout* products have an exceptionally high level of chemical damage resistance. If, for example, you were developing a chemical laboratory as a business in your basement or garage and wanted to protect the floor, wall, and counter tile installation areas against chemical spill damage, these mortars and grouts would be ideal for the job.

Furans in the structural makeup of these adhesive and grout products are concocted from furfural alcohols. They are resistant to inorganic chemicals, and most organic corrosive solvents as well. The mortars and grouts are mixed by combining a resin and a catalyst on the job as needed. They set rather rapidly and require handling skill.

Furan mortars and grouts are costly but as they serve a particular installation purpose, cost may not be a vital factor in the consideration.

Application Tips: *If you are using furan mortar to cover a concrete surface, an asphalt membrane is necessary between the base concrete and the furan mortar. If the mortar is to be placed over a wooden surface prior to tile installation, however, no membrane or separation material is required for the job.*

If the correct epoxy mortar is used for the tile underlayment and furan grout is used to complete the tile installation, no waiting time between application and subsequent use is required. Other forms of mortars, epoxy systems, and grouts require drying and sealing periods ranging from hours to days.

Fungus- and Mildew-Resistant Grout

This type of grout has been formulated to resist the growth of most active types of fungus and mildew in many home environments. In addition, the grout has the capacity to resist the so-called black molds, which have a tendency to discolor standard grouts and to make a tile installation appear dirty.

Although the active ingredients in the formulation are reported to be ecologically safe, most manufacturers of this type of grout suggest that it not be used where food is prepared.

Available in an assortment of colors, fungus- and mildew-resistant grout is particularly useful in baths and shower rooms. Installation for this grout product follows the same general rules as other grout products.

Application Tip: Fungus- and mildew-resistant grout can usually be put into use after 48 hours, although it takes seven days to cure thoroughly. Some manufacturers suggest a 3-day wet cure and a 4-day dry cure to increase the hardness of this type of grout.

General Tips for Grouting

- Purchase a sufficient supply of grout to cover your project. This is especially important if the grout is to have a special coloring.
- Always read and follow the manufacturer's instructions. These techniques have been tested, tried in the field, and have proven useful.
- Before you begin a grouting job, remove all installed spacers or other items you have used to mark or hold tiles.
- Be sure that tile areas are clean before you grout. Wipe the tiles thoroughly to remove accumulated dust and dirt. These items can contaminate the grouting material.
- Check the areas between the tiles which are to be grouted. These areas must be free of dirt, water, or any substance that may be covered with grout.
- Always use clean containers and tools for mixing grouts.
- There are chemical preparations available to make grout installation easier. A commercial grout release placed on tiles before grout installation is helpful during the cleanup process. Another commercial preparation cuts down on the development of grout haze.
- When doing the actual grouting work, be sure that you spread the grout over the joint surfaces until it is flush with the surrounding tiles.

- If a grout joint is over ⅛ inch, always use a mortar-based grout.
- Pack each joint between tiles completely to be sure that all air pockets are completely eliminated.
- Keep off the grouted tiles until the adhesives or dry-set have had ample opportunity to dry or cure thoroughly. Manufacturer's directions will suggest drying or curing times. Curing is the length of time it takes for the moisture in the adhesive to evaporate completely.
- Always keep the room in which tile has been bonded well ventilated.

Finishing the Job—Caulking

When a secure, permanent, waterproof sealant is required around or between a sink, bathtub, shower, plumbing fixture, or expansion joint, the most effective method is caulking. Silicone rubber or vinyl acrylic caulking are good choices. These caulking products are pliable, putty-like, and work equally well on indoor or outdoor installations. Caulking is flexible enough to flow into, around, between and under fittings and objects of all kinds. This material also serves as a protective buffer between expansion joint materials that do not contract or expand

Table 6–1. A Handy Grout Reference Chart

Type of Installation	Grout Application
Glazed Wall Tiles	1/3/4/6
Glazed Floor Tiles	2/3/4/5/6
Mosaics	1/2/3/4/5/6
Floor Mosaics	1/2/3/4/5/6
Wall Paver-Quarry Tiles	1/2/4/5
Floor Paver-Quarry Tiles	1/2/4/5
Constantly Wet	1/2/3/4/5/6
Intermittently Wet	1/2/3/4/5/6
Exterior Tile	1/2/3/4/5

PRODUCT KEY
(1) Commercial Portland Cement Grout
(2) Sand-Portland Cement Grout
(3) Dry-set Grout
(4) Latex-Portland Cement Grout
(5) Epoxy Grout
(6) Silicone Grout

at the same rate of speed or distance, and require this type of filler material.

A caulking product is generally applied using a caulking gun, a piece of equipment designed specifically to handle prepackaged caulk cartridges. The caulking is premixed and used without any additives exactly as it flows from the container or cartridge. The size of the cut made on the cartridge's nosepiece or nozzle and the pressure applied on the levered handle of the applicator determines the quantity and thickness of the caulk bead that flows from the cartridge onto the work area.

Both silicone caulking and water-based vinyl caulking are available in clear, white, or shades to match most grout colors.

Vinyl acrylic caulking is a little easier to work with than its silicone rubber counterpart. Any excess vinyl caulking can be cleaned up using water while silicone caulking must be scraped away. No matter which type caulking is used, the application area must be absolutely clean and dry. It should also be oil-or grease-free to insure a strong caulk bond.

Sample Product Information Tables

The following reference charts are samples of those available from industry suppliers. They cover the use of mortars, adhesives/mastics and grouts. Product information charts of this type are usually available on request. Names and addresses of these companies are in the supplier section of this book.

Table 6–2 suggests mortars and additives for wall installations while Table 6–3 reviews similar information for floor tile installations.

Table 6–4 is a Quick Selector adhesive/mastic chart for wall tile jobs.

Table 6–5 covers the selection of adhesives/mastics for floor tile installations.

Table 6–6 provides grout choices for wall tile installations.

Table 6–7 discusses grout selection possibilities for floor tile installations.

There are a reasonable number of application options to select from in each category. If product information is available, it is suggested that these sources be checked.

Table 6–2. Quick Selector Mortar and Additive Chart for Wall Installations

Subsurface Material	Location	Area Condition	Type of Tile	Suggested Treatment or Product Mix
Concrete Concrete Block Masonry	Inside	Damp/Wet Area	Vitreous, semi-vitreous, non-vitreous	Dry set mortar/dry set mortar with polymer additive
Concrete Concrete Block Masonry	Outside	Damp/Wet and Dry Areas	Vitreous tile and certain mosaics; porcelain tile	Dry set mortar/dry set mortar with Polymer additive
Concrete Concrete Block Masonry	Inside or Outside	Wet Area	Vitreous tile, certain mosaics	Dry set mortar with Latex Additive
Backer Board Surfaces	Inside	Wet or Dry Areas	Vitreous, semi-vitreous, non-vitreous tile	Dry set mortar Dry set mortar with polymer Priming/leveling additive where required
Gypsum Wallboard	Inside	Dry Area	Vitreous, semi-vitreous non-vitreous	Dry set mortar Dry set mortar with polymer Priming/leveling additive where required
Older Ceramic Tile Already in Place	Inside	Glazed Tile Subsurface Unglazed Tile Subsurface	All types of tile except impervious porcelain	Dry set mortar Polymer additive

Table 6–3. Quick Selector Mortar and Additive Charts for Floor Installations

Subsurface Material	Location	Area Condition	Type of Tile	Suggested Treatment or Product Mix
Concrete	Inside	Light to medium wear/traffic	Vitreous	Dry set mortar Dry set mortar with polymer additive, also latex and acrylic latex additives
Concrete	Inside	Medium to heavy wear/traffic	Vitreous	Dry set mortar Dry set mortar with polymer additive, also latex and acrylic latex additives
Plywood-Exterior	Inside	Residential	All types of tile	Dry set mortar Dry set mortar with polymer additive
Older Ceramic Tile Already in Place	Inside	Glazed tile Subsurface Unglazed tile Subsurface	Vitreous except porcelain	Dry set mortar Dry set mortar with polymer additive, also latex additive

129

Table 6-4. Quick Selector Adhesive Chart for Wall Tile Installation

Subsurface Materials	Location	Current Surface Condition	Type of Tile	Suggested Adhesive
Concrete/Masonry	Inside	Wet	Vitreous Semi-vitreous Nonvitreous	Multipurpose mastic adhesive " "
Concrete/Masonry	Inside	Dry	Vitreous Semi-vitreous Nonvitreous	Multipurpose mastic adhesive " "
Gypsum/Wallboard	Inside	Dry	Nonvitreous Semi-vitreous Vitreous	Multipurpose mastic adhesive " "
Backerboard	Inside	Wet	Vitreous Semi-vitreous Nonvitreous	Multipurpose mastic adhesive " "
Older Ceramic Tile Tile Already in Place	Inside	Wet or Dry	Nonvitreous Semi-vitreous Vitreous	Multipurpose mastic adhesive " "

Table 6–5. Quick Selector Adhesive Chart for Floor Installation

Subsurface Materials	Location	Current Surface Condition	Type of Tile	Suggested Adhesive
Concrete	Inside	Light use / No heavy foot traffic	Vitreous Semi-vitreous Suggest flat back tile	Multipurpose mastic adhesive
Plywood-Exterior Grade	Inside Floor	Dry	Vitreous Semi-vitreous Nonvitreous Suggest flat back tile	Multipurpose mastic adhesive
Plywood-Exterior Grade	Inside Countertop Areas	Dry	Vitreous Semi-vitreous Nonvitreous Suggest flat back tile	Multipurpose mastic adhesive

Table 6–6. Grout Selection Chart for Wall Installations

Location	Suggested Joint Width	Types of Tile	Suggested Treatment or Product Mix
Inside	1/16"- 1/8"	Nonvitreous, glazed tile	Acrylic latex additive, Unsanded mix (glazed tile)
Inside	1/8"-1/2"	Vitreous tile, mosaic	Portland cement, acrylic latex additive
Outside	1/8"-1/2"	Vitreous tile	Portland cement, acrylic latex additive

Table 6–7. Grout Selection Chart for Floor Installations

Surface Material	Location	Suggested Joint Width	Type of Tile	Suggested Treatment or Product Mix
Concrete	Inside	Use 1/8" minimum joint width	Vitreous Nonvitreous	Portland cement blend acrylic latex additive
Plywood	Inside	Use 1/8" minimum joint width	All types of applications	Portland cement blend, epoxy mortar mix, acrylic latex additive
Old /In-Use Vinyl	Inside	Use 1/8" minimum joint width		Portland cement blend, epoxy mortar, acrylic latex additive
Metal	Inside	Use 1/8" minimum joint width		Epoxy mortar mix
Kitchen Counters	Inside	Use 1/8" minimum joint width	Stain resistant types of tile	Epoxy mortar mix

CHAPTER 7

Laying Out the Tile Job

Layout Preliminaries

The tile, adhesive, and grout have been selected and purchased. The tools are neatly in place and ready. The room has been cleared of all hangings, furniture, and other impediments that might slow down the installation. It is now time to get down to work and map out the job.

A few words of caution first. Working with tile can create a great deal of fine dust, since mixing, cutting, chipping, sawing, and sanding will be involved. If possible, put up barriers between the areas where work will be done and other areas to reduce dirt infiltration. A large piece of plastic tacked to the door frame can be used as a flexible barrier.

Always use safety glasses when doing any cutting or grinding. Small pieces of glass- and stone-like tile can break off and move with incredible speed and pressure when tile is nipped, crushed, or sawed. This safety precaution should never be ignored.

In the mixing process, ingredients in grouts and adhesives can sometimes get on the hands and body. Any residue should be washed off with clean water as soon as possible. If there is any possibility of an allergic reaction from exposure to the chemicals in the mixes, plastic or rubber gloves should be worn. A dust mask should also be used when mixing materials and sanding or sawing. Before any adhesive product is even opened for use, it is always wise to read the manufacturer's instructions and cautions printed on the bag or pail.

Plans

There are sound reasons for developing room layout plans before starting an installation. In complicated plans, layouts are imperative to achieve the look and quality you want (Fig. 7–1). The working lines that result from such a plan can be extremely useful in determining wall or floor reference and focal points. Tile layouts can be tested, and if necessary, changes and adjustments can be made in the layout before permanent installation takes place. The layout will also provide an indication of how much tile cutting will be necessary on the job, and will pinpoint areas in the installation where cut edges will be the least noticeable.

Fig. 7–1. Over 20 different types of ceramic tile ranging in size from 1 inch to 12 inches; 4" × 8"; 8" × 12" squares and rectangles are used in this dining environment. Covered with tile are walls, floor, stairs, pool, furniture and columns. *(Courtesy Italian Ceramic Tile)*

> **Installation Tips:** *Develop a floor or wall tile layout plan that uses as many full tiles in the installation as possible. Tiles will have to be trimmed on every job because no room is perfectly square. Where possible, place cut tiles where they will be noticed the least. The most visible focus point in any room is the area directly opposite the doorways. In bathrooms, the focal point is usually just above the sink or bathtub.*

Tools

The most useful tools for laying out wall and floor lines include a plumb bob, carpenter's square, chalk line, ruler or measuring tape, marking pencil, a straightedge and/or a layout stick.

Laying Out the Floor Tile Installation

It is assumed that the preliminary floor preparation has been completed. Earlier chapters have been consulted and the subsurface is now adequate to handle the forthcoming tile installation.

If there were sagging spots in parts of the floor, the section has now been adequately supported. If necessary, the floor has been leveled properly. If a new subfloor was needed, it has been installed. If the subsurface is concrete, any depressions and rough areas have been taken care of. Floor sanding and priming work, if required, have been completed. The floor area is ready to be marked up for the actual tile installation.

The Working Lines

There are a number of systems that are used to center tile installations, provide evenly-sized borders, etc. Tile craftspeople use whatever system they are most comfortable with. Indeed, some will simply start in one corner of a project and keep going until they are finished, regardless of the fractional tile pieces required at the end of each row. More aesthetic results can be achieved, however, by utilizing working chalk lines as discussed below.

Chalk lines should be considered as the basis and beginning of a complete floor tile installation. In order to lay ceramic tile, working lines are recommended to insure a neat, orderly installation and provide a practical working guide. To create working lines for your tile installation, follow the steps below.

1. Locate the approximate center of the floor. Clearly mark the area with a chalk or pencil cross.

2. Position and secure a chalk line from one side of the room to another through the center point mark. Snap the line so that a chalk line marks the floor from room edge to room edge.

3. Move, position, and secure the chalk line again so that it runs from one side of the room to another through the center point mark at right angles to the chalk line just made. Snap the line so that a chalk line marks the floor from room edge to room edge going in the opposite direction. The chalk lines on the floor will cross each other at right angles. The room where the installation is to take place will now be visually divided into four parts (Fig. 7–2).

Be sure that the lines, where they intersect on the floor, are at an exact 90-degree angle. This can best be accomplished using a carpenter's square. The square is placed alongside the marked lines to prove the angle measurement.

If the room is out of square, set up your working chalk lines using

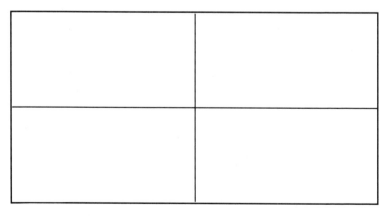

Fig. 7–2. Strike a vertical chalk line across the floor from one wall to another through the center point mark, at right angles to the existing line.

the following process. Place the carpenter's square down on the floor in the squarest corner. At the inner or bisecting point of the carpenter's square, secure one end of the chalk line. Use the carpenter's square on the adjacent corner of the floor. Secure the other end of the chalk line in the inner portion or bisecting point of the carpenter's square. Snap the line so that a chalk line marks the floor. Repeat the procedure until all four corners of the room are squared off with chalk lines. The intersecting chalk working lines can be put in place either before or after the room squaring process has been completed.

The resulting job of squaring will leave uneven portions of flooring alongside the walls which must be tiled. The tiles can be cut to fit the uneven sections against the walls after the main section has been tiled.

4. Lay a test row of tile along the chalk line that runs from the center of the floor at the marked intersecting point. Carefully lay this row of tiles, dry without any adhesive, along the working chalk line that goes from the center to one room edge. Leave space for projected grout joints or tile spacers between tiles as they are temporarily placed.

Some chalk line position changes may be required after this test layout. If the last or finishing tile that is placed in the test line must be cut to less than half its size to fit in the row, the chalk line can be readjusted and restruck so that the last tile in the row is at least a half of a full tile. This may not always be possible, but it should at least be a potential target. This process can be accomplished by measuring the remaining space in the row of tiles. Divide the measured distance in half. From the chalk center line, use this figure to make a new mark on the floor to the left of the original chalk line. Strike a new line and lay out the test line of dry tiles and joint spaces again. Note: If the test tiles are laid down from the center to the left side of the room instead of the right, the new chalk line would be to the right of the original line.

The line adjustment, right or left of the center line, will affect the size of the opposite layout square and the tiles it contains. The chalk line adjustment should now permit a half tile (more or less, based on measurements) to fit comfortably at the end of the row in the quarter section being worked on. Tiles in the opposite chalk-marked quarter will fit accordingly.

5. When the first tile layout test has been done and the chalk line on the floor properly adjusted, if necessary, for the balance of the tile installation, it is time to lay a test line of tile along the opposite chalk line. This is the line that runs at right angles to the first line. Repeat the

procedure outlined above making the necessary changes in grout space or readjustments in the chalk line to fit the tiles in place. Once all of the tiles are placed and fit satisfactorily, the test tiles can be picked up and the permanent installation of tiles begun by filling the squares created by the chalk lines. Spread adhesive material in the work area and install the tile permanently.

Floor Tile Layout Systems

There are a number of actual layout techniques that may be used to set ceramic floor tile in place. The names of the systems reflect their appearance when viewed from above. They are generally referred to as the *step* system, the *pyramid* or *running bond* technique, the *grid* or *graph* installation method, and *corner wall* system. There are other installation techniques available as well as variations to those systems described below.

The Step Tile Installation System

In the step system, tile is installed in quarter sections of the floor. This method uses the working chalk line divisions of the room as guides.

The installation starts with three tiles. Tile 1 is butted up against the chalk angle marking the exact center of the floor. Tile 2 is installed alongside the first, on the horizontal chalk marking line. The third tile is set in place above tile 1, butted up against the vertical line which forms a right angle. Visually, the tiles have formed their first step.

> **Installation Tip:** Remember to put the spacers between the tiles or leave space for grout rows.

The third, fourth and fifth tiles are placed next in the step system. Tile 4 abuts tile 2; tile 5 is placed above tile 2 and abuts tile 3; tile 6 is placed above tile 3. Tiles 4, 5 and 6 now form the steps. Another layer of tiles, 7, 8, and 9, are set in place next. Tile 7 fits above tile 6, abutting one side of the right angle chalk line. Tile 8 fits above tile 5 and abuts tile 6; tile 9 fits above tile 4 and abuts tile 5. The step layout design is enlarged with each diagonal row. The process continues until all of the tiles are placed in the section. The tiles that must be cut around the edges are left to last so that the entire cutting project can be completed at one time.

After the tiles are completely set in the first quarter of the floor, the process is repeated on the second, third and fourth quarters.

The Pyramid Tile Installation System

The running bond, or pyramid, tile installation technique also begins by using the horizontal chalk line as a guide. This technique works with half of the floor at a time, as opposed to one quarter as with the step system.

A stepped pyramid, which is built initially by using six tiles, forms the visual base. The tiles are laid against the horizontal chalk floor line with the first tile centered so that the chalk line runs through the center of the tile. Tile 2 abuts tile 1 on one side, while tile 3 abuts tile 1 on its other side. This makes a single row of three tiles centered on the chalk line.

Tiles 4 and 5 are then centered and placed exactly above the midpoint of tile 1. Tile 4 is set on one side of the chalk line and tile 5 is placed along the other side. Tile 6 is centered on the vertical line, as was tile 1, and sits above tile 4 and 5. The next three tiles, 7, 8 and 9, continue to form steps. Tile 7 abuts tile 2 on the horizontal line. Tile 8 is centered and fits above tiles 2 and 7; tile 9 is centered on tiles 4 and 8 and abuts tile 6. In every other course, the chalk center working line runs through the center of a tile.

This process continues on both sides of the horizontal line until it reaches the edges of the three walls. The tiles that must be cut around the edges are left to last so that the entire cutting project can be completed at one time. After the first half of the floor is completed, tiles are installed on the second half.

The Grid or Graph Tile Installation System

Most people are familiar with the standard sheet of graph paper where evenly-sized boxes or squares cover the page. These sheets can be used to plan room layouts, produce lettering of one size, or perform

Installation Tip: When using the pyramid or running bond system, as in all other layouts, remember to use tile spacers or to leave sufficient room for the grout between tiles.

No matter the installation technique used, be careful not to walk on or disturb freshly-placed tile. If work must be done across the installed tiles, either wait for the adhesive to dry thoroughly or use a board to support body weight.

many functions requiring repetitious measurements. When a picture is copied, for example, each of the squares represents a portion of the whole picture. Graph squares can be of varying sizes: small squares like those on school graph paper, or one-inch or larger squares. The lines that form graph paper are generally referred to as grid lines.

Another method for laying out a floor for a tile installation is the grid or graph system. In this system, the floor of a room is divided into squares using horizontal and vertical grid lines. Tiles are placed within these premeasured lines.

To use this system, the floor is first measured and the longest wall is selected as a starting point. The center of this long wall is located and marked. From this point, a chalk line is snapped on the floor across the room at a 90-degree angle to the wall. Starting at the center wall marker, a test/measurement row of dry tiles is laid out on the floor along the wall. The grout spacing (approximately ⅜ inch between tiles) must be factored into the space measurement. If the last test tile, the one that reaches the corner, is less than a half-tile width, calculate the space and divide the measurement. Snap a new chalk line to the left of the original line using this measurement. Remember to erase the previous chalk line to eliminate confusion. The new chalk center line should now be half a tile to the left of the original chalk marking line. This will provide even, uniform-appearing tiles at the end of the rows when the final installation is made.

The next step is to move to a wall adjacent to the one used for the original measurement. Repeat the measurement process by locating the center of the wall, snapping a chalk line across the floor at a 90-degree angle. Once again, start at the center point on this line and lay out tiles toward an adjacent wall. Include the grout spacing between each tile in the measurements. If the space between the last tile in this row is less than one-half a tile's width, snap a new chalk line as above. Remember to erase the previous chalk marking line to eliminate confusion. Move the new chalk line half a tile to the left of the original chalk line. This should provide evenly-sized end tiles when the tiles are permanently installed.

Beginning at the first chalk center line, lay down three tiles with grout spacing along the wall. Place one end of the chalk line at this measured point. At this point, set one side of a metal carpenter's square, on the wall, and line up the other side with the vertical center line. From the edge of the third tile, snap a chalk line along the edge of the square across the room at a 90-degree angle to the wall. Repeat this process every three tiles (plus three grout lines) along the entire first or long wall. Repeat the three tile plus grout line process along the adjacent wall.

When the entire floor has been marked off, the floor will look like a giant sheet of graph paper with grid lines every three tiles (plus grout lines) horizontally and vertically.

Some rooms are not perfect rectangles. Square off the room making the wall that catches the eye first, the most visible wall, the starting wall.

Installation Tip: *If you want to make sure that the initial courses of tile installed on the chalk lines are aligned, use a temporary wood working guide. Lightly nail down thin, perfectly straight pieces of wood along the chalk working lines where the tile installation is to begin. These short strips of wood are known as wood battens. Set the tile along the chalk lines abutting the aligned wood battens. After the tiles are installed, remove the wood strips. If you want to check the installation alignment, renail the wood battens anywhere along the chalk lines and repeat the above procedure.*

The Corner Wall Tile Installation System

Traditionally, when tile is set over a mortar bed, the corner wall tile installation system is used. This method, working from one end of a room, was probably used because it caused the least disturbance to the leveled mortar bed. In addition, only two sides of the room need have tile cut to fit. The other two sides are started with whole tile.

To start with, the walls in the room are checked to be sure that the corners are relatively square. If they are not, a squaring up process must be initiated.

Single square tiles are placed on the floor in the four corners of the room where the installation is to take place. The outside edge of the corner tile is used as a marking point. A defining mark is made on the floor. The measurement process is moved to the adjacent corner tile where once again the outside edge of the tile is used for a defining mark on the floor. Next, a chalk line is secured between these two marked square points and the line snapped to produce a marking on the floor. The procedure is moved from corner tile to corner tile until the four corners of the room are completed.

Next, the chalk lines are checked with a carpenter's square to make sure that the corner lines intersect at right angles. If there is a variation, the lines have to be adjusted and chalked. This will require rechecking the previous procedure until the corner lines intersect properly.

If at least two of the adjoining walls are square, that is, meeting at a 90-degree angle, the tile laying can begin. It is wise to set up a practice run of tiles to visually see how they lay out. For this process, place the tiles in position dry so that you can evaluate and are satisfied with the positioning.

Once you are satisfied with the layout, pick up the set of test tiles that are abutting the two adjacent walls. Nail batten strips on the floor along the wall side of the chalk lines. Check to make sure that the batten boards are at right angles when they are installed. Use the wood as a firm guide for the tiles during the tile installation procedure. Lay the tiles and then remove the wooden battens.

Laying Out the Wall Tile Installation

Wall installations are subjected to much closer visual scrutiny than floor tiles. The reason is obvious: most people usually do not focus their attention on a floor when they enter a room. Their visual attention is drawn to areas that are approximately at eye level. This presents some interesting challenges and establishes a number of ground rules for wall tile installation.

Installation Tip: *If the tile installation is to be made over an interior concrete slab, you may want to double check the floor area for dampness before starting the job. If the concrete floor is damp, tile will not adhere properly.*

If you are absolutely certain that the concrete floor always remains dry, move on directly to the tile installation. If you have any doubts, conduct a dampness test. Test results usually show up within a day. If you have the time, wait for a rainstorm, or better yet, a rainy period, before testing. The test will not only indicate whether there is a problem with installing tile, but may also tell you if proper ground barriers and drainage systems were initially installed.

To do a simple dampness test, cut out a number of small two- or three-inch squares of plastic wrap. The type of plastic used for wrapping food will suffice. Place the squares at various points on the concrete floor. Seal each square tightly to the floor using a cloth adhesive type tape on all four edges to let in as little air as possible.

Allow twenty-four hours, then lift the individual squares. If the underside of the plastic wrap is wet, damp, or even foggy, there is a moisture problem which must be addressed before tile can be installed. You may have to seek professional assistance to cure the dampness problem.

Secrets of Visual Perception

With visual harmony the key, the wall tile should be installed in such a way that when viewing all sections of a room, there is a continuous horizontal line rather than choppy distracting lines.

There are several installation errors that can disturb this visual harmony. If, as a result of a particular wall height requirement, tiles are cut a quarter or a half of their original size and then installed within the line of a person's vision, the harmonious line created by row after row of full tiles is broken. To remedy this difficulty when tiles must be cut to satisfy a measurement requirement, the row of cut tiles should be placed as close to the floor or base course as possible.

This next rule to assure visual harmony is to avoid making tile cuts too severe. If possible, make sure that standard tile pieces are always at least two inches in width. If the cut size is very close to two inches and this visual installation difficulty occurs, a possible remedy would be to make the grout line a bit wider next to the cut tile. This may compensate for a portion of the two-inch requirement and still provide reasonable visual harmony. The same rule holds true for trim tile: try not to reduce the width.

Wall Tile Layout Planning

Just as with floors, there are a number of layout systems following the same procedures that may be effectively used for walls. Each requires the development of horizontal and vertical wall lines to serve as guides for tile placement. Each of the line systems is designed to make sure that the completed, installed tiles are level, perpendicular, and visually pleasing.

When installing any ceramic wall tile in a room, the initial step is to set up a working wall map. When completed, this map will tell you exactly where the tiles are to be placed so that everything is in visual order. Many of the same tools used to create the floor installation lines will be used for the wall map. If the wall area to be worked on is particularly large, section it off into squares. Always be sure that the horizontal marking lines are drawn in one continuous line around the room.

Layout techniques for walls where no obstructions like bathtubs, sinks, or other fixtures exist will be discussed first, then techniques for bathrooms or rooms with other obstructions will be dealt with at the end of this chapter.

Establishing Wall Horizontal Lines

It it important to establish horizontal and vertical working lines on all walls where tile will be installed. The horizontal lines are used for the even vertical (up and down) spacing of the tile, and the vertical lines are used for even horizontal (side to side) spacing. Both are necessary for the most pleasing installation. Wall tiles are usually installed from the bottom up. The first working line, therefore, that must be established in the room is the horizontal line.

1. Begin at the floor. Use a level to locate the lowest point. Mark this low point where it meets the wall edge.

2. Place two dry ceramic tiles one against the other on the wall at

this marked lowest point. If you will be using cove tiles, you may use the cove tile at the floor level and one flat tile above it. If a spacer is not an integral part of the tile, place a tile spacer on the top edge of each tile.

3. Mark the area directly above the spacer lug of the second tile. Working from this mark, use a level and straightedge to scribe a line clockwise around the room. This will be the wall's horizontal baseline.

4. At this point, check to see if tiles will have to be cut in the area between the horizontal base line and the floor. This determination can be accomplished either by individually placing a full tile in each area and visually checking for size and position, or by using a layout stick if one has been marked up for the job. If the measurement shows that full tiles can be placed under the horizontal baseline area, there will be no additional installation concerns with these sections. If the distances under the horizontal baseline show that full tiles will not fit, the second course, that is, the course above the primary or cove tile pieces, will have to be individually measured and cut as it is installed.

5. Once the walls have been marked with horizontal working lines, batten strips (1″ × 2″ wooden strips) can be nailed along the marked line edges. The battens can be used as an installation working guide when the tiles are installed. The tiles are butted up against these edges for a perfectly level installation.

Establishing Wall Vertical Lines

In laying out tile, either in a pattern using colors or design, or in a single color installation, the objective is to get a visually pleasing result. When measurements are such that a given number of whole tiles with joint spaces for grout will fill a row evenly across a wall from corner to corner, getting an orderly effect is easy. In actual practice, however, wall sizes and sections are irregular. There are also doorways, windows, and cabinets which have to be considered. Important in planning layout, too, is the perspective from which a wall or a section will generally be viewed.

Measurement systems offer a number of options to find the vertical line. The important thing is that when all measurements are complete, the marked line is absolutely perpendicular.

The simplest way to locate the vertical line of a wall is with the use of a plumb bob and a chalk line. This technique has been discussed previously in connection with wall surface repairs but is worthwhile to review.

1. Start the process by locating and marking the center of the wall to be measured. On the ceiling, about one inch out from the wall, attach the string of the plumb bob. Drop the weighted bob but do not let it touch the floor.

2. When the bob stops rotating, mark the wall in back of the string at the top and the bottom of the wall. Stand away from the wall and look at the string. The small marks that you have made behind the string should not be visible. If they do show, readjust them until they cannot be seen when you stand back and look at the string.

3. Then, using small nails, tacks, or hooks, attach a taunt chalk line at the top and bottom markings and snap a chalk line.

4. On the floor, under the wall you have marked, place a row of dry tiles (without adhesive) from the vertical line to one corner of the room. Be sure to allow joint spaces for grout between each tile. If, when you reach the corner, there is room for less than a whole but more than a half tile, you can divide the measurement of the fractional part of the tile needed and move your vertical chalk line a corresponding distance. This will give you evenly-sized tile pieces on both sides of the wall.

Installation Tip: *If the measurement is less than a tile, consider whether a small increase in the grout spacing will make up for it.*

If fractional tiles must be used, a decision should be made as to whether they should be equally-sized on both sides of the wall and in adjoining corners or whether they should be used in a single vertical row. There are no set rules about these options. It is simply a matter of visual preference.

In every instance, however, it is important to establish a perpendicular vertical line on the wall to assure that the up and down placement of tiles is absolutely straight. Establishing the vertical line is also helpful in determining tile layout across the wall for visual satisfaction.

An Alternative Vertical Line Layout

If you wish to have full tiles in each of the corners, you can use an alternative vertical line technique.

Starting from one corner, lay out a single row of dry tiles on the floor along the wall, leaving space for grouting joints between each tile. If, when you get to the second corner, there is not room for the full tile you want in that corner, you will have to adjust the layout to place fractional tile(s) within the layout itself. If you opt for this adjustment, the general practice is, once again, to divide the measurement of the fractional tile in half and insert pieces of this size on the inner side of the corner tiles.

The option you select depends on what you find visually pleasing and/or the room layout. If, for example, a door might obscure the view of an adjacent wall, it might be more acceptable to keep the fractional tile adjoining the door.

No matter which option you choose, it is essential to use a plumb line to establish the vertical line, so that the tiles will run in a straight up and down row. Remember that this procedure establishes the first line up and down and if it is continued in plumb will assure that the horizontal placement is also correct.

To get tiles straight in their courses, use horizontal lines or batten strips for the horizontal dimension, and vertical lines or batten strips for the vertical dimension.

Installation Tip: *A layout stick may also be used to determine which of the options you would want to pursue to correct irregularities. These options are: to adjust grout line width, to divide fractional tile and install equal pieces on both sides of the wall, on the inner sides of the corner tiles, or between tiles to form a narrow vertical line, or to keep the entire fractional tile on one side.*

Laying Out Bathroom Walls

Bathrooms, or other rooms with wall and floor obstructions, require a somewhat different approach. The tub, sink, toilet tank, medicine chest, linen cabinets, and other fixtures represent obstructions to normal wall measurement procedures. In bathrooms, all horizontal and vertical lines do not flow simply from floor to ceiling, and arrangements must be made to compensate for these problem areas. Small ceramic accessory fixtures such as toothbrush, soap, and towel holders that will be installed must also be considered in plans and measurements. Open tile spaces must be left so that any accessories can be installed after the wall tiles are placed. In some jobs, any of these units may already be in place. When horizontal and vertical lines are drawn on bathroom walls, the areas where the accessories are to eventually be placed must also be clearly marked and accurately measured.

When a tile bathroom project is undertaken, decisions have to be made about the height of the tile to be installed in the bathtub section. In many older bathrooms, tile was often used only to cover the area from bathtub lip about three-fourths of the way up the surrounding tub walls. Today, the tile goes from the bathtub lip to the top of the wall. Often, tile also covers the bathtub ceiling area.

Installation Tips: Some tile accessories are recessed; that is, they do not extend out from the wall, but fit into the wall. A recessed soap dish is an example. Once you have measured the wall and determined the exact position of the recessed accessory, cut the wall area to fit the item. Do not tile before making the necessary wall cuts.

Use regular tile mastic adhesive for setting the tile accessory items if on a sheet rock backing, thin-set adhesive if on wonder board to provide a better bond.

Horizontal Lines for Bathroom Fixtures

The first step in preparing to tile around a bathtub is to lay out horizontal and vertical lines on the walls where the tile will be adhered. Before these lines are drawn, the level of the bathtub must first be determined. If the tub is level, to within ⅛ inch, the working horizontal line should be measured from the high point of the tub lip. If the tub is out of level by more than ⅛ inch, the working horizontal line should be measured from the low point of the tub body. If the distance is greater than ⅛ inch, the bottom row of tiles will probably have to be cut to fit. If the distance is ⅛ inch or less, the level can be achieved by compensatory grouting.

Once the tub level has been decided, lay a dry tile on top of the marked spot. Mark the wall area at the top of this full tile, plus ⅛ inch for grout spacing. Place a level on the mark and draw a horizontal line the length of the bathtub using a straightedge. If the tub is installed in a corner or end wall position, continue marking the horizontal line all the way around the tub enclosure.

After the line is drawn, nail 1″ by 2″ wood battens below the horizontal line to serve as installation guide lines. These battens can be removed after the upper tiles have been installed and the adhesive dried. The course of tiles adjoining the tub can then be installed.

The vertical line in a bathtub installation can be determined the same way as vertical lines are plotted for other walls. In this instance, the horizontal line at the back of the tub is used as a starting point for the dry test tiles. Find the center of this horizontal line and mark it. Place a row of dry tiles along the back of the bathtub, leaving spaces for grout joints. If the center point does not line up with a grout joint, make the necessary adjustment to bring it over to a grout line, following the procedure previously explained for the end tile widths. Use a level and a straightedge at the midpoint mark in the horizontal tiles to mark the vertical line above the bathtub. The line should be double-checked with a plumb bob and chalk line.

If there are end walls in the bathtub installation, they are usually laid out after the back wall has been tiled. The horizontal line which was marked around the bathtub during the preliminary process will provide the measurement base for the end wall lines. Using the same centering measurement as with other walls, place a row of dry tiles along the base of the bathtub end walls. Locate the center of the tiles, marking sure that the center line falls on a grout line. Mark the spot. Be sure that the end tiles fit properly. If the spaces for the end tiles are at least a half a tile width, proceed with the vertical line marking. If the spaces for the end tiles are less than a half tile width, make a new mark, a half tile in width, to one side or the other of the center line marking. The purpose of this marking change is to eliminate end tile cuts that are too narrow.

After the center point is determined, use a level and straightedge to draw a vertical line on the wall. This line should be checked with a plumb bob and chalk line for accuracy. When the dry tiles are removed, wood battens can be tacked below the horizontal line as a tile installation guide. If there are accessories or fixed items in other rooms to be tiled, use the same horizontal and vertical wall marking procedure designed for bathtub tiling.

CHAPTER 8

Installing Floor Tile

FLOOR TILING PRELIMINARIES—A REVIEW

The longest journey or the toughest job always starts with the first few steps. In previous chapters, the initial steps of a tile installation were discussed. In this chapter, a step-by-step sequence will be offered as a review and a guide.

1. To begin, the development of a checklist can save a great deal of time on the job. List the necessary tools, equipment, supplies, and work processes in a column on the left side of a lined sheet of paper. On the right side, leave a checkoff space to indicate whether the material is in place or a particular job function undertaken. Any space on the checklist which lacks a check mark shows that some work area requires attention. To provide the checklist with additional clarity, use horizontal lines under each work subject.

2. The floor areas to be tiled must be measured so that the number of tiles of various sizes required can be calculated.

3. It is always practical to develop a sketch or rough plan for each area to be tiled. The sketch should contain floor and wall dimensions and such other details as door areas or floor and wall obstructions. It should be as complete as possible, and ideally, to scale on graph paper when completed to serve as an installation reference guide, for ordering necessary materials, and for discussing the installation with any technical people.

Consult chapter 7, *Laying Out The Tile Job,* for more detailed information on this subject.

4. Purchase the tile. Logically, the entire supply needed should be purchased before the job is begun. Except for space requirements, there are no special storage or longevity problems with tile. It is also possible, of course, to do the initial preparation work and get the tile later, though most do-it-yourselfers want to get right on with the job and complete it from start to finish.

It is always wise to get in writing a delivery date, the agreed price, and an agreement that the tile will be as ordered. If your order is a particularly large one, you may also have to wait until the store reorders and receives a new supply of tile from the manufacturer.

Consult Chapter 2, *The World of Tile,* and Chapter 4, *Purchasing Tile,* for more detailed information on these subjects. Chapter 2 talks about the range of tile colors, glazes, and styles, while Chapter 4 discusses many of the tile shapes and accessories available.

5. The last basic step covers floor preparation, tools, and adhesives. Consult Chapter 7, *Laying Out the Tile Job,* for more detailed information on this subject.

A number of tools are designed specifically for tiling and other common household tools can be adapted for tile installation. Consult Chapter 3, *Tools and Equipment,* for more detailed information.

Consult Chapter 5, *Adhesives, Mortars and Grout,* for more detailed information on this subject. This chapter describes the products designed to hold every tile installation together.

Some Installation Techniques

Trowel Techniques

Trowel techniques and the type of trowel used differ with the type and brand of the adhesive and mortar, the kind of tiles installed, as well as with the individual doing the work. If, for example, large tiles are being place, a trowel with large V-notches will be used. The large notches make wide and deep troughs in the adhesive for the best adhesion of large tiles. Most standard tile installations use a trowel with ¼ inch notches. Consult the glossary section of Chapter 1, *Introduction to Tiling,* for more detailed information on this subject.

Begin standard trowel use by scooping up a quantity of adhesive from the pail and spreading it across the floor section to be covered with the flat edge of the trowel at approximately a 30- to 35-degree angle. Bring the adhesive up to the working chalk lines previously marked on the floor. Do not cover these lines as they will be necessary for other adhesive and tile placement. Watch out for any air bubbles in the adhesive—disperse them by running the trowel over the adhesive mixture in the problem areas.

The adhesive already in place is then drawn or combed across the floor at approximately a 45-degree angle using the V-notched portion of the trowel. Use two 45-degree passes in each section to complete this combing process. Move the trowel in an opposite direction for each pass, so that the result is a floor area covered with small, even rows of adhesive running in two directions, or cross-hatched.

Using the chalk line layout, place the adhesive in one small area at a time so that errors can be corrected more easily. Some adhesives have to set for a few minutes, while other adhesives can take the tile immediately. Consult the manufacturer's specification sheet or printed instructions.

If the tile is extra thick or has a deep pattern, spread adhesive on the back of each tile as well as on the floor. This process, called *buttering*, assures a more secure adhesion of tile to floor surface (Fig. 8–1).

To check for proper application, place one tile in the recently-spread adhesive. Push down lightly and apply a slight twisting motion to the tile. Now, remove the test tile from the floor. If the reverse side of the tile is evenly covered with the adhesive, you are ready to move ahead with the actual tile installation. If any of the reverse side of the tile shows through the ridges of adhesive, an additional supply of adhesive must be layered onto the floor.

The tile back adhesive test may also point out another installation error. The ridges created with the trowel may be much too deep for the tile installation. Bringing down the angle at which the adhesive is drawn across the floor with the trowel should correct this problem.

To practice your trowel technique, use a small piece of scrap plywood, and pencil in several lines to mark off the area to receive adhesive. Remove a small quantity of adhesive from the pail and go through the 30-degree adhesive layout and the 45-degree adhesive combing steps.

> **Installation Tips:** *If wood battens have been tacked down to align the first tiles in the installation grouping, be careful how you apply the adhesive. Bring it close to, but not onto, the wood strips.*
>
> *Apply adhesive to only a small section at a time when you first start a tiling job. As you move along with the project, you will gain confidence in your ability to handle the product and you will be able to apply the adhesive to larger sections of the floor.*

Laying the Floor Tile

There are four major steps to any tile-setting installation. Once the surface is prepared, the adhesive is applied, full tiles are set or placed in their proper positions on the floor (and all joints are accurately aligned and excess adhesive wiped off tile faces); necessary cuts are made to fit room edges (and any areas requiring less than full tile place-

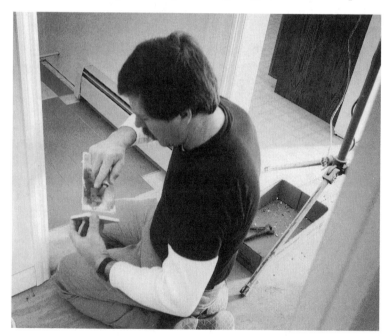

Fig. 8–1. Back buttering a piece of tile with adhesive.

ment); and the tile surfaces are grouted (and tile joints are compressed and surfaces cleaned of excessive grout).

Consult Chapter 5, *Preparing For a Tile Job*, for detailed information.

Applying the Tile Adhesive

In most cases, you will be using thin-set adhesive. Additives like latex can be introduced into the thin-set adhesive if required. Once the adhesive container has been opened and mixed, allow it to sit for about 10 minutes before applying.

Consult Chapter 6, *Adhesives, Mortars, and Grouts,* for more detailed information about types of adhesives and guidelines for selecting the proper adhesives.

The adhesive should be applied to one section of the floor at a time (Fig. 8–2) based on the floor layout plan. Work from one area

Fig. 8–2. Placing thin-set adhesive on a floor with a "V" notched trowel.

to another without disrupting tiles already in place. Working on a small area at a time also lets you work with the adhesive while it is still pliable, before it dries or becomes hard. Most adhesive manufacturers provide label information detailing the amount of time you have to set the tiles in the adhesive once it has been spread on the floor. This working period is sometimes referred to as *open time.* Make it a practice to stir the adhesive in the pail regularly.

Consult Chapter 7, *Laying Out a Tile Job,* for more detailed information on actual floor installation layouts.

Always follow the manufacturer's instructions printed on the can or bag of adhesive. Some manufacturers recommend that their adhesive product be spread in a circular pattern while others suggest that their adhesives be moved across the area of coverage with the trowel at an angle.

Setting the Tile

After the adhesive material is applied according to the chalk-lined floor layout, the first section is ready to accept the actual tile installation. Wood battens temporarily nailed into place help with the proper alignment of the initial tiles. Select tiles from each box so that if there is any color shading, the differences will be mixed through the installation. Stack the tiles in a place convenient to the installation. A wet cloth and a pail of clean water should be available to wipe away any excess adhesive from the newly installed tiles.

Place the very first tile in the adhesive along the marked guideline, against the batten strip, in accordance with the floor layout plan. Give the tile a slight twisting or wiggling motion as you place it in the adhesive. Press the tile firmly in place but not too hard or the adhesive may bubble up into the grout area or work its way up wall surfaces. Be firm but gentle in this procedure. Always leave joint spaces between the tiles. Joint spacers are pre-fired onto some tile bodies so that the joint spacing is automatic. Other tiles require that properly-sized plastic joint spacers are set between each tile to allow even joints. Make sure that a sufficient supply of these tile spaces is available for the job, if they are necessary.

Continue the tile placement, following the floor plan until all of the tiles have been placed in the section of the floor where the adhesive has been applied (Fig. 8–3).

Inspect the tile work you have completed in the first section. Make

Fig. 8–3. Tiles are placed into the adhesive material on the floor. Once tiles are put into place, a beater block and mallet are used to set them firmly into the adhesive.

sure that every course of tile is straight and even. Line up each row with a straightedge and square. If any adjustments are necessary, straighten out the line before the adhesive hardens. Wipe off any excess adhesive on the tile surfaces.

If all of the tiles in the section are in square and lined up properly, the next step is to be sure that every tile is seated securely and evenly in the adhesive. Use the beater block and rubber mallet or hammer to do this. Place the carpet- or heavy-material-covered beater block over a row of tiles diagonally to the tile joints, and lightly tap it with the mallet or hammer. Move the beater block from one set of tiles to the next until this work is completed.

As more tile is laid out, less and less open floor space will remain in the room. Do not walk directly on the tiles that have recently been set in the floor adhesive. There will, however, come a time in every installation when end, corner, and specially-sized tiles, cut to fit a job, will have to be set in the adhesive and placed in position to finish the installation. These specially-sized pieces of tile can be set without damage to the work already done by placing a large piece of flat board on the completed area. Walking on this board helps to distribute body weight and permits crossover without damage to the installed tiles (Fig. 8–4).

Fig. 8–4. Specially sized tiles are cut to fit around areas such as toilet bowl opening and radiation. Note the board used across tiles to spread the installer's weight evenly.

Always be sure that the adhesive has dried thoroughly before proceeding to the next step—be sure you know how much time should be allowed for this.

There will always be at least one point where the floor tile installation in one room must join with the floor of another room, depending on the number of room entrances. The point at which two rooms converge is generally covered by a piece of material called a *sill*. Both the tile on one side of the sill and the floor covering of the adjacent room are installed so that both abut the doorway sill. Sills are usually one piece and composed of a marble slab, wood, or the like. If marble is used, sills can be installed with an adhesive. If wood is used, the sills can either be bonded to the floor surface with an adhesive and/or with wood screws used to secure the sill to the floor surface. When wood is used for the sill, protect its surface when grouting the tile. Always leave joint space between the tile and the sill. Fill the space with grout or caulking compound.

Tile can abut wood door frames if fitting preparations are made in advance. Place a piece of corrugated cardboard on the floor against each side of the door frame. Set a tile on top of the cardboard. Rest a well-sharpened saw on top of the tile and cut away the bottom of the door frame. Clear out the sawn area, slide the tile to the wall, and cement the tile in place. Repeat the process on the opposite side of the door frame.

Installing Mosaic Tile Sheets

If mosaic tiles are used instead of individual tiles, the same preliminary techniques are necessary. When laying out a floor plan for mosaic installation, adjustments should be made in the chalk layout lines so that there will be a minimum number of tile cuts. The first few mosaic sheets should be set in the adhesive and checked to be sure that the installation is even and square. Once the check is satisfactorily completed, the balance of the mosaic sheets can be installed on the floor section where adhesive has been placed, being careful to match edges and check the direction of each mosaic sheet.

Once the mosaic sheets have been placed, the beater block and mallet should be used to assure that they are even and firmly set. Any small tile pieces that must be cut and set in place should be installed.

If it is necessary to cross over installed sheets of mosaic tile to work on a section requiring completion, use a weight-distributing piece of board. Wait for the adhesive to dry thoroughly before doing any additional work on the mosaic tile sheets.

Cutting Floor Tile

At some point in almost every installation, some tiles will have to be cut. Tile edges, corners, or centers will have to be gently removed, or nipped off, so that you get a piece that fits the required space. Consult Chapter 3, *Tools and Equipment,* for more detailed information on available tile cutting devices.

Most do-it-yourselfers leave the cutting and trimming of tile pieces for last. This is fine as long as it does not interfere with the correct placement of tiles in other portions of the floor.

There are several types of tile cuts you can expect to use. The simplest and the most frequently needed is the *straight cut.* This cut can be accomplished in one stroke, straight across the file face with a cutting tool. The tile(s) to be cut should be marked. Cutting tools include a hand tile cutter or snap tool; a tub or wet saw, if one is available on the job; or tile nippers. If no specific tile cutting tools are available, a line can be firmly scribed on the face of the tile with a glass cutter. The tile is then placed over a dowel stick or a round pencil with the scribed line directly over the round section. Pressure is exerted on both wings of the tile until it snaps along the scribed line.

A *short cut* goes across the tile face in the same manner as the straight cut, except a smaller section of the tile is cut away. If, for example, a tile is 4 inches square, a straight cut would go down the exact center providing two, 2 inch pieces upon completion of the cut. A 4 inch tile undergoing a short cut might end up with one 2½-inch and one 1½-inch piece upon completion of the cut (Fig. 8–5).

If a *diagonal cut* is required, the same marking process is used, and the tile can be cut with a wet saw or with the snap cutter. Make sure the piece of equipment you are using has the proper bed and scribing device to make a good cut.

There a number of techniques to make a *round cut* on a piece of tile. Clearly mark the tile face indicating the required circumference of the circle. If a suitably-sized diamond- or carborundum-treated round cutting blade is available, install the blade in your electric drill and drill the round piece of ceramic out of the tile. An alternative is to drill a series of small holes around the marked circle with a carborundum bit. Then, insert a tile-cutting hacksaw blade in

Fig. 8–5. Using a tile snapper to trim tile to size.

the drilled area and work the blade around the marked hole until the tile is all cut away.

A method which may be used with equally effective results was discussed earlier in this book. Mark both the required circle and a center line on the face of the tile. Cut the tile in half using the straight cut method. On each half of the tile, make small holes with a carborundum bit around the circumference of the marked semicircle. Use the tile nippers to nip away to the marked line on both tile halves. It may be necessary to use carborundum sandpaper on the areas of tile that have been drilled or sawed to smooth the surfaces (Fig. 8–6). For safety, always secure the tile before doing any drilling. The tile can be placed in a vise or on a board surrounded by nails to hold it securely in place.

There are a number of other cuts which may be needed to make

Fig. 8–6. Some tile cuts requiring sanding with carborundum laced paper to smooth off plier-nipped edges.

a tile fit. A small piece of one or more *tile edges* might require nibbling away with a pair of tile nippers. Tiny bites are carefully taken out of the tile until the marked area is reached and the cut tile fits perfectly into the installation (Fig. 8–7). A *small round area* may have to be cut out of a piece of tile if it must fit around a water or heating pipe. This marked area would also receive a nibbling treatment with pair of tile snippers. A *corner cut* is sometimes required. This is a small right angle cut on one corner of a piece of tile. Mark the right angle on the tile then cut along both arms of the angle with

---

Installation Tip: Remember to use a fine felt tip pen to clearly mark the cuts required on glazed tile. Do not use a felt tip pen on unglazed tile as the surface will absorb the ink and mar the tile. For marking unglazed tile: a sharp nail or pointed object can be drawn across the surface or a piece of adhesive tape can be placed along the cut line.

Fig. 8–7.   Tile nippers allow you to take small, irregular pieces out of a piece of tile.

a wet saw (Fig. 8–8). A tile snapper can also be used, but this may be harder to handle. Cuts around irregular areas and angle cuts can be measured and marked using the contour gauge and the sliding level square.

Grouting Tile

The most important requirement in the grouting procedure is patience. Allow the tile adhesive to set completely, at least 24 hours, before beginning to grout. If the individual spacers between tiles are not an integral part of the tiles themselves, remove them before starting the grouting job. While some installers suggest grouting over the plastic spacers, there is a dual danger in this procedure. The grout may discolor unevenly, and weakness may develop in the grout-covered spacer areas.

Grout has a number of specific uses. If a line of tile is installed incorrectly, the grout installation can provide minor correction. It also

Fig. 8–8. A tile or wet saw can speed up the tile cutting process. As the diamond impregnated blade cuts, water automatically flows onto the blade and tile.

helps contain moisture seepage and prevents dampness from permeating from the subsurface to the adhesive-setting beds. The hardened grout also protects tile edges from damage.

Consult Chapter 6, *Adhesives, Mortars, and Grouts,* for more detailed information on grout selection and use.

Before applying the grout, clean out anything which has fallen into the joints. A grout release can be applied to the tiles before the grouting process begins. This will make the cleanup process easier after the grout dries.

If you are applying colored grout, mix a small batch and let it dry to make sure that the grout dye matches the tiles you have installed. Place a test quantity across the face of a piece of scrap tile. Check the tile for any staining caused by the grout. If there is a color match or staining problem, change the type of grout used.

When you are ready to begin, mix the group according to the manufacturer's directions. If you are mixing a liquid with a dry grout powder, check to make sure that the mixing process has been complete, and that there is no dry grout left on the bottom or sides of the mixing container. Mix the grout thoroughly so that there are no lumps. Always keep the mixing stick deep in the grout mixture to cut down the chances for air bubbles to form. After stirring, let the grout set for about fifteen minutes.

Grout is ready for use when the mixture has reached the consistency of well-beaten egg whites or mashed potatoes. The mixture should maintain peaks just like beaten egg whites and have a definite body structure when scooped for use from the container.

Start the grouting procedure by scooping out a quantity of grout from the container with a rubber squeegee, hard rubber float, or non-metal grout trowel. Use a generous quantity, and work on only one small section at a time, limiting the area to about 4 square feet, a 2′ by 2′ section. If the grouting procedure is done on too large a portion, the grout may dry out and cause a problem.

Hold the rubber float or squeegee at approximately a 30- to 35-degree angle, moving the entire grout mixture diagonally across the installed tiles (Fig. 8–9). Move the float across the tile joints a number of times, pressing down so that the grout is compressed into the joints. Move the grout across different portions of the work area every time you make a pass. If the rubber float or grout trowel cannot reach into a particular area where tile joints must be filled, use your hands. Remember to use rubber gloves if there is any danger that you may be allergic to the grout. Once the joints have been completely filled and compacted, the excess grout should be moved off the tile field. Change the position of the grout squeegee so that it now wipes across the tile at about a 90-degree angle, pulling the grout before it. When the pile of grout reaches a drop-off point, use the float or trowel to remove it from the tile surface. Return it to the grout container for later reuse. At this point, dry grout powder, if available, can be sprinkled on top of the grouted tiles to help draw the moisture from the joints. Use the rubber float to resmooth the joint areas after the dry grout is sprinkled.

Each type of grout dries at a different rate of speed. Some may take 10 minutes; others may require 20 minutes to set up. The particular brand of grout, the grout mix, the outside temperature, and humidity all may affect drying time.

Fig. 8–9. Packing tile joints with grout after tile adhesive has dried thoroughly.

Once the grout has set up, initiate the preliminary finishing process with a sponge or cheesecloth and clean water. Soak the sponge in the clean water, wring it out thoroughly and very gently wipe it across the grout-covered tile surfaces (Fig. 8–10) with a circular motion. Continue to rinse out the sponge between each set of circular passes over the tile. Change the water so that you are always working with clean water. Continue the process until the tiles shine through and all traces of grout film have been removed (Fig. 8–11). Three or four washings should do it. At this point, all the grout lines between tiles should be smooth and even with the tile surfaces.

If any grout pulls out from between the tile rows during the rinsing process, you may not be wringing out the sponge sufficiently and the dry grout is receiving too much water. Squeeze out the sponge more thoroughly. Grout lifting may also occur if the grout has not had enough time to set up. Let the grout dry a little longer before washing

Fig. 8–10. After the tiles are grouted, excess grout is washed off the tiles.

it down. If some grout has pulled out from between the joints, hand-press it back into the joints.

Once the preliminary wash has been completed and the grout is still pliable, the next process is trimming the joints between the tiles. Floor tile joints do not usually require trimming. The grout will generally be flush with the tile face. If slightly concave joints are required, use the wet sponge or cheesecloth to make gentle passes down the joint lines. Using this procedure will cut down the amount of grout in the joints.

If you want to make even deeper cuts in the grout joints, use the handle of an old toothbrush or a special joint margin tool to accomplish this procedure. Run the narrow edge of the toothbrush handle or margin tool across (up and down) all of the grout joint rows to make an indentation in the joints. On most joint widths, the design of the toothbrush handle or the margin tool will not permit too great an indenta-

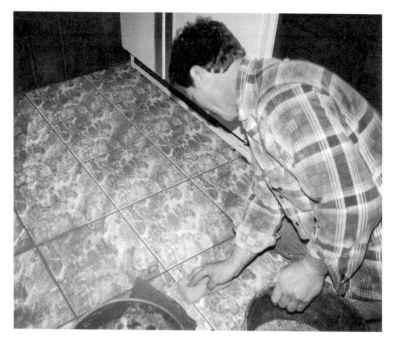

Fig. 8–11. It takes a number of passes with a sponge and clean water to thoroughly clean grout off the tiles. The sponge must be wrung out so that excess water does not loosen up the joints.

tion. If too much flexibility of the grout joint is noted, however, wait for the grout to dry a bit longer.

If the installed tile has shaped edges or rounded corners, a great deal more attention will have to be paid to the joint trimming procedure.

After the joints are trimmed, another light wash should remove any pieces of grout that may have accumulated on the tile surfaces. Use a plentiful supply of clean water and wring out the sponge completely. When this last wash dries, a light grout haze may form on the tiles. This can be wiped off with a dry towel, or a grout haze remover can be applied to the grouted tile surfaces. The haze remover usually comes in a spray container and is easily applied.

Manufacturers sometimes recommend that a *damp curing process* be used with grout. This means that after the grout is installed, it is kept moist by misting daily for about three days. The misting work can be cut considerably by misting once and placing a plastic sheet over the tile for the same time period. Damp curing is usually used on installation where dampness or excessive use may be a consideration.

Do not use any type of grout sealer for at least a month so that the curing process can mature fully. After a sufficient curing period has elapsed, the grouted joints may be sealed with a penetrating-type of sealer available in tile supply stores.

Installation Tips: Grout can stain wood and other surfaces. If the grouting is to take place near a wall, wood floor or other surface subject to discoloration, use tape paper to mask over these surfaces before grouting. The tape may be removed after the grout has dried thoroughly. Grout joints will usually leach out a white haze as the grout dries. This comes from salts contained in the grout and in some adhesives. These salts rise to the grout surfaces but will easily wash away with water. Be sure to give this white haze an opportunity to come out before you place any sealer on the grout.

Floor Tile as a Heat Collector and Diffuser

In warm areas, tile is frequently used because of its capacity to cut down on generated heat by diffusing it. In cooler areas, a tile floor installation in a greenhouse, sunporch, or other sun-exposed or skylighted room can be beneficial and cost saving.

Tile is an effective and efficient solar energy collector. It can store solar heat during the daylight hours and return the stored-up energy to the residence in the cooler evening hours. The floor's subsurface composition and design can also add to heat retention and release. A similar heat collection and return system is generated around radiators and wood stoves when ceramic floor tiles are installed beneath these units. The warmth produced by the radiation is captured by the tiles when heat is produced and returned to the room for a considerable period afterward.

CHAPTER 9

Installing Wall Tile

Wall Tiling Preliminaries

Tiling a wall requires the same careful consideration and preparation given every other type of tile installation. No matter where the tiles are to be placed, if the job is to be long lasting and attractive, the undersurfaces have to be fully prepared to accept the tiles before the very first tile is adhered. Specific concerns include the overall stability of the wall surface, the ability of the wall structure to support any additional load or stress, and the visual impact of the completed job.

The load factor of a wall tile installation includes the weight of the tiles plus installation adhesive and grout. A weak wall, lacking proper substructure, will not support a good job. It would be equally incorrect to attempt to install tiles on a wall that is subject to excessive dampness unless it is bolstered or replaced with waterproof backing board. If a wall is uneven or its level is seriously in question, this condition, too, must be remedied. In addition, there always exists the minute possibility that a wall surface can react negatively to an adhesive or other substance used in the installation. In most instances, the possibility of this can be checked with the product manufacturer's instruction sheet beforehand. For the strongest, most effective tile installation, wall surfaces must be clean, dry, flat, waterproof, straight, plumb, and secure.

Consult Chapter 5, Preparing For The Tile Job, for more detailed information on preparation techniques.

> **Installation Tip:** If both floor and walls are to be tiled, always complete the wall installation first.

Tile Installation Preparation

Checklist

A working checklist, as previously mentioned, is invaluable for a wall tile installation just as for other tiling jobs, starting with the layout of the room and ending with the final tile polishing or sealing. On one side of the checklist, each activity is described simply. On the opposite side is space for a checkoff as tasks are completed. Areas that still require attention and completion are left unchecked. A swift review of the checklist will indicate progress and the areas requiring further attention. For example:

ACTIVITY	TASK COMPLETION
Purchase: 500 4″ × 4″ white tiles	X
Purchase: 25 pounds of adhesive	X
Purchase: 15 cove tiles / white	X
Purchase: One inset soap dish	X
Use plumb bob on wall	X
Mark wall with chalk line	X

Preparing to Lay Wall Tile

Once the wall subsurfaces have been structurally prepared, then a layout should be created. The wall areas to be tiled are measured, and a sketch or rough plan is drawn up, ideally to scale. From this sketch the number and sizes of tiles to be purchased are calculated. Always be sure to purchase enough tiles to allow for breakage, shading differences, and future repairs. The last preliminary step concerns assembling the materials that you will need, tools, adhesives, layout plan, tiles, trim pieces, and accessories. Tiles should be unpacked and inspected to minimize shade differences. These steps are covered in more detail in Chapter 8, *Installing Floor Tile;* and also in Chapter 4, *Purchasing Tile;* Chapter 5, *Preparing for the Tile Job;* and Chapter 7, *Laying Out the Tile Job.*

The first work on the actual wall surface, apart from repairs, is to remove all picture hooks, nails, and other wall obstructions. If any other holes develop in the removal process, they should be patched before the adhesive is applied.

Electric wall switch and receptacle plates must also be taken off (Fig. 9–1). If they are to be replaced after the tile is installed, it is a good idea to keep the plates and the attaching screws in an easily identifiable box or sealable clear plastic bag.

If the room requires additional electrical receptacles or switches, the time to call an electrician is before the tile work is started and while the wall studding is easily accessible.

In order to tile the walls behind radiators and baseboard heating, these units should also be temporarily detached. It is recommended that you call a heating professional to handle this job.

If the tiling is to be installed down to the floor line, the baseboard or molding must be removed. If this is done carefully, the material can be installed later.

The next step in preparing the wall surface is to develop and mark the vertical and horizontal lines that will be used to lay the tile. Chapter 7, *Laying Out the Tile Job,* gives complete instructions.

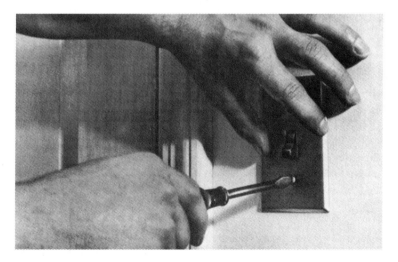

Fig. 9–1. Remove light fixtures and plates from switches and outlets. *(Courtesy Benjamin Moore)*

Laying the Wall Tile

Wall Tile Adhesive

Once the walls are marked, the next step is to apply the adhesive. In most instances, thin-set adhesive or mastic will be the choice for home wall installations. When the adhesive container is opened for use, allow it to sit for about ten minutes before applying to the wall. A trowel with relatively small V-notches will be used to apply the adhesive to wall surfaces.

Installation Tip: A reminder—adhesive trowels come in a number of sizes depending on the width and depth of the V-notches. The notches range in size from $3/16$-inch for standard tile installation use to $1/4$-inch and $3/8$-inch notches for larger tile. A combination of the notch sizes and adhesive application technique controls the depth of adhesive rows.

Select the starting point on the wall. Remove adhesive from the container with the trowel. Use the trowel's flat edge to spread the adhesive across the wall in the marked installation space. Next, using the V-notched portion of the trowel, comb the adhesive, working it in a criss-cross pattern. Make sure that the adhesive completely covers only the marked work area. Do not let it flow onto the batten board guides which will be removed later. When working on the horizontal line with the wood strips, bring the adhesive carefully near the line or backbutter each of the tiles before fitting into place.

If too much adhesive is placed on the wall, exposed and allowed to dry, it may have to be chipped away before a fresh layer is laid. If not, the tile levels may be uneven.

Consult Chapter 6, *Adhesives, Mortar, and Grout,* for more detailed information about wall tile adhesives.

Placement of Wall Tile

Install the individual tiles carefully on the wall in their preselected, prepared order according to your layout. If the individual tiles already have pre-fired, built-on spacers, no additional spacers will be required between tiles to form the joint rows. If not, plastic spacers will have to be installed between each tile. Make sure that the wet adhesive is not forced up into the joint areas. This can happen if the file is moved around too much during placement.

It is helpful to nail batten boards or thin wood strips at the beginning horizontal chalk line marked on the wall so that the horizontal alignment of the tiles is absolutely accurate. Double check the batten board line with a carpenter's level and square. Check the horizontal line continually as you install the tiles. Batten boards can also be used along the vertical chalk line.

You can start above the horizontal base line or below. If you start above the horizontal line, complete the tile installation along the various wall sections and then return to the areas below the horizontal base line.

When cove tiles are to be the first course on the wall, begin by installing the cove course of tile to the floor line. The base of the wall may not be absolutely level. Place as many of these tiles as possible without trimming the individual tiles.

As the cove tiles are installed around the wall, the work should proceed toward the room corners or edges. If there is not room for a full cove tile when the line reaches any corner, you have to decide what systems to use to size the tile segment or segments you will need. A wet saw is preferable to a tile snapper for cutting cove tiles. Because of their design, they are difficult to cut with a tile snapper and may easily be broken.

There are a number of measurement methods that can be used. The open space from last tile to wall edge can be measured with a ruler and the necessary distance marked on the tile face. The tile can then be cut along the markings.

Another space measurement uses two dry tiles, without any adhesive, placed directly on top of the last full tile that has been installed. The top tile is then slid over to the corner and the remaining dry tile is marked with a fine point marking pen. The marked tile is then cut with a tile snapper or saw.

After cutting, the tile piece is cemented and set into the wall in the appropriate position, completing the line of tile to the wall edge. Always insert tile spacers between the tiles to form the necessary tile joint lines. If spacers are already fired onto the tiles, plastic spacers will not be necessary.

In placing the first line of tiles in a confined space, take care to use tile adhesive only in the areas where the cove tiles are to be installed.

The second course of tiles is placed above the cove tiles, but below the horizontal line that you have taken care to make absolutely level. As a result, you may have to cut tiles to fit the possible unequal space between the cove base and the horizontal lines. This is where the level of the installation is corrected. After this step, check with level and square.

You can now proceed to tile up to the height your design calls for. If, for some reason, the tile installation is not designed to begin at floor level, it can begin at the intersection of the vertical line and the horizontal base line at the appropriate height. Once the initial guiding tiles are put in place, the entire wall installation can continue until completion. A level and square should be used as any installation proceeds.

A useful technique for placing individual tiles is to flop each one into place in the adhesive from its bottom edge, then seat with a slight pressure and a twisting motion.

Continually check the horizontal and vertical alignment of the installation as you place the tiles on the wall. After sections of tiles have been placed, use a clean damp cloth to wipe away any excess adhesive that may have worked its way on to the tile surfaces.

When installing wall tiles, try to make sure that the bottom and the top courses are never less than half a tile in width. If wall measurements cause this to occur, install the half tiles at the bottom of the wall just above the cove tile course. In this way, the half tiles will be out of a viewer's direct line of vision.

Consult Chapter 7, *Laying Out the Tile Job*, for more detailed information on wall layouts.

Installation Tip: *Always start tiling a wall from the bottom up and constantly use your level and square to keep the courses true.*

Cutting Wall Tile

Individual tile cuts may include straight, short, diagonal, corner, and round cuts as previously described. A tile snapper, nipper, wet saw, or combination of these tile tools may be used to cut them.

For more detailed information on the methods used to achieve each of the cuts and for the tools used to cut them, consult Chapter 3, *Tools and Equipment,* and the preceding Chapter 8, *Installing Floor Tile.*

It is generally convenient to do all the required tile cuts at one time. After the full tiles have been placed into the adhesive in each wall section, the wall end areas requiring less than a full tile must be measured. Mark the measurements to be cut on the face of each wall tile with a fine felt tip pen and cut the tile according to instructions.

Grouting Wall Tile

Allow 24 hours for setting before grouting, then follow some preliminary steps. If there are plastic tile spacers, they should be removed before grouting. Make sure also that the joint spaces are clear of any debris. Tape or otherwise protect any wood that may come in contact with the grout during its application, as wet grout can stain wood surfaces. A grout release can be used on the tiles before grouting to speed up the cleanup process.

Select the correct type of grout for the wall installation. If a colored grout is to be used, test it to make sure that it does not stain the tile surfaces. This is particularly important if you are using unglazed tile. If any test produces staining, change to either a plain mixture or a grout that does not damage the tile when tested.

Mix the grout well before use as described in Chapter 8, *Installing Floor Tile,* or purchase ready-mixed.

Scoop out a small quantity of grout with a rubber application float, and apply the grout to the wall surface diagonally, drawing and pressing it at about a 45-degree angle. Fill joints in a small section of wall, approximately four square feet at a time, using techniques described previously.

The grouted wall will dry somewhat in about ten minutes, depending on the grout brand, room temperature, and humidity. Some grout may take a little longer. After the grout has firmed or set up, dry grout should be rubbed along the joint rows to draw out additional moisture.

Use a sponge or cheesecloth pad and clean water to remove the excess grout form the tiles, again using techniques described previously.

Allow the grout to dry a little longer and then trim the joints. This procedure must be done after the grout has set up but while it still retains some pliability. The trimming procedure will provide a finish for the tile with a very minor indentation along joint lines. Make sure that the trimming process is not done too soon or the grout may pull or roll out of the joints. Use the handle of an old toothbrush, a popsicle stick, or a margin tool to run up and down every joint (Fig 9–2). If the tile has rounded corners or edges, the grout trimming process may have to be done tile by tile.

Once the joint trimming has been completed, the tiled wall should receive another clean water wash. The sponge or pad must be squeezed thoroughly before passing it over the tiles. Continue the washing process until the tiles dry without a heavy film. If a light haze forms on the tile faces, use a turkish towel or other heavy-bodied soft cloth to polish it away. A grout haze remover can also be used on the grouted tile to clean up the tile surfaces quicker.

Do not apply any sealant to the tile surfaces until the grout has had a sufficient time to dry completely. The grout drying process may take a month or even longer depending on weather conditions. Humidity will slow down the process while warm, dry weather can speed it up.

Fig. 9–2. Striking joint lines on a wall of tile. A tile tool or toothbrush handle can be used for this job. *(Courtesy Summitville Tile)*

Consult Chapter 6, *Adhesives, Mortars, and Grout,* for more detailed information about grout.

Special Installations

Wall Mosaic Tile

Using mosaic tile in squares or sheets can speed up an installation. While the composition of a mosaic may be half-inch, one- or two-inch pieces, or 3″ × 3″ or 4″ × 4″ tiles, a complete sheet of mosaic tile might contain one, two, or three square feet of tile. Mosaic tile sheets are installed in almost exactly the same way as standard individual tiles. Some sheets of full size tile are pregrouted, while most sheets of mosaics must be grouted after installation. All of the rules for preparing the wall surfaces and drawing layout lines on the walls are similar for mosaic tile. Use the same procedure to make sure all of the sheets of tile are horizontal and vertically aligned.

Wall Tile Trim

There are a large number of trim tile options available for wall installations (Fig. 9–3). Each of these is designed to make the finishing job easier and the results more attractive.

If the tile work must go around corners, there are round-out, round-in, and square-in corners. Each type permits a smooth transition from one wall to another. Stretcher tile of all sizes and shapes, cove, bead, and edging caps, as well as a complete range of bullnose tile shapes, are also available to trim an installation.

Wall Tile Accessories

Space needed for accessories built into or placed on the wall must be planned. Electric light switch plates and electric receptacle plates which are initially removed can be put back, or new matching or complimentary ceramic plates can be installed in their place.

If the tile installation is in the bathroom, a variety of useful accessories might be considered, such as towel racks, toilet paper holders, soap dishes, robe hooks, toothbrush and tumbler holders, magazine

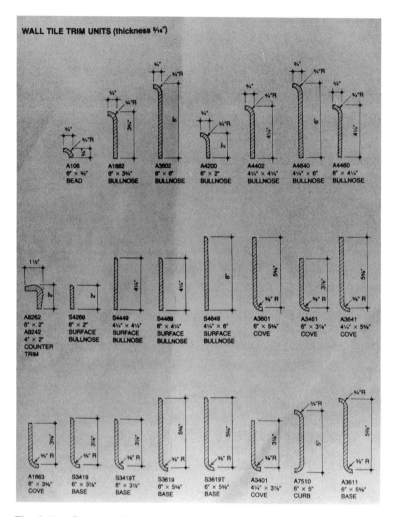

Fig. 9–3. Some of the wall tile trim units available to finish off a tile job. *(Courtesy Tile Council of America, Inc., American National Standard Specifications)*

racks, etc. Some of these accessory items may be affixed to the wall with an adhesive designed for this purpose, while other require measuring, cutting and fitting into the wall. Some may also be attached to the tile with screws and clip-on plates.

Installation Tips: *Always leave space for accessories when installing wall tiles. Do not use the regular tile mastic adhesive to secure the accessory items—use acrylic adhesive instead.*

CHAPTER 10

Installing Ceramic Patios and Other Outdoor Areas

Preliminary Considerations

In earlier chapters on indoor tiling, the importance of a firm, level subsurface was discussed. Outdoor patios require the same preparatory treatment. Foundations must either be built or renovated so that they are smooth, level, and solid.

There are other important considerations in the patio planning process. When selecting tiles for the patio, choose those with slip-resistant surfaces to help protect against accidental falls on wet surfaces.

Always use a carpenter's level to make sure that the site has a suitable, built-in slope away from building foundations. This should be approximately ⅛ inch per foot in most cases so that the patio surfaces will drain properly. A slope toward a building creates the potential of flooding and foundation damage. In addition to ground-level tile patios, outdoor tile patios can be installed on balconies two or more stories above street level or on a roof if there is sufficient architectural support (Figs. 10–1 through 10–4), and as long as community building codes allow this type of installation. Lightweight, thin-set adhesives can be used where weight bearing may be a major concern. If you are considering a project of this type, check with an experienced architect or engineer.

Fig. 10–1. Ceramic tile can be installed on outdoor patios in high-rise building providing the structure is designed to handle the additional weight and all codes and regulations are adhered to. The installation procedure is similar to placing a tile floor. It includes putting down the proper adhesive. *(Courtesy Ro-Tile, Inc.)*

Fig. 10–2. Setting the tile, grouting the joints. *(Courtesy Ro-Tile, Inc.)*

Patio Tile Selection

Nonvitreous or semi-vitreous tiles require sealants of some type to remain stain free and stand up to outdoor weather conditions. The sealant must be applied at regular intervals, especially if the installation is in a region subject to frost.

Vitreous tile, both glazed and unglazed, does not require sealants. It is also stain-resistant and weather-resistant. They are freeze-proof

Fig. 10–3. Washing down the completed project so that the tile is residue-free. *(Courtesy Ro-Tile, Inc.)*

and resist thermal shock. This means that they can be used in any climate, and will hold up well in successive exposure to cold and heat.

Make absolutely sure that the manufacturer recommends the tile for outdoor .se. Some tiles are suggested for both indoor and outdoor installation while others are definitely not recommended for outdoor use. If the patio will be in a region subject to frost, check

Fig. 10–4. The finished patio provides enjoyment. *(Courtesy Ro-Tile, Inc.)*

manufacturers' specification sheets carefully to determine if the tile is guaranteed to withstand wintry conditions and thermal shock.

The two tiles most often recommended for patio installation are known as quarry tile and paver tile. Quarry tile is made by an extrusion process; paver tile is created by pressing. Quarry tiles are available glazed or unglazed, and can be fired to high temperatures to produce a vitreous, moisture-proof, and stain-resistant surface capable of surviving in frost-prone regions. Paver tiles are also available glazed or unglazed, but they are not fired to a vitreous finish. While they are suitable for some patio installations, they should not be used where there is danger of frost or thermal shock. They generally must be sealed to protect and preserve the surfaces.

Both paver and quarry tiles are durable, thick, and available in a selection of earthtone and other colors. Colors in both paver and quarry tile, incidentally, are run throughout the tile bodies and are not merely on the surface. Glazed tiles offer decor options because of glaze texture and color variations. On the other hand, glazed tiles can prove slippery in wet areas and are not recommended for patios.

Remember that most unglazed tiles, unless fired to a vitreous finish, are affected by moisture and freezing temperatures.

Preparing the Patio Foundation

If a new base has to be built for the patio, there are several steps to follow.

Site Designation

The area selected for the patio must be designated and the site laid out. Some patios are level with an existing lawn, or on grade, while others require a base constructed that is even with a section of the adjoining foundation.

If the patio base is to be situated on grade or not more than 6 to 9 inches above ground level, two sets of wooden markers should be used to mark the base boundaries and clearly define the work areas (Fig 10–5).

A first set of four wooden marking pegs should be sunk in the earth at the four corners of the proposed base, approximately 6″ outside or away from the measured base dimensions. String should be attached to these pegs so the digging perimeters are clearly indicated.

The second set of eight marking or control stakes should be installed in the area of the base to monitor the exact planned measurements of the base. These stakes should be sunk in the earth about one foot away from all corners of the digging site outside of the first stakes, but in line with the original foundation measurements (Fig. 10–6).

When the marking stakes and string are in place, the sod and topsoil should be removed from the base area. If there are large stones within the marked-off area, these too should be disposed of.

Excavation

Now, excavation work for the patio base should be initiated in the marked area. The depth to which the base must be dug is often governed by municipal building codes. Always check for building permits before work begins. Some towns require the submission of complete

Fig. 10–5. One set of four marking pegs should be sunk in the earth at the four corners of the proposed base, approximately six inches out from the measured base dimensions.

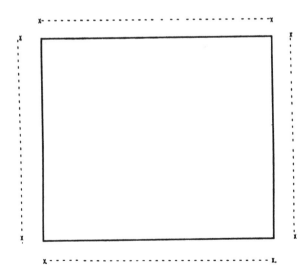

Fig. 10–6. The second set of eight marked pegs should be installed in the area of the base about one foot from all corners of the digging site.

plans before a job can be initiated. Remember that each town or city building code may differ.

If the weather conditions in an area are generally frigid during the winter months, the base must be excavated below the region's frost line. If the excavation is in a temperate zone, a base depth of 4 to 6 inches below the earth/grass line level is usually sufficient. When excavating the base, all earth corners must be squared and earth walls cut vertically. The walls of earth should be perpendicular and not allowed to bevel in or out. Save the earth dug out of the patio base hole for any backfilling required later.

Filling the Excavation

After the excavation has been dug, the foundation hole should be filled with small stones in a variety of sizes. The excavation is filled with gravel in levels, usually including fieldstone, then progressively smaller sizes of bank run gravel. The purpose of the stone fill in the foundation excavation is to provide satisfactory drainage.

The cubic quantity requirements for gravel to fill the excavation can easily be calculated by multiplying the *length* of the excavation times the *width*, times the *height* to which the gravel will be placed. For example, an excavated base 12 feet long by 10 feet wide and 2 feet deep would required 240 cubic feet of stone to fill the measured space. A cubic yard, the measure by which stone or gravel is generally sold, is 27 cubic feet, so you would divide 240 by 27 to get the basic yardage you need.

Stone or gravel compacts as it settles, so when calculating necessary quantities, plan on ordering up to two times the estimated measured quantity.

Wood Forms

After the gravel fill has been put in the excavation, a $2'' \times 4''$ wood form should be constructed around the base layout. This form should follow the line and dimensions of the marking stakes previously put around the perimeter to mark the exact dimensions of the proposed base. It will define the area into which the cement will be poured and leveled. A carpenter's square should be used to assure that all corners of the form have been squared, and a carpenter's level can be used to make sure that the wood form for the base has the correct pitch, about ⅛ inch to the foot, inclined away from the foundation.

For example, a 2″ or 3″ × 8″ to 10″ hole is dug around the perimeter of the base. The wood planking, cut to size, is placed in the dug out area and nailed together. Be sure the four corners of the wood form are square. Also be sure that the pitch of the framework does not tilt toward the building foundation. Secure the wood form with pegs so that there is no movement during the cement pouring process. The pegs can be placed at a number of points along the frame. If a foundation with greater depth is desired, you can create a form using 2″ × 12″ lumber, the type usually used for floor beam construction.

Pouring Cement

After the cement has been properly blended and mixed, it should be poured into the foundation form. Make sure that the pouring process does not disturb the framing. When the form is completely filled, the cement must be leveled off. Use a piece of wood a bit longer than the width of the form for this procedure. In one continuous motion, draw the piece of wood back and forth across the framing. Any excess cement will spill off the form onto the ground. After the cement poured into the foundation frame has thoroughly dried and matures, the wood frame can be removed and earth backfilled around the base to the required height.

Expanding an Old Foundation Base

If an existing cement foundation base can be used for the proposed new tile patio, it may only be necessary to make some additions, or repairs.

When an existing base must be expanded, calculate the additional space requirements. One or more sides adjoining the existing cement base may have to be dug out to make room for the wood extension form.

After excavating, wood forms of the proper size should be put in place, leveled, and graded to match the existing base. The excavation should be filled with stone and bank run gravel to the preselected base level. A small section of the old cement base abutting the new section should be roughened to improve adhesion qualities. Reinforced wire can be installed on both the loose stone filling the excavation and on the framed roughed-up section of the old cement base. The wet concrete should then be poured over the framed-in area of the old foundation and into the wood form. The cement should be allowed to dry thoroughly before installing any tiles. Use standard alternate wet down and drying techniques during the cement curing process. After the cement has dried completely, the wood forms should be removed and the area around the base backfilled with earth to the desired height.

Installing Patio Tile

Install patio tile using the same procedures as for floor tile (Chapter 8). Thin-set adhesives can be used on top of the cement foundation to adhere the tiles. The tile pieces can be cut, trimmed, and then set properly to form the completed patio design. After allowing the adhesive time to dry, the tiles can be grouted with a sand-Portland cement mixture. If desired, the grout can be mixed with a color to match or compliment the tile.

The choice of whether to use a sealant for the tile depends on the type of tile used. There is a variety of tile types available in many sizes, shapes, and qualities. Consult Chapter 4. *Purchasing Tile,* and chapter 3, *Tools and Equipment,* for more detailed information on this subject.

Installation Tip: The cement base and the tiles which are to be installed on the patio should strongly adhere when they are finally bonded together. A tight, secure bond is insurance against the invasion of moisture. One method to assure this bond is to score or "screed" the level cement face of the patio before the concrete has had an opportunity to set thoroughly. Screeding is simply making slashes in many different directions across the entire cement surface. The slashes, while not very deep, will take in some of the bonding material when the adhesive is put down to adhere the tiles. When the adhesive dries, the adhesive-filled slashes and surface adhesive form strong interlocking surfaces.

Using Tile for Steps

Safety, attractiveness, and longevity are the main considerations for using specific types of tile for installation on outdoor steps.

If frigid weather is expected in a region, the tile selected should be vitreous. A glossy tile, while it has attractive qualities, is not a good choice for step surfaces because of its slippery finish.

For safety, the horizontal section of each step (tread) must be tiled with slip-resistant tile. Vertical risers do not require slip resistance, but tiles used on the riser and step surfaces should have visual compatibility. Bullnose tile, or trim tile with rounded, finished edges, can be used to finish off the stair treads. If, for some reason, trim tile is not used, always install the vertical tile risers first and then the horizontal step tiles. The tread tiles, in this instance, should overlap the riser tiles.

Step Construction

A basic set of steps can be constructed from a variety of building materials, including wood, concrete, and metal. If the project is completely new, building materials may be selected to suit the particular job. If, on the other hand, the framework of the steps already exists, the material choices are limited. The least expensive framework for a set of tile steps is generally wood, while the most expensive is usually concrete.

Installation on Existing Concrete Steps—Before installing new tile on the framework of existing concrete steps, there are a number of areas to check and if necessary, correct. The steps, landing, and all supporting concrete areas should be completely free of cracks or fissures (Fig. 10–7). Oil film, wax, grease, or other such substances must be removed from all the surfaces with an appropriate cleaner. If the concrete has any curing compound on its surface, this too must be removed before the installation is started. If the surface of the concrete steps is smooth, it must be roughened before work is begun. This is usually accomplished mechanically.

Check each step with a carpenter's level to make sure there is a slight grade away from the riser to allow any water accumulation to run off. If the grade or pitch is not adequate, correct it when installing the cover mortar bed. Consult Chapter 5, *Preparing For The Tile Job* (section on cleaning concrete surfaces). The installation sequence for installing tile on top of cement stairs would be: Level 1—concrete steps currently in place; Level 2—mortar bed; Level 3—bonding or adhesive coat; Level 4—the selected tile. A framework of wood may have to be designed and built on each stair level to contain the mortar bed.

Installation on Existing Wood Stairs—As with concrete steps, use a carpenter's level on the landing and each individual step to be sure that a slight grade exists to allow water accumulation to run off, away from the riser. If a problem with grade is located, make the necessary repairs. Carefully check all portions of the framework of the stairs to

Fig. 10–7. Epoxy patcher and adhesive can be used to repair steps and other areas before installing tile. *(Courtesy Sears)*

make sure that a good background support is in place. If any weak spots are located, provide the proper bolstering. Remember that tile and backing material will place additional weight on the steps.

Inspect any areas of the wood steps that are in contact with ground or concrete surfaces. Wood should be properly treated against rot and insect damage before any tiling takes place. In order to protect wood from moisture damage, install a waterproof membrane against wood surfaces before the metal mortar-holding lath is installed on the steps. A heavy, nonbiodegradable plastic can be used for this process. The installation sequence for installing tile on wood steps should be: Level 1—wood steps currently in place; Level 2—waterproof membrane; Level 3—metal lath; Level 4—mortar scratch coat; Level 5—mortar bed; Level 6—bonding or adhesive coat; and Level 7—the selected tile. A framework of wood may have to be designed and built on each stair tread to contain the mortar bed.

Installation On Existing Metal Stairs—Check the level of the treads for a slight grade. If there is none, prepare to make any necessary alterations in the mortar bed that will be installed on top of the mesh and metal surface so that water accumulations will run off away from the risers. When placing reinforcing mesh on the metal stairs, use tack welds, if possible. If equipment is not available to weld the mesh, figure out some other means to lock the mesh securely into the metal stairs. If possible, cut through the mortar bed and metal reinforcing material where the stair treads meet to permit flexibility.

The installation sequence for placing tile on metal steps should be: Level 1—metal steps currently in place; Level 2-reinforcing mesh; Level 3—mortar bed; Level 4—bonding or adhesive coat; and Level 5—the selected ceramic tile. A framework of wood may have to be designed and built on each stair tread to contain the mortar bed.

New Steps—If the framework of the steps is to be completely new, some people may prefer to do the framing themselves. The alternative, of course, is to bring in a professional carpenter or mason to do the basic structural work.

Steps in Laying Outdoor Tile

Use the same techniques and systems used to lay out, measure, adhere, and grout tiles to floors and walls to set tiles securely on steps, patios, and other outdoor installations.

1. When planning the tile layout, make all of the necessary measurements using carpenter's squares, levels, and rulers to assure accuracy. Mark clear working lines in the areas where work is to proceed.

2. Dry test the tiles in the actual position they will take in the project. If there is any problem at this point, changes can be made effortlessly. The dry test will also alert you to the number of tile cuts that may be necessary on the job. If a large number of tiles need to be cut, a tile saw can be rented.

3. The next step in the process is to place the adhesive or bonding material on the marked surfaces. Bonding work should proceed a small section at a time. This assures that the adhesive will not dry out and gives better control.

4. The tiles should now be accurately and firmly positioned in the adhesive. Thin-set adhesives, usually latex or acrylic bonding material, are generally used for outdoor installations. If a block of recently installed tiles must be crossed to work on another area of tile, place a large wooden board over the tiles to spread the weight and stress.

Use a damp cloth to clean off any excess adhesive that may be on the tile surfaces. Once all of the tiles have been put in place, allow the adhesive to dry thoroughly before proceeding further with the job. Consult the manufacturers' directions for adequate drying time.

5. Grouting follows the bonding process. The selected group, usually a sand-Portland cement mix, should be prepared according to the

manufacturer's directions. If a colored grout is desired, the color should be added to the mixture during the preparation. Apply as previously described.

6. If the tiles require sealing, allow the grout to mature or work for about a month before applying any sealant. During the maturing process, the grout may continually give off a material that causes a haze on the tile surfaces. This haze can be wiped off easily and should be before the sealant is applied. A haze-clearing product will rapidly clear up this condition.

Other Outdoor Tiling Possibilities

Tile adapts very well to outdoor installations. It is practical and can be used as decoration on a great many different outdoor items. If the proper type of tile is selected, it is long-lasting and will remain attractive despite all types of weather conditions. Tile is easy to take care of and requires only minimum maintenance.

There are many other outdoor items that lend themselves to tiling. Outdoor dining tables and benches can be tiled with plain, pattern or decorative tiles. Large concrete planters, dividers, or walls (Fig. 10–8) used to separate or decorate lawn sections are good candidates for tiling, as are fountains (Fig. 10–9). Decorative tile in a variety of colors to compliment patios areas (Fig. 10–10), or full sheets of standard or mosaic tile can simplify and speed up these installations. Barbecue or fireplace units can also be tiled. If sections of the barbecue unit that come in contact with food are tiled, mildew-resistant grout should not be used as it may have harmful chemical components. Entranceways (Fig. 10–11), hot tubs (Fig. 10–12), and pool areas (Fig. 10–13) also lend themselves to tiling.

The one rule that must be followed with all of the tiling projects discussed is that the tile work should only be applied to a strong, secure foundation. Otherwise, the completed work may look attractive but have only a limited lifespan. Check the foundation thoroughly before beginning the tile job. If you notice any structural weak points, make the necessary repairs first.

Fig. 10–8. Tile can be used to form a very decorative wall in a garden setting. A sound background for support, design layout, and tile choice are all that is required

Fig. 10–9. Water fountains also lend themselves to decorative tile designs.

Courtesy Epro Tile　　　　　　　　*Courtesy Mannington Tile*

Fig. 10–10. There are many layout, design, and tile color selections that can be made when developing a patio to complement a home. Figs. 10–11, 10–12 and 10–13 demonstrate some of the available options.

Courtesy Mannington Tile

Fig. 10–11. A tiled outdoor entranceway. *(Courtesy Epro Tile)*

Fig. 10–12. Tile, used in and on a colorful, king-size octagonal hot tub can last indefinitely. There are many tile fashion colors to select from. *(Courtesy Summitville Tile)*

Fig. 10–13. A tile patio surrounding a pool and adjacent to an outdoor sun deck can be a homeowner's and a decorator's delight. *(Courtesy Metropolitan Ceramics)*

CHAPTER 11

Tiling Countertops and Special Areas

Preliminary Considerations

A countertop tile installation probably offers more decorative challenges than any other type of home tiling job. Tiled countertops may be in a kitchen, den, or bathroom; on a buffet, bar, vanity, or part of an individual shelf or series of shelves. Although it is always easier to start new and begin from an uncluttered fresh base, new tile can be installed over existing tiles and older laminated plastic or formica surfaces, as long as the old tiles or laminates are completely secured to the base or subsurface area and are properly prepared by sanding and priming before new tiles are set in place. Information on the methods for handling this preliminary work is located in another section of this book.

Sink, basin, and backsplash considerations are only necessary in kitchen, bathroom, or bar countertop installations. When the countertop involves a sink, there are three sink setting options. You must decide on which option to use before any part of the work can be started.

Preparing Countertops for Sinks

Decisions on the methods for setting a sink or dual sinks into a tile-covered countertop depend on both practicality and aesthetics.

The first step is to decide where the sink is to be positioned. A hole is then cut to accept the unit.

Most new sinks come with paper templates provided by the manufacturer. When the template is positioned on the countertop, it serves as a guide for proper measurement and cutting.

If a sink template is not available, one can be made. To make a template, use a large sheet of plain paper. Start by placing the basin, rim side down, on the paper worksheet. With a pencil, draw the outline of the sink by tracing around the rim or entire outer circumference. This sketch is used as a reference line.

A normal sink rim will extend outward from the sink body a certain distance, based on design. Measure the width of the rim, the area necessary to fit over and hold the sink in place permanently on the countertop once the unit has been installed. Measure in, the width of the rim, from the initial sink outline, and draw another line around the entire sink outline at the new inner measured point. This will be the designated cutting line for the countertop template.

Before cutting out the template, while the paper is still whole, draw a set of guidelines on the paper sink outline. These lines will visually divide the entire sink bowl in half vertically and horizontally. These guidelines will help align the sink so that it is accurately and evenly placed into the countertop.

If dual sinks are to be used, a template should be made for each.

Sink Setting Options

Once you have cut the properly-sized opening, or openings, to accept the sink body, the various setting options can be considered.

One option is to complete the tiling, including bonding tiles to the countertop surface and grouting, before physically setting the sink. The tiling is done directly up to the edge of the hole cut for the sink body. The basin is then set into the designated area and rests on top of the tiles. This type of sink-countertop setting provides a neat installation with no visible raw tile edges around the basic area. The tiles and joints between the sink and the countertop must be well caulked. Caulking serves as a water seal between tile and sink and limits water seepage which can be destructive to the adhesive and grouting material. Water piping and waste lines are connected to the sink in the usual manner.

A second option is to insert the sink body into the countertop wood support framework before the tiles are put into place. After the sink is hooked up to the plumbing fixtures, the tiles are bonded to the countertop surface right up to the sink's rim and then grouted. The area around the entire rim is caulked to prevent moisture from seeping under, behind, or around any of the tiles. This installation process depends more on the grout and caulking for a neat visual finish and generally will not produce tile edging as neat as the previous system.

The third option utilizes a special metal edge trim. This metal rim is attached to the area which has been cut out of the wood countertop to receive the basin. The sink is set onto the metal edge, which supports the sink body. The supply and waste pipes are attached to the sink and then the tile is bonded to the countertop against all sides of the metal frame. After the adhesive has dried thoroughly, the tiles are grouted and the balance of the installation completed. This metal edge trim system assures a neat, professional-looking finish and reduces the possibility of sink weight damaging tile surfaces.

Choosing Countertop Tile

Since most countertops will be subjected to moisture, choices should generally be made from glazed tile. Tiles should be checked for resistance to moisture, strength, and durability. Sheets of small tiles in colors or mosaic design may be used. However, it is usually impractical to use pregrouted sheets for countertops since it is not always possible to match grout when trimming is done.

Glazed tile is available in many colors. Pastels, vivid or deep hues, patterns and designs are all available from various manufacturers. Countertops should be designed to be compatible with the style and coloring of the entire unit, as well as the room (Figs. 11–1 and 11–2).

In an earlier chapter, the possibility of obtaining color-coordinated tile, appliances, fixtures, and wallpaper was discussed. In the supplier section of this book are the names of manufacturers who produce equipment and coverings that match tile color selections.

Trim Choices

Trim pieces, the tiles or other materials selected to go around, or serve as facing for countertop and sink edges, are also available in many aesthetic and practical options.

Fig. 11–1. A variety of tile shapes can be used when installing a countertop. *(Courtesy Epro, Inc.)*

The least expensive way to the countertop edging is with the *same color and type of flat tile* used for the installation. No special finishing trim is used. To finish off the counter edge, the flat horizontal countertop tiles are placed over the vertical tiles that run up to the countertop edges. These vertical tiles are bonded to the counter framework first. Using this system, one portion of the countertop will always display a visible raw tile edge. Horizontal and vertical tile edging pieces should, of course, be grouted following standard procedures.

A more effective edging can be achieved with *sink caps.* These individual pieces of ceramic trim are designed specifically for countertop jobs. They come in colors to match or coordinate with tiles used on counter surfaces. Sink caps are also designed to direct any flow of water back onto the countertop rather than letting it drip over the edges and onto the floor.

Another edging option is *bullnose tile.* Bullnose tiles have a rounded, finished edge at either one or both ends. They can be used along both the vertical and the horizontal edge surfaces of the countertop to give the countertop edge a fine, finished appearance. Bull-

Fig. 11–2. Basic floor and countertop tiles are the same color in this kitchen. A combination of single and multiple tiles are used to create the backsplash. *(Courtesy Metropolitan Ceramics)*

nose tiles can also be used directly against and around the sink body to provide an equally attractive finish to the sink. Sink cap tile and bullnose trim tile can be combined and used jointly on countertop edges, backsplashes, and around sink installations.

Quarter round trim tile, in colors to match the flat tile already in place on the counter, can also be used for countertop edging. When installed, this type of trim tile can span or cross small sections of the countertop's horizontal and vertical edges. One part of the quarter round tile fits on and completes the vertical section of the counter edge while the other part abuts the horizontal surface or flat tile section of the counter edge.

Wood or plastic edgings are other choices for countertop finishing. These edging materials are installed along the countertop edge before tile placement. When flat tiles are put in place, the top portion of the flat surface tiles is usually level with the top portion of the wood edging.

This measurement adjustment must be taken into consideration when the edging is installed. Although wood edging can be extremely attractive, it is liable to chipping, cut marks, and other surface damage from food preparation work.

Before grouting the tile, it is a good practice to protect the wood edging to eliminate the danger of staining from the grouting process. Edge grouting can be eliminated if a caulking material is used between the tile and wood surfaces instead. It is also good practice to use a number of coats of good water sealant on the wood surfaces before installing. To assure a neat job, recess the screw holes used to attach the wood edging, then fill these holes with wood plugs or wood filler material.

Decorative Inserts or Borders

Countertop tile can be plain or decorated. Designs can be inset into the surface or backsplash sections. They might be used, for example, to border a mirror or a cabinet door. Decorative tiles can be placed in a pattern or inset in any section of the counter.

A practical approach to design installation is to plan and lay out the pattern design in advance. A piece of graph paper, marked with the size of the proposed countertop installation, can simplify the job. The printed squares on the graph paper can represent the tiles—use them to indicate the position and number required of each of the design tiles and provide guidance during installation.

It is always good practice to lay out the dry tiles on the counter surfaces in a test run before bonding them. In this way, any necessary changes or problems can be detected in advance and corrections can be made easily.

There are many decorative options for tile countertop installations. Complimentary or contrasting tiles can be selected to define borders on either surfaces or backsplash areas. Special designs can be inset in other areas. Specialty or design tiles might include geometrics, florals, people, historical figures, animals, trees, birds, vegetables, ship scenes, or patterns identified with various cultures, countries, or eras. The design tiles may be installed singly on the counter tile surfaces and backsplash areas or inset in multiples of any number (Fig. 11–3).

Fig. 11–3. Counter tile can also extend down and around cabinet areas. *(Courtesy Epro Tile)*

It is important that design tiles be similar in size and thickness to the flat surface tiles planned for the job. If not, there will be difficulties with the installation. It is also practical to order the special or design tiles well in advance of the installation starting date, so that they will be available when needed.

Countertop Tile Installation

Preparations

In this section, we will assume that the countertops to be tiled are either on a newly-constructed plywood base and ready to accept the tile, or, if on an older countertop, all surfaces have been prepared to accept the new tile. If the project is new countertop, the area where the sink is to be placed must be cut out. If the job is an older countertop, all loose tiles or laminate surfaced must be rebonded then sanded and primed. All kitchen equipment and other articles must be removed. A new wood countertop framework may either be built by the home handyperson using plans available in many home decorating booklets, or by a woodworking contractor.

If the tile backsplash is to be installed near or over electrical outlets, the covers of the outlets must be removed. The outlets may require reseating if they are sunk in the wall too far for covers to be effectively reattached after the tiles have been put in place. An electrical contractor can be called in to handle this job.

If there is no difficulty with the electrical fixture depth and the tiles must simply fit around the fixture, there are several ways to handle this process. The tile can be cut in half and the opening nibbled away with a tile nipper, a hole can be cut in the tile, or the tiles can be measured and sawed or snapped to the required size.

Laying Out the Countertop

Although the instructions which follow focus on kitchen countertops, the same instructions apply to counter surfaces without sinks.

The countertop tile installation job is started by laying out the trim tiles. These are the edging or sink caps that will be used to finish off the countertop edges.

Locate the center of the countertop, or the center of the installed sink or sink opening, and mark this point. Take one piece of this trim tile and center it on this mark. The tile should be placed dry on the edge of the countertop in the same position where it will be permanently placed. The longest portion of the trim tile will face toward the floor and away from the countertop surface. The shorter portion of the trim tile will overlap the counter surface. With marking pen or pencil, mark the countertop surface along the edge of this trim tile (Fig. 11–4).

Select other spots a few feet from both sides of the initially marked countertop position and make marks along the edge of the trim tile. Continue this marking procedure all around the surface edge of the countertop. When this initial marking is completed, join all of the marks on the counter together using a straightedge. An even line should now extend completely around the countertop surface edge. If the countertop is "L" or a "U" shaped, continue the trim tile marking and subsequent line extension. Use a carpenter's square to make sure the turns for the "L" or "U" are square.

Lay out the dry edging tile that will be used all along the marked line from one end of the countertop to another. Place a spacer, usually ⅛-inch,

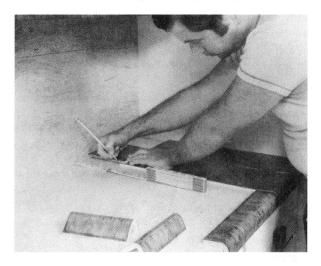

Fig. 11–4. Lay the front-edge trim down without glue, starting from the center of the countertop. Then lay out tile and tile spacings.

between each tile to simulate the exact layout when tiles are permanently bonded to the counter surface. These spacers mark the grouting joints.

If, after all of the edging tiles have been laid out, the distance remaining at the ends of the countertops is less than one inch, slightly shift all of the joint spacers to compensate. The purpose for the shift is to make sure that measurements at both ends of the counter are now at least one inch. Anything less than one inch may not be attractive.

The edging tiles around the front of the sink will probably have to be cut to fit if they hang over the sink. When all of the dry trim tiles are in set along the front edge of the sink, check for those that extend over the sink edge. These must be marked for cutting. Scribe the underside of the trim tile with a pencil mark. Use the sink or metal frame as a guide. These trim tiles can be cut immediately or any time before installation.

Once the front row of tiles has been placed, the edging tiles on the sink marked, and all working lines established, the tiles which fit the rest of the way around the sink can be placed.

Use the trim tiles on the sink's edges as a guide and lay out the dry tile along the left and right side of the sink. Include ⅛-inch spacers between each tile. When a tile extends over the sink edge, mark the tile to be cut on the underside. Continue tiles and spacers around to the back edge of the sink, marking the tiles where cutting will be necessary. These tiles can either be cut immediately or just before permanent installation.

Mitered corner trim tiles should be used for inside corners. If the mitered trim tiles are longer than the flat countertop tiles, position each mitered tile to allow space for a grout joint. If a piece of L-shaped trim is to be used on the job, center the trim piece on the corner and work edging trim tile from both sides. Set the trim tile pieces in place dry so that positioning of all edging tile can be checked before permanent installation proceeds.

Finishing the Countertop

Once the edging trim tile positions have been clearly lined up and marked, guidelines for the flat or countertop surfaces should be marked for tile installation, lined up with the trim tiles.

A carpenter's square and straightedge should be used to mark full layout lines along the flat surfaces of the counter. These marks must be aligned with the row of trim tiles on the front edge of the countertop.

After the necessary guidelines have been scribed, it is good practice to place the balance of the dry tile, section by section onto the countertop to make sure of alignment, spacing and visual effect (Fig. 11–4). Either single tiles or sheets of tile can be used to dry-test the layout. Once the tile layout is satisfactory, remove the dry tiles and start the permanent bonding to the countertop surface.

Any of the trim or flat tiles requiring a reduction in size should be trimmed using available cutting equipment. After cutting a tile to the required size, it is good practice to mark its permanent position clearly on the countertop. This can be done by making a pencil mark on the reverse side of the tile.

Start bonding the tiles by individually backbuttering the trim edging tile with mastic adhesive. Use a V-notched trowel to apply the adhesive in the manner described previously (Fig. 11–5). Set all of the trim tile edging in place along the front of the countertop first. When the edging is completed, move on, section by section, to the main portions of the counter surface. Begin the flat tile installation at an inside corner of the countertop. The bonding process for flat tile is similar for single or multiple tiles in sheets.

Use the V-notch trowel to apply the mastic adhesive to each section of the countertop surface. Adhesive placement methods described in earlier chapters should be followed.

Fig. 11–5. Apply the adhesive with a V-notched trowel. *(Courtesy American Olean Tile)*

Lay the flat tile using both the edging tile and countertop marking lines as guides. To set individual tiles, carefully lower one end of the tile into the adhesive and then the other end (Fig. 11–6). Give the tile a slight twisting motion as you move it into position thus embedding it firmly in the adhesive. Do cut tiles and irregular areas after the main part (Fig. 11–7). When all of the tiles in one section of the counter are in place, use a beater block and mallet to set the tiles securely into the adhesive. Place the beater block at an angle to the tiles. Use a damp cloth to clean up any extra adhesive on the tile surfaces.

Continue placing the tiles until all flat and trim tiles are bonded to the surface of the countertop. Allow the adhesive material and newly-installed tiles to dry for at least 24 hours, or longer, if suggested by the manufacturer's instructions.

Backsplash Installation

A countertop backsplash usually runs the full length of the counter and is made up of one or more rows of flat tile and/or a row of trim tiles. The topmost row is generally a bullnose or other trim tile. Based on the type of installation, a cove tile may be used for the bottom tile. Use of trim tiles assures a smooth finish to the job and eliminates any rough, unsightly tile edges.

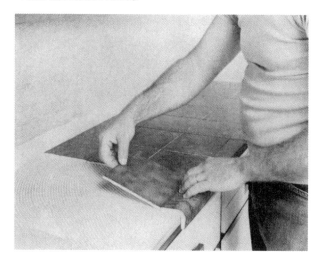

Fig. 11–6. Lay the tiles in place and press them firmly down. Keep the spacing and joints even. *(Courtesy American Olean Tile)*

Decorative tiles are often selected for a backsplash. They can serve as a design or a border. For accuracy in ordering and placement, the number and position of these decorative and border tiles should be indicated on the preliminary reference worksheet.

When permanently installing backsplash tiles, the flat tile positions and joint lines on the installed countertop surfaces should be used as a guide for tile layout (Fig. 11–8). When the job is completed, the grout

Fig. 11–7. Do edges and cutouts after you finish the main part. *(Courtesy American Olean Tile)*

Fig. 11–8. Do the backsplash after you finish the countertop, making sure that the joint lines are evenly aligned. *(Courtesy American Olean Tile)*

lines on the flat countertop tiles surfaces should match up with the grout lines between the backsplash tiles.

Start the layout by determining the height of the backsplash. Assume the total height will be three tiles—two of the tiles will be flat and a trim tile will be used on the top row. Place the three dry tiles plus appropriate joint spacers against the wall. Make a mark at this point. Use a level and straightedge, with the mark as a guide, to establish a horizontal line along the entire wall. Any irregular backsplash tile should be cut and permanent positions marked in pencil on the reverse sides.

Once the tile positioning is satisfactory, the dry tiles can be removed, adhesive placed along the marked horizontal line and the flat tiles and top trim tiles permanently set in place (Fig. 11–9).

Fig. 11–9. Add bullnose trim to the backsplash after the rest is done. *(Courtesy American Olean Tile)*

The next step in the installation process is to grout the tiled countertop and backsplash surfaces. Use the grouting procedures described in earlier chapters. A technique that may be useful when grouting counter edges is to use masking tape along all of the bottom edges of the sink caps or other trim tile. The tape will retain the grout in the joints while it is drying and it can be removed when the job is completed.

Remember not to use a grout containing chemicals that inhibit the growth of fungus if food preparation is to take place on the tiled surface. If, however, the countertop being tiled is a vanity in a bathroom area, a fungus-resistant grout is acceptable.

After grouting, wash the tile down with clear water and a well wrung-out sponge to remove all excess grout from the tile surfaces.

Allow the grout to begin to set up. Use a striking tool or toothbrush handle to trim the grout joints so they are level or even slightly concave. Wash the surfaces again with clean water and a well wrung-out sponge. Polish the tile surfaces with a dry cloth (Figs. 11–10, 11–11, 11–12, 11–13).

Fig. 11–10. Mix the grout and work it into the joints. (*Courtesy American Olean Tile*)

Fig. 11–11. Strike off joints with a wooden stick to leave them rounded. *(Courtesy American Olean Tile)*

Fig. 11–12. Clean off the grout film with a damp sponge. *(Courtesy American Olean Tile)*

Fig. 11–13. Wipe off haze with a soft rag. *(Courtesy American Olean Tile)*

Range Hoods and Other Applications

Tiling the hood of a kitchen stove, or tiling above and around other appliances, follows much the same procedure as tiling a wall. The hood or appliance is first measured and the exact center determined and marked. Place a level on this center mark and draw a vertical line up and down the hood surface. The bottom of the hood is used to establish the horizontal base line. Check with a level to make sure that this line is truly level. If there is any deviation, try to compensate for the difference using the installed tiles and grout lines.

Once the layout lines have been established, select one of the wall tile installation techniques described earlier in this book to handle the bonding, grouting, and finishing. Make sure that the adhesive and grout recommended for the job can withstand any surface heat that may develop. A thin-set epoxy resin mixed with its catalyst and epoxy grout can be used for the job.

Always use full tiles on the bottom or horizontal base line. When cut tiles are necessary, install them at the highest point on the hood.

Tile a small section of the hood at a time so that you maintain control of the work. Allow sufficient time for both the adhesive and grout to dry thoroughly.

If both sides of the hood are to be tiled, complete the inside first. Trim tiles should be used to finish off the edges.

CHAPTER 12

Tiling the Shower Stall

Preliminary Considerations

There was a time, not too long ago, when tiling a shower stall was considered a fairly massive and complex undertaking. It still is not the simplest of projects, but with waterproof backer board, mastic adhesives, waterproof shower pan membranes, and full sheets of tile, the job has become less complex and certainly within the scope of an able do-it-yourselfer. There is one caveat: if there is any part of the shower installation which you are not completely qualified to do, like the carpentry, masonry, electricity, or plumbing work, call in the appropriate contractor to handle it. If, for example, a light is to be installed in a shower stall, an electrical contractor should be called in to make the necessary electrical hookup before you proceed with the tile work.

There are many choices of patterns, layouts, and colors as with any other tile installation. Some examples of what can be done in bathrooms and shower stalls are shown in Figs. 12–1 through 12–4. Fig 12–5 shows how to measure the shower stall to compute your tile needs.

Once the shower stall position has been selected and planned out, the wall studded and stall-related carpentry completed, and the piping including the drain installed, the next step is to create a solid base for the stall. There are a number of options. If the floor where the shower is to be installed is level and structurally sound, an appropriately sized piece of exterior grade plywood can be used to start. If the floor requires leveling or buildup, you will need to build a mortar base.

Fig. 12–1. 6-inch by 6-inch tiles were used on shower walls and 1-inch mosaic tiles on shower floor. *(Courtesy American Olean Tile Co.)*

Building a Mortar Shower Base

Begin by constructing a wood base form of the appropriate size and shape in the stall. The mortar will be poured into this form. This form should be designed to permit a slope of ¼ inch per foot toward the weep holes in the drain. The cement from might be 1½ to 2 inches

Fig. 12–2. Classic black and white ceramic tiles are used in this free-standing shower. *(Courtesy Italian Ceramic Tile)*

in height, or more, depending on the particular design. Seal off the shower drain opening carefully so that when mortar is poured into the form, it does not block the drain fitting. Allow this mortar base to dry thoroughly before proceeding any further. When it is dry, remove the wood form and the protective drain covering.

A second mortar layer will be spread after the shower pan mem-

Fig. 12–3. Tile used in this shaped shower stall compliment floor and bath tiles. *(Courtesy Dal Tile Corp.)*

brane has been set in place and other work completed. This second layer will also be spread or worked toward the drain.

The mortar bed is designed to provide a basic barrier against moisture. It will also serve as a firm, solid surface for the shower floor tile.

Building a Shower Curb

The next step is to build a shower curb at the front entrance to the stall to serve as a barrier against water flowing out of the stall, and also as the bottom base for a shower door, if one is to be installed. Shower curb installation is relatively simple. Scrap pieces of backer board are set in place across the entire front of the shower stall to create a form for cement. The form should be approximately 6 inches high and 4 inches wide. The structure should be leveled and firmly supported so that it will be immobile when filled with cement. The mixture, consist-

Fig. 12–4. Tile designs and colors are used in a decorative scheme in this bathroom. Shower tiles match those used on the bathtub and is part of design pattern. *(Courtesy Dal Tile Corp.)*

ing of Portland cement, sand, and water in proportions as directed on the package, should be poured into the form. The wet cement in the form should be chopped or sliced through several times with a trowel to eliminate air pockets. Finally, the cement should be leveled and allowed to dry completely before the forms are removed.

Installing Waterproof Membrane

A waterproof fabric is required as a moisture barrier between the layers of mortar and the rest of the system. There are a number of different types of shower pan membranes that can be selected; one is a waterproof membrane made of a plastic material known as CPE, or chlorinated polyethylene.

The first step in the installation of the shower pan is marking the

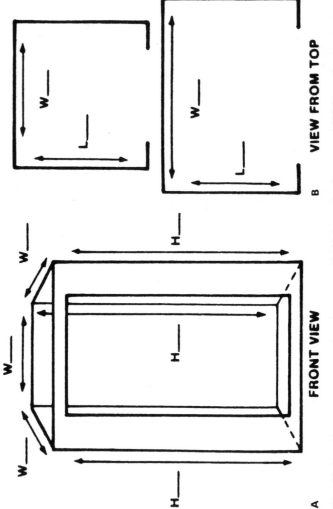

FRONT VIEW

VIEW FROM TOP

A

B

Fig. 12–5. How to measure the shower stall (A) from the front, and (B) from the top to compute tile needs.

dimensions of both the shower bed plus an allowance of several inches on the CPE material that will be placed up the shower walls. The membrane should be installed approximately 3 inches above the shower stall curb. If there is no curb, the shower membrane should be installed 6 inches above the floor line.

Cut the membrane material to the proper size. Crease along the inner dimension markings and fold it so that it can be easily handled and moved to its position on the shower stall.

Clean up any loose dirt on the mortar bed—make sure there are no nails, screwheads or protruding bits of mortar that can damage the shower pan material. Spread a ready mixed-organic mastic adhesive over the entire mortar surface to bond and secure the shower pan fabric.

Starting at one corner of the shower stall, lay the shower pan material into the adhesive-covered mortar or wood frame. The creases in the shower pan layout mark the supply of additional material that was cut to be positioned up the walls of the shower stall. Press down and smooth out the CPE material on the floor to seal it thoroughly to the adhesive on the mortar bed.

The additional CPE material to be placed up the shower stall studs should be unfolded and secured with roofing nails ot the wood studding at it highest point (3 inches high if a shower stall curbing is in place, 6 inches up from the floor without a curbing). When you get to the corners, fold the membrane material in behind and nail these corner pieces to the wood studding at the highest point to hold them securely in place. The section of the membrane that fits against the curbing can be nailed to the corner studding and cemented to the mortar curbing.

If, at any point, the shower pan membrane consists of more than one piece, it is good practice to use a solvent cement to weld the two pieces together. Place the solvent cement on each piece, wait several minutes and then press the pieces together for a secure fit.

Once the shower pan fabric has been set in place on the bonding adhesive, holes must be cut for the drain and flange bolts. Feel around for the drain hole and carefully make a slice in the material with a utility knife. Cut the material around the diameter of the drain to open a hole for the drain fixture. Feel under the shower pan fabric for the flange bolt holes and then cut openings for the bolts. Trim the material so that the flange will fit securely.

Lift the cut edges of the shower pan material and squeeze caulking under the pan to seal the CPE material to the flange. Set the bolts in place.

Now slide the upper part of the flange down over the bolts and tighten them securely. Finish the installation of the shower pan by screwing down the strainer.

After the cement shower curb has dried thoroughly, the area should be swept clear of all debris and the drain capped. A thin layer of cement mortar should be spread across the entire surface of the shower pan material. The mortar is spread or worked in such a way that a gradual grade from the wall areas down to the drain is developed. The objective is for all running water in the shower to flow back toward and out the weep holes of the drain. The original mortar form was designed with a slope of ¼ inch to the foot so that both the shower membrane and the topping layer of mortar would naturally follow this format.

Before installing backer board and tile, it is a good practice to test the drain fittings and shower pan to make sure they are completely waterproof. Fill the shower pan with three or four inches of water, and let the water stand for about a day. If there is no water loss, the job is secure. If there is leakage, look for the source and repair it.

Another Waterproof Membrane Option

Another shower stall membrane installation material makes use of a white, high bond strength, flexible, trowelable, two-component waterproof membrane and adhesive. The product may be used over cured concrete, exterior grade plywood, existing ceramic tile, bare steel, and a number of other potential shower bases.

Before beginning work on the shower stall base, make sure the drain is covered. As discussed previously, design the shower base so that when the membrane is installed, there will be a floor pitch of ¼ inch per foot toward the drain.

When you are ready to put the waterproofing compound into the stall base, mix the two parts that make up this product to achieve a homogenous paste consistency. The mix should be used within one hour.

A ³⁄₁₆ inch V-notched trowel is used to spread the mixture over the shower base. Smooth the mixture immediately with the flat edge of the trowel. Compact the product membrane in all openings, cracks, and around all orifices.

After thirty minutes, the membrane material should not be re-worked. Allow the product to set 12 to 24 hours before proceeding further with the shower job. After the product has set and a stall curbing is in place, test to be sure that the completed base is waterproof. Fill the area with water and allow to stand for a few hours, checking for any change of water level or leaks. If there are any air bubbles or pin holes, use a second coat of the membrane mixture to seal up any defective areas in the base. Once the membrane is waterproof and satisfactory, the floor tile installation can proceed.

It is best to check with the various manufacturer's specification and instruction sheets for precise information when using specialty products. The company instruction sheets will detail compound mixing details, installation techniques, and other information relating to this process.

Prefabricated Shower Pans

Shower pans made of fiberglass can be purchased. They are made to be set in place over a drain pipe. The drain built into the pan is then connected to the drain-and-trap, which comes out of the subfloor.

Installing Backer Board

Backer board is a strong, water-resistant wallboard material that serves as protection against moisture damage. Used extensively in bathroom installations, backer board protects the subsurface on which it is applied, closes in the framework, and provides a sound, moisture-resistant surface on which to apply tiles. There are different types of backer board. One company, for example, produces a product called Wonder Board.

Before installing backer board, staple strips of builder's felt to the studding to fur out the front of the stall studs. The felt is similar in thickness to the shower pan membrane, so it builds up the studs to match the overlapping membrane pan edges on the corners. The backer board is also a little thinner than drywall material, so the felt strips will make the backer board surface flush with the drywall at the edge of the shower.

Lay down a protective covering over the shower base and drain before installing the backer board. Start by nailing the backer board to the bottom of the back wall, then work upward. Using roofing nails, nail at or above the top of the shower pan to keep nails from puncturing the fabric at vulnerable places. The first sheet of backer board should go right over the lip of the fabric pan. Use ½ inch spacers to keep the bottom of the backer board above the shower pan material.

When laying out the backer board to fit in the shower stall, cut the sheets of material in such a way that there will be as few vertical seams as possible. Complete the back wall using a piece of backer board measured and cut to fit flush between the previous sheet and the drywall of the ceiling. Repeat the installation procedure with the backer board on the two side walls of the shower stall. When measuring and cutting, try to plan the backer boards so that there is an exact fit to the drywall on the outside of the stall.

When you have to cut out of the board for the water valve stems and the shower control mechanism piping, take measurements of the positions of each of these fixtures. Then transfer the measurements to the piece of backer board that has been cut to fit in the wall space where the piping goes. Drive a nail into the exact center of the measured and marked hole in the backer board. The holes for the piping can now be redrawn on the reverse side of the backer board. Use the nail hole as a marker and with a compass draw the appropriate-sized marking holes. Where the fixture holes are marked, score the mesh (which is part of the backer board), front and back, with a carbide-tipped knife, then knock out the pieces with a hammer. Slide the board over the stems and nail it to the wall.

If the openings cut out of the backer board are not perfectly clean, there is no need to be concerned. When the wall is completed, the openings will be covered with a handle flange and tile.

After all of the backer board has been installed, the next step is to ceramic mud and tape all of the separations or seams between the installed pieces. When taping the stall walls, the most effective way is to start by spreading a layer of thin-set cement, or mud, on the horizontal seams. Place a layer of mesh tape over these cemented seams. Use a tape knife to embed the mesh into the mud and smooth out the entire seam line. Continue working around all of the shower stall walls, placing the thin-set cement and tape on each of the backer board joints until the seams in the entire stall are smoothed.

When taping the corners, lay the thin-set cement into the seam joints, working from both walls. Use your fingers to wedge tape into these seam joints and make several passes with the tape knife over them.

Installing Tile and Grouting

The quickest way to tile a shower stall is to use prespaced sheets of tile which also provide the installation with a bit of flexibility. These sheets, in a wide variety of colors and tile sizes, come with tile pre-attached. The logical choice for shower stall tile is a glazed porcelain tile, vitreous or impervious to moisture. Tiles for the shower stall floor should be slip-resistant.

Begin by laying out the tiling lines in the shower stall as if you were working on a wall installation in any other part of the house. Consult Chapter 7, *Laying Out a Tile Job,* or Chapter 9, *Installing Wall Tile,* for more detailed information. After the lines are all in place, bring the tile and other equipment into the work area.

Use a mastic adhesive to bond the tile sheets to the wall. For information about adhesives and their application and for more detailed information about bonding the shower stall tiles, consult Chapter 6, *Adhesives, Mortars, and Grout.* Install tile as described for wall tile installation, then use a carpenter's level to make sure that each of the sheets of tile, or individual tiles if used, is perfectly level. Make the necessary tile cuts around the piping and fixtures so that these cut tile pieces fit and look well.

Start the tiling at the back wall of the shower stall and then complete the side walls. Use full tiles at the bottom of the walls on all sides. If, because of measurement problems, tile cutting is required, be sure to place the cut tiles at the top of the shower wall where they are not as visible. For a neat finished appearance, use bullnose tile along the edges where the backer board and drywall meet, and also on the curb.

If a tile shelf, soap dish, or a combination of both is to be installed, calculate the exact positions on the shower walls and leave a number of tiles out of the initial installation to allow space. Accessories can be installed after the wall tiles are all in place. When setting in the accessory items in the shower stall, use a thin-set adhesive for backer board bonding. If accessories are to be installed elsewhere in the bathroom on sheetrock, use a mastic adhesive. Twist the items slightly as you place them into the wall for a secure seating. Use a piece of tape across the face of the accessory items and several adjoining tiles to secure them until the adhesive sets thoroughly.

Some shower stalls also have tiles installed on the ceiling. The installation process is similar to setting wall tiles. Draw the layout lines, make sure that all lines are square and that ceiling tile and grout joints match up with the adjoining wall tiles. Follow the standard adhesive and grouting procedures.

Allow the adhesive to dry thoroughly before grouting. Consult Chapter 6, *Adhesives, Mortar, and Grout* for more detailed information on grouting the shower stall walls. Follow the manufacturer's directions for selecting and using grout. You may want to use an antimildew type of grout in the shower installation to inhibit mildew growth.

Closing Off the Shower

There are several ways to finish off the shower opening, one of these being a purchased door. These doors come with built-in frames which simply screw to the walls with the bottom edge resting on the top of the lip of the floor flange.

A second method is the build stub walls on either side of the shower opening. These must be built before the shower is tiled, then they are tiled at the same time as the rest of the shower. When stub walls are used, a low threshold joins the bottoms of the two walls. A door can be installed between the stub walls, or a shower curtain can be hung from a rod suspended between the two walls.

Project Sequence

The following is a checklist that you may want to follow for your shower installation.

(1) Select the position in the bathroom for the shower stall.

(2) Complete plumbing and electrical work for the shower.

(3) Use either a plywood sheet or build a mortar base for the stall floor.

(4) Build a masonry shower curb for the stall.

(5) Install the waterproof membrane.

(6) Place the secondary layer of masonry on the membrane.

(7) Test out the base to make sure that it is waterproof.

(8) Build stub walls if they are to be used.

(9) Place backer board on walls of stall.

(10) Seam the backer board.

(11) Install the tile on backer board.

(12) Install stall floor tile.

(13) Grout the tile.

CHAPTER 13

Tiling Fireplaces and Hearths

Safety Precautions and Building Codes

The first important preliminary step that should be taken when working with any type of combustible equipment or surface is always to check your community's fire safety and building codes to determine if regulations about fire-resistant materials and their installation exist. If specific rules appear in the municipality's code books, secure a copy, and follow the rules. This is particularly important, not only for safety purposes, but also when considering home fire insurance coverages, liability, and protection.

The use of an air channel behind fireplace tile is a case in point. This type of system, required in certain municipalities and under certain installation conditions, uses special noncombustible air channel construction spacers attached directly to the fireplace surfaces. Noncombustible building material, composed of a glass-mesh mortar body, is then attached to these spacers, forming an air channel. The facing tile is then bonded to the noncombustible material instead of directly to the old fireplace surfaces. Other code regulations that should be considered include wood stove clearance distances. Municipal codes often set the number of inches a wood stove must be from the ceiling and from front, side, and rear wall areas.

Building codes in some areas require that a hearth slab must be constructed of brick, concrete, stone, or some other noncombustible material (Fig. 13–1). Codes also set slab dimensions. Four inches is the usual thickness. The depth of a hearth slab, the area from front to back, generally runs from 1-½' to 2' while its width must extend at least 9" past each side of a fireplace.

Installation Considerations

To most people, a fireplace is utilitarian as well as a significant design feature of a room. The addition of tiles, in colors, designs, or shapes, can add to the attractiveness of both inset and free-standing fireplaces. Tile, on the face of the fireplace, the mantel, and/or the surrounding hearth, can enhance the area as a focal point for a room (Fig. 13–2).

The installation of tile on any of the fireplace surfaces follows much the same pattern as tile placement on walls and floors. When tiles are placed in a horizontal hearth area, the process follows floor layout procedures. If tiles are being set along the face of a fireplace or its mantel surfaces, wall tile installation techniques should be used.

There are some specific installation considerations that must be

Fig. 13–1. Tile can be set into the hearth area of a fireplace serving both a decorative and protective purpose. *(Courtesy Italian Ceramic Tile)*

Fig. 13–2. Custom-painted tiles accent a hearth in a country house. This motif is American songbirds. *(Courtesy Summitville Tiles)*

taken into account. It is particularly important when working with fireplace adhesives to check the manufacturer's specification sheets. Before beginning the project, the heat resistance and maximum temperatures to which the bonding material can be exposed should be determined.

If the fireplace surface is masonry, the tiles should be bonded to these surfaces with a cement-based adhesive. If the walls of the fireplace or the mantel are not constructed of a masonry material, a mastic may be used to adhere the tiles. If the tiles are to be placed anywhere inside the heat-emitting surfaces of the fireplace, a cement-based adhesive must be used. Organic mastics and many thin-set adhesives should be avoided when tiling fireplaces.

Even with extensive surface damage, a stone or brick fireplace can be tiled and renovated. All loose stone or brick should first be cemented in place so that the entire surface is solid. A smooth, leveling coat of plaster must then be applied to the rough brick or stone. After the plaster has dried thoroughly, tile can be adhered.

Tile and wood can also be used together on the front surfaces of a fireplace. It is suggested that fire-resistant wood be applied when using this decorative scheme. Holes should be drilled into the area of the fireplace with a masonry drill where the wood is to be applied. To make the wood facing absolutely secure, drill holes to at least ¾-inch into the stone facing. Lead expansion shields can be placed into the holes and the wood facing secured with masonry nails. Be careful not to drill too deeply into the stone facing as overheated nails can cause problems. If ceramic tiles are to be placed alongside any portion of the wood facing, it is a good idea to leave about ⅛″ to ¼″ of space between the surfaces. This area can be filled in with a caulking compound when the job is completed. If you intend to stain the fireplace facing wood, do so before you put the tiles in place. This will eliminate the possibility of any tile grout staining.

Tiling the Fireplace Surface

Soot can be damaging to an adhesive. The entire surface area to be tiled must be thoroughly cleaned to remove all soot and grease before any work is begun.

If the fireplace surface is not smooth, is seriously off level, or if the fireplace face has been marred and is no longer flat, damage must be repaired before tiling. If these repairs are not made and tile is installed, it will follow the natural surface lines and the defects will become obvious. Plaster, noncombustible framing, and other materials can be used to repair the surfaces.

When tiling a metal or free-standing fireplace, the metal surface, because of its relatively thin, flexible skin, should be strengthened with a covering layer of noncombustible material such as glass-mesh mortar-reinforced board. This covering should be bonded to the metal body, then install tile in the usual fashion. Tiles may be glazed or unglazed, textured, decorated, or plain.

Standard flat field tiles (Fig. 13–3), as well as a variety of trim tiles, including bullnose and double bullnose, etc., may be used for fireplace

Fig. 13–3. Tile can be placed internally and externally on a fireplace as well as on the hearth area. *(Courtesy Manning Ceramic)*

installations. Decorative tiles can also be used effectively on fireplace installations. These colorful tiles enhance room decor and if specially designed, painted, and fired, tell a story. Unique hand-painted tiles or design tiles may be interspersed with standard tiles to form patterns.

As with wall and floor installations, start by establishing vertical and horizontal lines on fireplace sides to assure that the tile courses are level in all directions. If possible, place at least one row of dry tile and accompanying joint spacers along the fireplace wall or side surface to determine the side width layout and to see if the tile must be cut to fit. Based on this visual sighting, any necessary adjustments can be made in the tile and/or grouting so that cut tiles can be positioned in the least obvious place.

Once the tile layout is satisfactory, the tile can be bonded, grouted, and the job completed. Grout colors to match the tiles may be used.

Fireplace mantels are handled in much the same manner as fireplace and hearth projects. To insure straight tile and grout lines, initial layout lines should be established on the mantel surface, then set up a test run of dry tiles and joint spacers to preview the layout. If the test run is satisfactory, permanent bonding and grout work can be completed.

Preparing the Hearth

A fireplace hearth is the area immediately in front of an installed fireplace or beneath a free-standing fireplace unit (Fig. 13–4). It can be flush with the floor or on a platform or step, and its purpose is to protect against the live logs or sparks which might fall from the fireplace and ignite a wood or carpet surface. It helps contain any soot, ash, and other dirt developing from the combustion process. In most instances, a hearth installation is a requirement for free-standing units.

The selection of the type of tile to be used for a hearth is important. Since areas of the hearth will have to bear the weight of stored fireplace wood, and may also be subjected to sharp, heavy blows from falling pieces of wood or tools, tile should be selected for structural strength and durability. Check manufacturer's specifications and choose a tile with a breaking test strength of not less than 250 pounds. An abrasion resistance in class 3 or 4 is a good safety measure.

Fig. 13–4. A living area floor, steps and fireplace all have received tile treatment in this home. This picture shows a standard tiled hearth. *(Courtesy Metropolitan Ceramics)*

The hearth surface will also be exposed to some foot traffic. If a slip-resistant tile is selected, make sure that its design allows for ease of cleaning. Fireplace ashes stick to surfaces and may be difficult to remove from some grooved or textured surfaces.

Some manufacturers recommend quarry and paver tile for hearth installations. Glazed or unglazed tile can be used if it meets the specifications outlined. Unglazed tile must be sealed and regularly treated to prevent it from staining. If possible, locate a tile that is multipurpose. There are tiles available from some manufacturers whose features include strength; a non-slip, waterproof, stain-free, and easy-to-care for surface; and availability in a variety of colors.

If the hearth is being constructed, the subsurface backing area can be strengthened and provided with some resilience with the installation of several sheets of noncombustible board. The board should be bonded together and the remaining hearth surface material put in place prior to tile installation. If the hearth area will come in contact with any wood floor section, a small space of about ⅛ inch should be left between the wood and ceramic tiles. This gap, approximately a standard joint space in width, can be filled with a caulking material. The spacing protects the wood against any possible grout staining or damage and the ceramic against wood expansion.

Tiling the Hearth

Calculate the number of tiles required for the hearth job, plus an additional quantity for job waste and for tile repair in the future. Based on the hearth layout, bullnose tiles or other types of trim tiles also should be purchased for the installation.

After the tiles are selected, job tools and supplies readied, and the hearth surface prepared to accept the tile installation, layout lines should be developed on the hearth's surface. The procedure is the same as installing tiles on a floor. Once the lines have been drawn on the working surface, lay a test row of dry tiles, including joint spacers, on the hearth. If the layout is visually pleasing, proceed with bonding the tile to the surface. If there is a problem with the layout, redraw the lines or reset the dry tiles until you are satisfied. Tiles that require cutting should be measured and then nipped using a tile nipper or cut with a snapper, wet saw, or other tile-trimming equipment. Place the shorter, cut tiles in the rear of the hearth so that they are not as visible.

Apply the tile adhesive material exactly as you would for a floor installation, a workable section at a time. Put the tile in place using any of the installation systems discussed in earlier chapters. Remember to use joint spacers, if necessary, and to set the tiles into the adhesive using a slight twisting motion. After the tiles are placed in the adhesive, use a beater board and mallet to set the tiles firmly into the bonding material. Allow the adhesive to dry thoroughly before beginning the grouting process. Use the appropriate matching grout for the hearth installation. Follow manufacturers' recommendations when making this selection. After grouting has concluded, wash down with clean water and a well wrung-out sponge. Use a grout striker or toothbrush handle to smooth out the grout lines. After a final washing, polish the tile surfaces with a dry towel or soft cloth.

CHAPTER 14

Repairing Tile

Preliminary Considerations

In addition to intrinsic beauty, a practical advantage of ceramic tile is that any damage that may occur to one or more tiles is usually repairable. It is important to recognize that an entire wall does not have to be replaced should one or even a few problem areas develop. If tiles need to be added to a current installation, this can also be done easily. When the repair or addition is completed, the new work is usually not even noticeable.

If a supply of extra tile was secured and stored when the tile was originally installed, tile of the right color and shading will be available when replacements or additions are required. Tile can be preserved indefinitely as long as it is stored safely. Throughout this book the purchase of an extra supply for future use has been stressed.

A tile repair job may be necessary for various reasons:

- Tiles can crack. A heavy item may inadvertently be dropped or may hit the surface of a tile at some stress point and cause a tile to crack or break.
- Tiles can become loose. An adhesive may dry out or an incorrect adhesive may have been used for the initial bonding. A problem may develop with wall surfaces behind the tile, or other circumstances may cause tile loosening or shifting.
- You may decide to expand the current tiled area by extending a tiled wall as part of a planned room redecorating scheme.

- A colorful new tile border, replacing plain edging tile, may be just one of many planned changes.

There may be other instances when replacement of tile on existing surfaces becomes necessary. The way to make these tile repairs or changes is discussed later in this chapter.

Poor Preparation Equals Future Problems

Something heavy dropped on a floor, something sharp hitting a wall, or man-made abuses can damage tile surfaces and grout joints. However, these strikes are not the only way that tiles and grout may be cracked or marred. More often than not, the damage, while not immediate, is the result of overlooked wall or floor subsurface or support problems. Improper backing materials and failure to observe instructions for placing fill, adhesives, or the like can also cause future difficulties. Walls and floors that are not properly leveled or supported eventually cause damage to tiles. The basic rule for a long-lasting tile installation is to attend to the background support system. Consult Chapter 5, *Preparing for the Tile Job,* for details about proper preliminary preparations.

Structural forces, such as normal settling conditions in many new homes, can also cause damage. The shifting may move a wall or floor and stress a tile layout until snapping or breakage occurs. In this instance, too, the background support has to be evaluated before repair work is undertaken.

Water can also damage a tile installation, weakening the tile backing and support surfaces. A broken water pipe, a roof drainage problem, or water seepage beneath the floor or foundation can be a serious cause for concern. These areas must be repaired as soon as possible, not only for the sake of the tile, but also to avoid serious structural damage.

Repairing Existing Tile—Typical Problems

Loose Tiles

If a tile is loose, the problem can be remedied. If many tiles are loose, this too can be corrected. The proper approach to the problem, however, is first to determine the root cause of the difficulty and to correct it.

Some warning signs will be obvious and others not as evident. Several possibilities to investigate include inner wall or subfloor dampness, poor initial wall or floor preparation, an improper adhesive or a breakdown of older adhesive, or vibration problems. As a rule of thumb, if only one or a few tiles are involved, some external problem or force was a contributing factor. If, on the other hand, a complete row or section of tiles suddenly cracks or breaks loose, the trouble is probably structural in nature. Another indicator of the type of problem is the way tiles break. If the tile crack appears concave, the chances are something has struck the tile and caused the break. If the break looks more convex, that is, bulging outward, some pressure behind the tile is pushing it out. In either case, the tile must be repaired. In the convex instance, however, the source of the problem must be located before tile replacement is initiated.

Once the tiles to be replaced are removed from the wall or floor, a little scraping and poking around will often reveal if a water condition exists. A powdery, flaky condition of the old adhesive on wall or floor surfaces indicates that the adhesive has dried out. A vibration problem becomes fairly obvious when you analyze external conditions. For example, a door that constantly slams and causes heavy thumping in the area of loose tiles is a likely suspect.

Start the repair process by removing any tile that is loose or broken. Dig out all of the surrounding grout using a nail, sharp knife, pointed pry-type can opener, or other pointed instrument. Remove old adhesive with a putty knife or chisel after loose tile has been removed.

All of the subsurfaces must be repaired or replaced before the new tile bonding can begin. If the damaged area is minor, a simple repair can be made to the surface. If an entire floor or wall section must be replaced, all of the tile, even though not loose, should be removed so that the subsurface repair can be completed.

Consult Chapter 5, *Preparing For The Tile Job,* Chapter 8, *Installing Floor Tiles,* or Chapter 9, *Installing Wall Tile,* for more detailed information on subsurface repairs.

Minor Tile Replacement

If only a few tiles must be replaced, complete the necessary repairs to floor or wall surfaces. If backing is damaged, fill and smooth with patching compound. Do not fill too full. When the area is dry, prime

> *Installation Tips: If the difficulty is traced to inner wall dampness or the development of a wet wall condition, install backer board on the wall area before reinstalling the tile. If the difficulty is traced to a floor dampness condition, after removing the tiles, conduct a test of the area beneath the tiles for seepage through the concrete floor. If dampness is found, a contractor familiar with this type of condition should be called to make repairs before tile is reinstalled.*

with latex primer. Allow the primer to dry. Clean all loose debris from the back of the tile. Gently scrape off or sandpaper any of the old, loose adhesive. Set the old tile into the newly-repaired area to make sure of the fit. *Backbutter* the tile with adhesive and put it in place. Tap the newly installed tile gently with a board and mallet to make sure that it is secure. Allow the adhesive to dry thoroughly. Grout the joints. Use the same type and color grout that was applied in the original job. Wipe the surfaces clean of grout residue.

Major Tile Replacement

If it becomes necessary to replace a large section of tiles, complete the required repairs to the wall or floor, then prime the entire surface. Give this newly primed area time to dry thoroughly. Clean the reverse side of each tile that is to be reinstalled. Remove all debris and sand the old adhesive off the tile.

New chalk level lines may have to be struck or lines scribed from existing tiles to assure that the tiles will be level when replaced. Spread the adhesive in the areas to receive the tiles. Fit the tiles using installation, cutting, and trimming techniques discussed in previous chapter. Tap the newly-installed tiles gently with a board and mallet to make sure that they are securely in place. After the adhesive is allowed to dry thoroughly, regrout the joints. Use the same type and color grout as in the original job.

> *Installation Tip: If the broken tiles are near water or drain holes, cover or block these openings with rags or paper before tile removal begins to protect them from possible damage or blockage caused by loose, cracked tile pieces, or other debris.*

Cracked Tile

A cracked tile presents a slightly different repair problem than a loose tile. Although it may be cracked in one or more places, the tile is probably still held securely in place by the subsurface adhesive. The objective is to remove the damaged tile or tiles without damaging any of the surrounding tiles. There are a number of ways to do this.

One technique to start the cracked tile removal process is to rid the surrounding area of grout. A nail, knife, pointed pry-type can opener or other pointed instrument can be used for this portion of the job.

Use a cold chisel and a hammer to break the damaged tile. A cold chisel is a tempered, heavy piece of steel ground to a sharp flat edge at one end and worked into a larger flat, striking area on the opposite end. A hammer is struck repeatedly against the flat end while the sharp end is positioned to break up or dig into objects.

The cracked tile should be broken into as many pieces as possible so that the pieces can be chipped or broken away from the subsurface. Dig and chip from the center of the tile, working toward the tile edges to avoid damaging any surrounding tile. After all pieces of the tile have been removed, clean the debris from the subsurface. Scrape out any remaining adhesive. Be careful not to damage the actual subsurface.

Another technique is first to clear out the surrounding grout, and then hammer a hole through the center of the broken tile with a nail set. A nail set is a metal instrument tapered almost to a point that is used to drive nails below the surface level of a piece of wood. Once a hole is cut into the tile, a cross is scribed from one corner to another on the tile face with a glass cutter. A cold chisel is then applied to the center hole and the broken tile chipped away. The debris is removed from the exposed subsurface.

Another removal process requires only a hammer. Grout is first cleared from the areas surrounding the defective tile. The center portion of the tile is struck with the hammer head until it shatters. Slowly and carefully, other sections are struck until the entire tile is cracked. The tile pieces are then loosened and removed from the backing.

Replacement tile is placed dry in the cleared backing areas to check the fit. If everything is satisfactory, a layer of adhesive is spread on the tile and it is permanently reinstalled. The newly-installed tile is gently tapped with a board and mallet to make sure it is securely in place. The adhesive is then allowed to dry thoroughly and the joints are regrouted. The same type and color grout installed with the original tiling job should be used.

If, in addition to a broken tile, a ceramic accessory item has been damaged and must be removed, the removal procedure is similar. Before initiating the repair procedure, the replacement accessory should be selected to check for correct fit. If the replacement differs in size from the original, surrounding tiles may have to be removed, or extra tiles cut to fit open spaces. If the replacement accessory is a glass, tissue or toothbrush holder or a similar article, it can be replaced in the wall with tile adhesive. If the device is a safety rack or bar designed to assist entry and exit from a bathtub or shower, the holder should also be anchored to a wall stud with screws since the tile adhesive alone may not sufficiently secure it.

Installation Tips: *Always wear safety glasses and an air filter mask when removing old or damaged tile. Tile chips can be dangerous to eyes, and ceramic dust can be injurious to the respiratory tract.*

If an insufficient number of matching tiles are available for replacement, check with dealers handling the particular brand of tile. If the tiles are not available, ask to see the dealer's "bone pile." You may be able to find a sufficient number of matching tiles from this source.

Mosaic Tile Repair

Damaged mosaic tile, installed on floors or walls, occasionally requires repair. The techniques suggested for individual tile repair also apply to mosaics. All loose, cracked, or broken pieces of the mosaic tile must be removed. However, when preparing to replace broken mosaic tile, examine the overall pattern of the damaged area of the mosaic. It may be easier and more effective to replace an entire section of the mosaic rather than just a tiny broken piece. Note how the mosaic pattern repeats itself to determine how to cut out the replacement tile from a piece of new mosaic saved from the original installation. When installing the new piece of mosaic tile, use the same bonding method that was applied originally. The newly-installed piece of mosaic will have to be grouted with the same type and color grout previously used.

Lost Grout Replacement

All wall, floor, and other areas that have been tiled also have been grouted to finish off the installation. In most instances, tile will need to be regrouted only if the grout is somehow seriously damaged or pieces are missing. Continuous abuse by the sharp pointed heels of women's shoes, for example, can damage grout. There are times, however, when colored grout is desired to produce a room decor change. In this instance, all of the aging, plain colored-grout on a job may be removed and replaced with a grout designed to complement the tile or match some particular object in the room.

There are also times when grout disintegrates and sections require regrouting. The entire defective joint must be cleaned out thoroughly to a point in the line where the grout is firm and no longer loose. A nail, can opener point, awl, or other sharp pointed instrument can be used to dig out the area completely. The area should be cleared as work progresses so that grout pieces and dust do not settle in the work area. When the clearing/cleaning job is completed, the joints can be regrouted. If the area to be grouted is large, the grouting procedure described in an earlier chapter should be used. The grout must be mixed and then wiped diagonally across joints and tiles with a rubber grout float. If the area to be regrouted is limited, mix the grout and hand press it into the joints. If allergies to potential chemicals in the grout present a problem, rubber gloves should be worn.

Adding New Tile to Existing Installations

Tile Extensions

The urge to remodel strikes many homeowners at one time or another, and drastic changes can be the order of the day. Entire walls of wallpaper can be steamed off and replaced; floor finishes may be changed and mixed or matched with a variety of products; room uses may be changed and tiled walls or floors may be added or replaced.

Installation Tip: *When tile adhesive is used, it must be permitted to dry or cure completely before grout is installed. If the drying process is not complete, the grout will not cure properly and sections of the joints may eventually fall out.*

Tile, because of its versatility and flexibility, can be modernized with minimum effort.

Any tile surface, wall or floor, can be extended even if the original tile color and shade is no longer available. Contrasting rows of tile can be placed between the old and new tiles. This procedure can create a visually pleasing horizontal or vertical extension of a particular wall. For example, prior to a wall extension, a tile wall might be installed only to wainscot height. The edging tile on the wainscotting can be removed and replaced with a few contrasting courses of tile. The new tile can then be placed above the contrasting course and installed as far up as you wish.

Another example might be a rug area surrounded by a tile floor. A new decor calls for a full tile floor. After the rug is removed and the subsurface area properly cleaned and measured, the section is primed and tile adhesive applied in the approved way. A pattern of tiles to complement the existing tiles is selected and placed in the space formerly occupied by the rug. When the work is completed, the finished tile job, either in special pattern or color, complements or blends with the original tile floor.

Tile Accenting

Room decor changes can also be as simple as installing accent tiles. An accent tile is simply a decorated tile or group of tiles with the same, contrasting, or complimentary background color as the tiles on the wall or floor. The designs may be initials, floral, birds, animals, trees, landscapes, figures, or any pattern that is pleasing. Accent patterns might even be individualized with the homeowner preparing the artistic layout and ordering the design to be fired onto the tiles at a local ceramic shop.

Accent patterns might flow along the entire ceiling edge of a wall. They can be used to form a design on a floor so that a particular group of tiles develops into a selected pattern. A set of accent tiles might adorn the kitchen backsplash, or be set into a wall as initials, for example. The installation process is started by deciding the location of the wall or floor accent tile so that it most effectively highlights the room. The use of accent tile can create a unique decor, and express the individuality of the homeowner.

If there is an existing tile installation in place, individual tiles or groups of tile may have to be removed to make room for the accent tile placement. Follow the procedures outlined previously for removal of broken tiles and reinstallation techniques.

Before starting the renovation process, make sure that the decorative tiles are available and will fit into your installation. Check to be sure that the tiles are the correct size, thickness, and number. If the accent tiles happen to be thinner, the backing wall or subfloor area can be built up with the proper setting material. Be wary of accent tiles that are too thick—if installed, they will not allow for an even surface.

Renovating a Tile Installation

It is possible to change the look of an existing tile installation without changing every tile in the room. If the tile job happens to be an older installation, new edging and trim pieces are now available that will give the job a more modern look. Kitchen countertops are special candidates for this type of renewal. Contrasting colors in tile trim and edging pieces eliminate the need to locate a perfect color match for existing tile. The job is started by removing the existing grout and then the trim or edging pieces. The area is cleaned thoroughly by scraping out any loose grout and broken tile pieces, then the old adhesive is sanded down. A putty knife can be used to apply new adhesive. The new edging or trim tile is set in place and allowed to dry thoroughly before regrouting.

Color Changes

Epoxy paint can be used to paint existing tiles. The tiles must be sanded with fine grade abrasive paper to provide a gripping surface for the epoxy. The entire area must then be thoroughly cleaned of accumulated dirt, grease, and oil before paint application. The surrounding grout will probably have to be painted the same color as the tile. Paint application information, drying times, etc., can be found on the epoxy containers. It is a good idea to paint a few sample tiles pieces before starting on a complete job to test the color, paint, and brush flow.

Epoxy painting the surface of tile is not an easy project and requires a steady and practiced hand to turn out a workmanlike job.

New Tile on Old

In an earlier chapter, the placement of tile on tile was covered extensively. This is a reminder that this technique of placing new on old can be used in an existing installation to change a color, design, pattern, or room decor. The face of existing tile must be sanded thoroughly and all dirt, dust, oil, or grease must be removed from the tile before the adhesive and the new tiles will form a firm and secure bond (Fig. 14–1).

Repairing Marble

Marble tiles share a number of characteristics with ceramic tile. In an earlier chapter on tile installation, for example, it was indicated that bonding and grouting techniques were much the same. On the down side, both ceramic and marble floor and wall covering may be subject to damage if punished with harsh use. Both also respond poorly to inadequately prepared surfaces.

When marble tiles crack or break, repair is possible. A broken marble tile can be almost completely repaired if all of the pieces are still available. Begin by bringing all of the damaged pieces together, reassembling them as you would a jigsaw puzzle. This is to make sure that all pieces are available. If everything appears whole, disassemble and wash the pieces and edges with acetone. This will remove accumulated dirt from surrounding edges.

Many supply or hardware shops have a special marble glue. If this glue is not available, use an epoxy-based adhesive. Use a small, inexpensive brush (the kind used with children's paints is ideal) to apply the adhesive. Paint the edge of each broken piece with the glue and fit the pieces together to reform the original. Press the edges together, maintaining the pressure for the time specified in the adhesive instructions. If excess glue oozes out, wipe it away before it dries.

Fig. 14–1. New tile can be installed on top of old tile. The cross section shows the existing tile sanded down and cleaned, adhesive, new tile and grout. *(Courtesy Summitville Tile)*

It is possible to repair a marble tile even if a piece is missing (Fig. 14–2). Most often, the damage occurs to corners and generally the break is not extensive. Start by framing in the broken corner with several pieces of wood the same depth as the tile. If you have some marble scraps from the original installation, break these pieces up into a fine powder. You can also go to a supplier and buy a single tile and break it up. Mix the powder into a paste with polyester resin glue. Fill the wood form you have created with the mixture and cover with paper so that it does not dry too rapidly. Allow the mixture to dry for 18 to 24 hours.

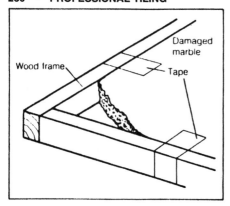

Fig. 14–2. Repair a broken corner on a marble tile with mixed polyester resin and marble dust placed in a form.

Remove the form and covering paper, then rub the new and old surfaces with a marble polishing powder.

A Final Word About Tile Repair

It bears repeating that the most important step to be taken in the tile repair process is to isolate the underlying cause of any problem. Except in rare instances, tiles usually do not drop off a wall or simply lift from a floor without cause. If the cause is obvious, the damaged tile can be quickly replaced after the proper adjustment is made. If, however, the root cause of the problem is not discovered, it makes little sense to replace a tile until the problem is found. Continue to search until a solution to the problem is discovered and solved. Then the tile can be replaced safely.

CHAPTER 15

Caring for Tile

Preliminary Considerations

Normally, tile requires minimal effort to keep it sparkling clean. A number of household products can be used to remove most stains. If stains are particularly difficult and not responsive to home cleaning products, there are commercial products that can be used effectively in the majority of cases.

As we have previously discussed, tile is either glazed or unglazed. Different levels of care are necessary depending on the type of tile. Glazed tile has a glass-like, protective finish developed during the manufacturing process, and thus requires less care (Fig. 15–1).

Unglazed tile, on the other hand, has a porous surface that often requires sealing after installation. Sealants come in either high gloss or dull finish. The main purpose of the sealant is to protect the unglazed tile from stains, though it may also be used to bring out natural color variations or to highlight texture. Sealers can also darken or lighten certain unglazed tile surfaces.

Like unglazed tile, cement-based grouts require sealant treatment; epoxy-based grouts, like glazed tile, do not require a sealant.

Fig. 15–1. Commercial tile is used extensively in restaurant kitchens. Strict cleanliness and maintenance requirements make tile an ideal choice. *(Courtesy Italian Ceramic Tile)*

Tile Sealers

When selecting the proper type of sealer for unglazed tile and cement-based grout, there are two basic sets of choices. The first is between water-, oil-, lacquer-, or silicon-based sealers. The second is between penetrating or coating sealers.

If the sealer is required to protect the tile only against potential water damage, a *water-based sealer* can handle the job. If, on the other hand, a sealer is needed to protect the tile against both water and oil damage, an *oil-based sealer* is preferable.

If the unglazed tile must be made water-resistant, a *lacquer-* or *silicon-based sealer* is a good choice. Such sealers can protect the tile from moisture and stains. Lacquer-based sealers are not as effective as silicone sealers in wet areas, but they can penetrate the pores of unglazed tile more effectively. Silicone sealers work effectively on cement-based grouts adjacent to the glazed tiles, since they separate easily from glazed surfaces and thus do not cause extra cleanup work. Silicone sealers are particularly useful when continuous grout staining is a problem.

The selection of a penetrating or a coating seal is dependent on other factors. A *penetrating sealer,* as its name implies, is actually absorbed into the tile and its accompanying grout and generally does not leave a sheen on the tile surface. The main function of the penetrating sealer is to reduce the absorbency of the unglazed tile surface and grout.

A *coating sealer* stays on the surface of the tile and leaves a glossy residue. It, too, is designed to reduce the absorbency of the tile and grout. Surfaces treated with coating sealers usually require waxing to strengthen and protect the sealing coat.

Common lemon oil, available in almost any store, is a natural grout sealer that is a good choice for use on kitchen countertop grout. Normally, sealers with a silicone base would be used to seal grout in areas subject to moisture, such as bathtubs, sinks, or backsplashes. Silicone-based sealers should not, however, be used on kitchen countertops or other food preparation areas.

Cleaning Tile

The standard and easiest way to clean tiles is to use a damp sponge, mop or cloth, clean water, and mild household detergent. Glazed or sealed tile is simply wiped or mopped until clean. Unglazed tile, once sealed, can be cleaned in the same way.

Countertops should always be cleaned with a sponge or soft cloth after food preparation, especially if acid foods have been prepared. It is a good practice to protect the countertops from such food acids, using a cutting board, an acrylic sheet, or a sheet of waxed paper, plastic wrap or foil.

Acid-based cleaners should not be used on glazed tile. The acid mixture may eat away at the glaze. Stick to water, washing soda, or detergents for this type of tile. Supermarkets have shelves of detergents such as Spic & Span®, Mr. Clean®, Liquid Comet®, Top Job®, Ajax Liquid®, etc., that can be used on both floor and wall tile. Always read product labels carefully for cautionary messages or special directions.

Wax should not be used on glazed tile. It can easily be spread over the tile face and it will not penetrate the surface. The residue can be picked up on shoes, creating a potential danger of slipping and spreading the residue to damage other floor surfaces or carpeting.

Wax should be used on unglazed tiles. There are a number of water-based waxes prepared specifically for this application. Sealer plus wax can combine to give unglazed tile an attractive and protective gloss. Always check manufacturers' directions on both the tiles and specific products to make sure that each product is acceptable for your specific brand and type of tile.

Abrasive cleaning powders, or acid-based liquids such as vinegar should never be used on unglazed tile surfaces. Steel wool pads should not be used on glazed or unglazed tile. The metal can scratch glazed tile or rust-stain the unglazed tile.

Use caution when applying a cleaning product that contains any color on unglazed tile. The porous tile body may absorb the color. It is always a good idea to test every product you intend to use on a spare tile or a section of tile not readily visible.

Commercial tile cleaning products may be used to supplement simple water cleanup, especially if a hard water condition exists. If a noncommercial cleaner is preferred for hard water areas, a 50/50 mixture of white vinegar and water may be used on glazed tile. Products containing caustic soda can also be used on heavily-soiled glazed tiles.

If the tiles are particularly dirty, a stiff-bristled brush or a nylon scrubbing pad may be used in the preliminary cleanup process, followed by a damp mop, sponge, or cloth, and clean water.

Although tile does not have to be damp-cleaned daily, it is a good practice to sweep regularly or vacuum any dirt that may accumulate on the floor surfaces. This will protect the tile from grit grinding damage. Be careful when using a vacuum cleaner so that the metal parts do not scratch or otherwise damage the tile.

Mosaic tile may be cleaned using the same products and procedures as other tile installations.

If applied wax must be removed from tile surfaces, hot water and detergents can be used. The old wax can also be cleaned off with a commercial wax stripper.

A Suggested Tile Cleaning Routine

Most cleaning jobs run more smoothly if a routine is developed. To maintain house tile in a like-new condition, a regular cleaning schedule and procedures should be maintained. Here are some suggestions.

If the Wall Is Composed of Glazed Tile . . .

- Clean regularly with an all-purpose household cleaning product. Use the cleaner with a damp, soft cleaning cloth to keep the tile surfaces bright and shining. An application of window cleaning solution or commercial cleaner, if available, for routine cleaning may also be used on glazed tile. After applying the cleaner, wipe the tiles with toweling or other soft absorbent cloth.
- If the glazed wall tile is very dirty, use an all-purpose household cleaner and a nylon, nonmetallic scrubbing pad or brush. Scouring powders may be used, but test the powder on a small section of tile to be sure that it will not damage surfaces. Nonscratch scouring powders may be used occasionally. Check with the manufacturers' directions to be sure that repeated use of scouring powder does not mar the tile finish.

If the Wall Is Composed of Unglazed Tile . . .

- Clean regularly with plain water and a soapless detergent such as Spic & Span. Dilute the solution according to package directions. After detergent application, wash or sponge wall tile with clean water. It is always a good idea to protect your hands by using rubber gloves when working with cleaning products.

- If the unglazed wall tile is very dirty, use household scouring powder that has been mixed with water to form a paste. Leave the paste on the tile surface for a short period of time and rub with a brush or nylon pad. Use clean water to rinse the tile surfaces and dry with an absorbent cloth.

If the Floor Is Composed of Glazed Tile . . .

- Vacuum regularly to remove sand, dirt, and grit before it scratches the surface or mars the finish. Clean regularly with a mop, sponge, or soft cloth wrung out of a non-soap detergent, such as Spic & Span, and water. Then, with clean mop, sponge, or cloth, wipe again with clean water to remove any detergent residue.
- If the glazed floor is very dirty, after vacuuming use a non-soap detergent and water. Increase the ratio of detergent to water to make a very strong solution, or use a commercial cleaner to loosen any heavy dirt accumulation. If glazed tile is heavily stained, use a household cleaning powder with bleach. Mix the powder with a little water to form a paste and apply to the tile surfaces. Allow the paste to remain for a short time before rinsing off and drying with an absorbent towel. If the tile is exceptionally dirty, a motorized cleaning unit may be necessary to scrub the tiles. After using the powder scrubber, wash the floor with clean water and dry. Be exceedingly careful with the mechanized cleaning device to avoid damage to the floor tiles.

If the Floor Is Composed of Unglazed Tile . . .

- After thoroughly vacuuming the floor, clean with a mop, sponge, or soft cleaning cloth and a solution of a non-soap detergent and water. After the tiles have been washed, rinse them with a clean mop, sponge, or cloth and clean water.
- If the unglazed floor is very dirty, make a paste mixture of a strong household cleaning powder and apply it to the tile surfaces. Allow the cleaning mixture to remain on the tile for a short period of time before brush-scrubbing the surface. After scrubbing, use clean water to thoroughly rinse the floor. Dry the tiles with an absorbent

cloth. If the floor is exceptionally dirty, a motorized floor scrubbing unit may have to be used. After the powder scrubber is used, wash the tiles with clean water and dry with an absorbent cloth. Before using cleaning powders on unglazed surfaces, test them on a spare tile or small section of the floor.

When Kitchen Countertop Is Glazed Tile . . .

- Clean regularly with an all-purpose household cleaning product. Use the cleaner with a damp cleaning cloth to keep the tile surfaces bright and shining. An application of window cleaning solution may also be used on the tile surfaces. After applying the cleaner, dry the surface with an absorbent cloth. A commercial cleaner may also be used for routine cleaning.
- If the glazed countertop tile is very dirty, use an all-purpose household cleaner or a nylon, nonmetallic scrubbing pad, but not steel wool. A non-scratch scouring powder may be used but it should be tested on a small section of tile to be sure that it will not damage the surface. Make sure that the cleaner residue is completely washed away with clean water so that it will not affect any food.

When the Tile in a Shower Stall Is Glazed Tile . . .

- Clean regularly with household bathroom cleansers labeled for use on tiles (Fig. 15–2). Wipe or spray the cleaner on the tiles and allow it to work on accumulated dirt for a short time. Wash the tiles with clean water. A 50/50 mixture of white vinegar and water may also be used to clean most glazed tile. However, vinegar can etch certain types of tile and erode certain grouts. Test a small section of the tile and grout to be sure that the vinegar mixture will not affect it.
- If the glazed shower tile is very dirty, several household products may be used. The tile surfaces may be washed down with either hydrogen peroxide or bleach. If the dirt still does not respond to either of these cleaning agents, mix some household scouring powder with water to form a paste. Select a powder that contains a bleaching agent. Apply the paste to the walls and leave it in place for 6–8 hours. Using a scrubbing brush on the tile surfaces to take off the dirt and caked paste. Wash the walls down thoroughly with plain water. Mildew in a shower usually responds to a bleach or ammonia

Fig. 15–2. When grout gets dirty, it can be cleaned with an all-purpose household cleaning product. An ordinary toothbrush can be used to scrub the joints. *(Courtesy Summitville Tile)*

wash. **Do not, under any circumstances, mix bleach and ammonia, or products containing them together, as they will react chemically and form a deadly gas.**

- If mildew affects the tile and grout around the base of a bathtub, an effective way to remove it is to use full strength bleach on the area. Fill a shallow pan with bleach, tear narrow strips of cloth, and then soak them in the pan. Lay the bleach-soaked strips along the tile and grout lines. Leave the cloths in place for 1 to 3 hours or until they dry moderately. Wash down the area after the strips are removed. The mildew should be gone. If this method is ineffective, use a commercial mildew remover.

Stain Removal Techniques

Most stains can be removed using standard household products. If the stain is particularly difficult to handle, a commercial stain remover can be used. Tile manufacturers like American Olean Tile Company, for example, have a general purpose tile cleaner, a tile and kitchen cleaner, a scouring cleanser, a mildew remover and cleaner, and other commercial cleaning and sealing products in addition to its line of tiles. Summitville Tiles markets a grout cleaner and mildew remover, a cleanup grout and tile cleaner, and other commercial cleaning and related products to support its line of tiles. Other manufacturers also offer a range of different cleaning products.

Stains of every kind can affect tiles and grout joints. The list which follows provides some of the most common staining problems and potential solutions.

Table 15–1. Tile and Grout Cleaning and Stain Removal Solutions

Problem	Remover(s)
Blood	B-C-G
Chewing Gum	H-J
Coffee	B-C-F-G
Dyes	C
Fats	E-M
Fruit Juices	B-C-F-G-I
Grease	E-K-M
Ink	B-C
Iodine	A
Lipstick	C-F-G
Mercurochrome	C
Mildew	A-B-C
Mineral Deposits	A-O
Motor Oil	K
Mustard	C
Nail Polish	C-L
Paint	J
Rust	B-N
Tar	H-J
Tea	C-F-G
Tough Stains	I
Vegetable oil	B-E
Water/Mineral Stains	O
Wax	H-J
Wet Paper/Corrugated Paper	C
Wine	B

Cleaners and Stain Removers

Most of the following items are regarded as household cleaning products and may be purchased at local supermarkets. Review the packaged directions before using any product for efficacy and safety.

A	**AMMONIA**	Comes in liquid form for cleaning purposes. Never mix ammonia of any kind with chlorine bleach. These products react chemically and release a poison gas. Always read product labels to be sure cleaners which you are mixing do not contain any ammonia or chlorine bleach.
B	**BAKING SODA**	Also known as Bicarbonate of Soda. Comes in powder form for cleaning purposes. Mix with water to form a paste.
C	**BLEACH**	Note caution under Ammonia. In addition, never mix bleach with acids of any kind. This combination can react chemically and be dangerous. Bleach, also known as chlorinated bleach and household bleach, comes in liquid form.
D	**CAUSTIC SODA**	A 5% sodium hydroxide solution.
E	**DETERGENT**	Common household cleaners available in all markets under various brand names. Both soapless, e.g., Spic & Span, and soap-forming detergents are available.
F	**HOUSEHOLD CLEANERS**	Include both detergent and nondetergent cleaners available in all markets under various brand names. Come in powder and liquid forms.
G	**HYDROGEN PEROXIDE**	Comes in liquid form. Usually sold in pharmacies or medication section of super-markets.
H	**ICE CUBES**	Can be made in the household refrigerator.
I	**OXALIC ACID**	A strong chemical bleach which should not be used with or confused with chlorine bleach. Oxalic acid comes in liquid form.
J	**PAINT REMOVER**	Commercial product available in liquid form in any paint or hardware store. Be especially

cautious when using this product. Some people are allergic to the chemicals in paint removers. It can also be highly inflammable.

K	**PLASTER OF PARIS**	A commercial product which may be purchased in any paint or hardware store. Available in powder form and mixed with water for cleaning purposes.
L	**NAIL POLISH REMOVER**	A commercial product available in the cosmetic section of department stores. Can be highly flammable. Comes in liquid form.
M	**SAL SODA**	This product is mixed with water for cleaning purposes.
N	**SCOURING POWDERS**	Available in most supermarkets under trade names such as Comet, Bon Ami, Ajax, etc. Always test on a small, sample section of tile or grout before using to be sure that the product will not scratch the surface.
O	**WHITE VINEGAR**	Always test a vinegar solution on a small section of tile before using as it can etch specific types of tile and also erode certain grout. Available in liquid form.

Cleaning Marble Tile

Marble tile, like ceramic tile, is subject to dirt and grime accumulations. It takes a little more attention to keep marble clean, especially when exposed to heavy dirt or staining conditions. In other chapters of this book, references have been made to the similarities between ceramic and marble tile installation. There are similarities in cleaning, but there are also some differences.

There are three distinct marble cleaning situations. The easiest problem to deal with is normal dirt accumulation. Daily cleaning tasks can generally be handled with standard household detergents or cleaning solutions designed for marble which are available in most supermarkets or tile supply houses. The marble should be wiped clean with a damp soft mop, cloth or sponge, and rinsed with cold water.

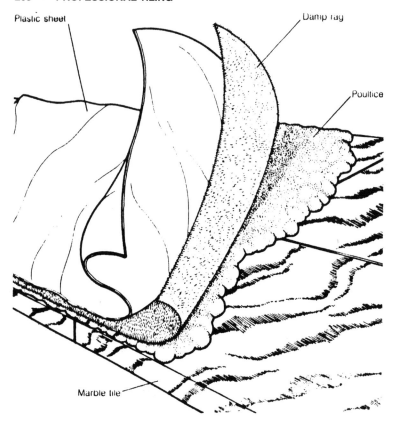

Plastic sheet

Damp rag

Poultice

Marble tile

Fig. 15–3. Cleaning heavy, ground-in, stubborn dirt from marble. Make a poultice of household detergent and water. Spread on area to be cleaned, place a damp cloth over it, then cover with a sheet of plastic. Allow material to "work" for at least 24 hours. Scrape mixture off gently with rubber scraper, wash with clean water, then polish with heavy dry toweling.

Always start with a small test piece of marble to make sure that the cleaning process or solutions causes no damage to the surface.

Heavy, ground-in dirt accumulations use the same cleaning solutions but require a different cleaning technique (Fig. 15–3). The heavy dirt category includes fat, grease, oil, or similar grime. The idea behind this technique is to give a solution time to work and to enhance its cleansing powers. Select a detergent, preferably a cleaner with a powder or paste base, and add sufficient water to develop a workable mixture. Spread a moderate amount of the paste or mixture over the stained area on the marble, allowing reasonably good coverage. Place a damp cover cloth over the area and a cover sheet of plastic over the damp cloth. Let the material "work" for at least a full day. The covering cloth and plastic will seal in the moisture. After 24 hours, remove the covering material and allow the cleaning mixture to air dry. Gently, with a rubber scraper, scrape the mixture off the marble, then wash the marble down with clean water. Polish the marble surface with heavy dry toweling.

Certain stains are more difficult to handle and require a different cleaning product but the same layered cleaning technique. If the stain is caused by spills from coffee, tea, cola, or organically-based dyes, soak a wad of paper towels or toilet tissue in a solution of 25 to 30% ordinary household bleach mixed with plain water. Place the bleach-soaked paper against the stained marble. Set a damp cloth over the top of the paper, and finally, a plastic cover sheet. This covering, depending on the magnitude of the stain, can remain in place for 12 hours to two days. When the time comes to check the effectiveness of the cleaning procedure, remove the covering and peel off the bleach-soaked paper. If the stain has been almost, but not completely, eliminated, the process may have to be repeated for a shorter time span: 1 to 12 hours should remove the balance of the stain. When finished, wash the marble surface with clean water and polish with a piece of dry toweling.

Test the bleach cleaning mixture on a small piece of scrap marble before moving forward with the entire project. This will alert you to any deleterious affects the bleach solution may have on the installed marble.

If a piece of marble has been scratched and you want to remove the blemish, this can usually be accomplished by gentle sanding. Sandpaper is rated by its grit number. The lower the number, the harsher the grit. Always start with a small test piece of marble to be sure the sanding process will cause no damage to the installed marble. An 80- to 100-grit paper is a good starting point. Sand the scratched piece of marble with this grade of paper, changing to progressively finer paper up to, for example, 350 grit. Once the scratch disappears from the marble, change to a really fine grit sandpaper, a 500- or 600-grit, and finish the job. A marble polishing powder can be purchased at most supply stores that will provide an even finer finish to the formerly scratched marble surface.

After all of the sanding and polishing processes have been completed, wash the marble surface with water and polish with dry toweling. There are wax sprays on the market that will provide an added degree of surface protection to marble.

Tile Industry Suppliers

The following is a list of some of the major tile manufacturers, industry suppliers, trade associations, and tile and decorating magazines. If you have specific questions about a company's products, require technical or specialized information, would like to know where a company's products may be purchased or receive a copy of the manufacturer's tile brochure, many of these firms would be pleased to respond to your request.

Note: If the manufacturer's name below is in bold type, the company or its representative has graciously contributed photographs or technical information for this book. The manufacturers listed below produce ceramic tile unless a different product line is noted alongside the name of the company.

Manufacturers

A C Products, Inc. (Accessory Items)
P.O. Box 518
4299 South Apple Creek Road
Apple Creek, OH 44606

American Olean Tile Company, Inc.
P.O. Box 271
1000 Canon Avenue
Lansdale, PA 19446-0271

Bon Tool Company (Tile Installation Tools)
4430 Gibsonia Road, Rt. 910
Gibsonia, PA 15044

Chapco Adhesive Products (Adhesives)
4658 West 60th Street
Chicago, IL 60629

Color Tile, Inc.
515 Houston Street
Fort Worth, TX 76102

Colorco - Masters of Mosaics
(Designed Murals, Mosaics, Patterns)
10 Evergreen Drive
Merrimack, NH 03045

Continental Clay Company
Kittanning, PA 16201

Dal-Tile
7834 Hawn Freeway
Dallas, TX 75217

Durabond Mortars (Adhesives and Grouts)
P.O. Box 277
Dayton, OH 45401

Ellis International Inc. (Brazilian Tile)
50 East Palisades Avenue, Suite 200
Engelwood, NJ 07631

Endicott Tile, Ltd.
P.O. Box 645
Fairbury, NE 68352

Epro, Inc.
156 East Broadway
Westerville, OH 43801

Felker Manufacturing Company (Tile Installation Tools)
17311 Edwards Road
Cerritos, CA 90701

Firebird, Inc.
335 Snyder Avenue
Berkeley Heights, NJ 07922

Florida Brick and Clay Co., Inc.
P.O. Box 1656
Plant City, FL 33564-1656

Florida Tile Division, Sikes Corp.
One Sikes Boulevard
Lakeland, FL 33802

Gilmer Potteries, Inc.
P.O. Box 489
105 Warren Avenue
Gilmer, TX 75644

Glen-Gery Corp.
Hanley Plant
Summerville, PA 15864-0068

Glessner Corp. (Grout and Sealers)
1301 Sansome Street
San Francisco, CA 94111

GTE Products Corp. (Glass Products)
P.O. Box 469
135 Commerce Way
Portsmouth, NH 03801

Goldblatt Tool Company (Tile Installation Tools)
P.O. Box 2334
511 Osage
Kansas City, KS 66110

W.W. Henry Company (Adhesives)
5608 Soto Street
Huntington Park, CA 90255

The O. Hommel Co. (Frit, Colors, and Coatings)
P.O. Box 16409
Pittsburgh, PA 15242-0709

Huntington/Pacific Ceramics Inc.
P.O. Box 1149
Corona, CA 91718

Italian Ceramic Tile (Italian Tile)
Italian Tile Center
Div. of the Italian Trade Commission
499 Park Avenue
New York, NY 10022

KPT Incorporated
P.O. Box 468
State Road 54-East
Bloomfield, IN 47424

Laticrete International, Inc. (Grout)
1 Laticrete Park North
Bethany, CT 06525

Laufen International
P.O. Box 6728
Tulsa, OK 74156

Lenape Products, Inc. (Tile Accessory Items)
P.O. Box 117
Pennington, NJ 08534

Lone Star Ceramics Co.
P.O. Box 810215
Dallas, TX 75381

Los Angeles Diamond Tools, Inc. (Tile Cutting Tools)
9722 Jordan Circle
Santa Fe, NM 90670

Ludowici Stoneware Co.
1650 Progress Drive
Richmond, IN 47374

MK Diamond Products (Tile Installation Tools)
12600 Chadrone Avenue
Hawthorne, CA 90251

Mannington Ceramic Tile
P.O. Box 1777
Lexington, NC 2729

Metropolitan Ceramics
Div. of Metropolitan Industries, Inc.
P.O. Box 9240
Canton, OH 44711

MAPEI (Mortars, Adhesives, and Grouts)
1350 Lively Boulevard
Elk Grove, IL 60007

Q.E.P. Company, Inc. (Tile Cutting Equipment)
Stony Point Industrial Park
P.O. Box 678
9 Kay Fries Drive
Stony Point, NY 10980

Quarry Tile Company
Spokane Industrial Park, Bldg. 12
Spokane, WA 99216

Ro-Tile, Inc.
1615 South Stockton Street
Lodi, CA 95240

Stiles
2700 Grand Avenue, Suite 300
Des Moines, IA 50312

Summitville Tiles, Inc.
P.O. Box 73
Summitville, OH 43962

Superior Tile Cutter, Inc. (Tile Installation Tools)
1566 W. 134th Street
Gardena, CA 90249

Target Products, Inc. (Tile Cutting Products)
4320 Clary Blvd.
Kansas City, MO 64130

Terra Designs, Inc.
241 East Blackwell Street
Dover, NJ 07801

The Tileworks
P.O. Box 160
Redfield, IA 50233

Trade Commission of Spain (Spanish Tile)
Home Furnishing Division
2655 Lejeune Road, Suite 1114
Coral Gables, FL 33134

The Willette Corporation
P.O. Box 28
Joyce Kilmer Ave. & Reed St.
New Brunswick, NJ 08903

Universal Quarry Tile
P.O. Box 469
Georgia Highway
Adairsville, GA 30103

USG Industries, Inc. (Tile Setting Products and Backer Board)
Durabond Division
101 S. Wacker Drive
Chicago, IL 60606

Wenczel Tile Company
200 Enterprise Avenue
Trenton, NJ 08638

Winburn Tile Manufacturing Company
P.O. Box 1369
Little Rock, AK 72203

Wonder Board
P.O. Box 216
Hamilton, OH 45012

Tile and Decorative Magazines

There is an abundance of magazines on the market from which home improvement ideas can be gleaned. When considering or anticipating a renovation or decorating change, it is a good plan to review as many sources as possible. Home decorating and home "how-to" magazines will generally represent a cross section of modern trends in the industry. If these magazines are regularly perused, they will also serve as idea stimulators. A few of the magazines are listed below.

Better Homes and Gardens
1716 Locust Street
Des Moines, IA 50336

House Beautiful
1700 Broadway
New York, NY 10019

Practical Homeowner
33 E. Minor Street
Emmaus, PA 18049

Select Homes Magazine
1450 Dons Mills
Ontario M3B 2X7
Canada

Tile and Decorative Surfaces
20355 Ventura Blvd., Suite 200
Woodland Hills, CA 91364

Tile News
Italian Trade Commission
499 Park Avenue
New York, NY 10022

Tile World
485 Kinderkamac Road
Oradell, NJ 07649

Walls and Ceilings
8602 N. 40th Street
Tampa, FL 33604

Yankee Homes
Main Street
Dublin, NH 03444

Your Home
Box 10010
Ogden, UT 84409

Trade Associations

There are a number of trade associations working with manufacturers and supporting the tile industry. These groups include:

Ceramic Institute of America
700 North Virgil
Los Angeles, CA 90027

Ceramic Tile Marketing Federation
1615 L Street, N.W., #925
Washington, DC 20036

Ceramic Tile Distributors Association
15 Salt Creek Lane, Suite 422
Hinsdale, IL 60521

Tile Council of America, Inc.
P.O. Box 326
Princeton, NJ 08542-0326

Index

AUDEL

These fully illustrated, up-to-date guides and manuals mean a better job done for mechanics, engineers, electricians, plumbers, carpenters, and all skilled workers.

CONTENTS

ELECTRICAL

House Wiring (Seventh Edition)

ROLAND E. PALMQUIST;
revised by PAUL ROSENBERG

5 1/2 × 8 1/4 Hardcover 248 pp. 150 Illus.
ISBN: 0-02-594692-7 $22.95

Rules and regulations of the current 1990 National Electrical Code for residential wiring fully explained and illustrated.

Practical Electricity
(Fifth Edition)

ROBERT G. MIDDLETON;
revised by L. DONALD MEYERS

5 1/2 × 8 1/4 Hardcover 512 pp. 335 Illus.
ISBN: 0-02-584561-6 $19.95

The fundamentals of electricity for electrical workers, apprentices, and others requiring concise information about electric principles and their practical applications.

Guide to the 1993 National Electrical Code

ROLAND E. PALMQUIST;
revised by PAUL ROSENBERG

5 1/2 × 8 1/4 Paperback 608 pp.
100 line drawings
ISBN: 0-02-077761-2 $25.00

The guide to the most recent revision of the electrical codes—how to read them, under-

stand them, and use them. Here is the most authoritative reference available, making clear the changes in the code and explaining these changes in a way that is easy to understand.

Installation Requirements of the 1993 National Electrical Code

PAUL ROSENBERG

5 1/2 × 8 1/4 Paperback 261 pp.
100 line drawings
ISBN: 0-02-077760-4 $22.00

A handy guide for electricians, contractors, and architects who need a reference on location. Arranging all the pertinent requirements (and only the pertinent requirements) of the 1993 NEC, it has an easy-to-follow format. Concise and updated, it's a perfect working companion for Apprentices, Journeymen, or for Master electricians.

Mathematics for Electricians and Electronics Technicians

REX MILLER

5 1/2 × 8 1/4 Hardcover 312 pp. 115 Illus.
ISBN: 0-8161-1700-4 $14.95

Mathematical concepts, formulas, and problem-solving techniques utilized on-the-job by electricians and those in electronics and related fields.

Fractional-Horsepower Electric Motors

REX MILLER and
MARK RICHARD MILLER

5 1/2 × 8 1/4 Har~~~
ISBN: 0-672-~~~
The i~~~ ~~~tenance, re-
pa~~~ ~~~e small-to-moder-
ate~~~ ~~~otors that power home
appl~~~ ~~~d industrial equipment.

Electric Motors (Fifth Edition)

EDWIN P. ANDERSON
and REX MILLER

5 1/2 × 8 1/4 Hardcover 696 pp.
Photos/line art
ISBN: 0-02-501920-1 $35.00

Complete reference guide for electricians, industrial maintenance personnel, and installers. Contains both theoretical and practical
descriptions.

Home Appliance Servicing
(Fourth Edition)

EDWIN P. ANDERSON;
revised by REX MILLER

5 1/2 × 8 1/4 Hardcover 640 pp. 345 Illus.
ISBN: 0-672-23379-7 $22.50

The essentials of testing, maintaining, and
repairing all types of home appliances.

Television Service Manual
(Fifth Edition)

ROBERT G. MIDDLETON;
revised by JOSEPH G. BARRILE

5 1/2 × 8 1/4 Hardcover 512 pp. 395 Illus.
ISBN: 0-672-23395-9 $16.95

A guide to all aspects of television transmis-
sion and reception, including the operating
principles of black and white and color re-
ceivers. Step-by-step maintenance and repair procedures.

Electrical Course for Apprentices and Journeymen
(Third Edition)

ROLAND E. PALMQUIST

5 1/2 × 8 1/4 Hardcover 478 pp. 290 Illus.
ISBN: 0-02-594550-5 $19.95

This practical course in electricity for those
in formal training programs or learning on
their own provides a thorough understanding
of operational theory and its applications on
the job.

Questions and Answers for Electricians Examinations
(1993 NEC Rulings Included)

revised by PAUL ROSENBERG

5 1/2 × 8 1/4 Paperback 270 pp.
100 line drawings
ISBN: 0-02-077762-0 $20.00

An Audel classic, considered the most thorough work on the subject in coverage and
content. This fully revised edition is based on
the 1993 National Electrical Code®, and is
written for anyone preparing for the various electricians' examinations—Apprentice,
Journeyman, or Master. It provides the li-
cense applicant with an understanding of
theory as well as of all definitions, specifications, and regulations included in the new
NEC.

MACHINE SHOP AND MECHANICAL TRADES

Machinists Library
(Fourth Edition, 3 Vols.)

REX MILLER

5 1/2 × 8 1/4 Hardcover 1,352 pp. 1120 Illus.
ISBN: 0-672-23380-0 $52.95

An indispensable three-volume reference set
for machinists, tool and die makers, machine
operators, metal workers, and those with
home workshops. The principles and methods of the entire field are covered in an up-
to-date text, photographs, diagrams, and tables.

Volume I: Basic Machine Shop
REX MILLER

5 1/2 × 8 1/4 Hardcover 392 pp. 375 Illus.
ISBN: 0-672-23381-9 $17.95

Volume II: Machine Shop
REX MILLER

5 1/2 × 8 1/4 Hardcover 528 pp. 445 Illus.
ISBN: 0-672-23382-7 $19.95

Volume III: Toolmakers Handy Book
REX MILLER

5 1/2 × 8 1/4 Hardcover 432 pp. 300 Illus.
ISBN: 0-672-23383-5 $14.95

Mathematics for Mechanical Technicians and Technologists

JOHN D. BIES

5 1/2 × 8 1/4 Hardcover 342 pp. 190 Illus.
ISBN: 0-02-510620-1 $17.95

The mathematical concepts, formulas, and problem-solving techniques utilized on the job by engineers, technicians, and other workers in industrial and mechanical technology and related fields.

Millwrights and Mechanics Guide (Fourth Edition)

CARL A. NELSON

5 1/2 × 8 1/4 Hardcover 1,040 pp. 880 Illus.
ISBN: 0-02-588591-x $29.95

The most comprehensive and authoritative guide available for millwrights, mechanics, maintenance workers, riggers, shop workers, foremen, inspectors, and superintendents on plant installation, operation, and maintenance.

Welders Guide (Third Edition)

JAMES E. BRUMBAUGH

5 1/2 × 8 1/4 Hardcover 960 pp. 615 Illus.
ISBN: 0-672-23374-6 $23.95

The theory, operation, and maintenance of all welding machines. Covers gas welding equipment, supplies, and process; arc welding equipment, supplies, and process; TIG and MIG welding; and much more.

Welders/Fitters Guide

HARRY L. STEWART

8 1/2 × 11 Paperback 160 pp. 195 Illus.
ISBN: 0-672-23325-8 $7.95

Step-by-step instruction for those training to become welders/fitters who have some knowledge of welding and the ability to read blueprints.

Sheet Metal Work

JOHN D. BIES

5 1/2 × 8 1/4 Hardcover 456 pp. 215 Illus.
ISBN: 0-8161-1706-3 $19.95

An on-the-job guide for workers in the manufacturing and construction industries and for those with home workshops. All facets of sheet metal work detailed and illustrated by drawings, photographs, and tables.

Power Plant Engineers Guide
(Third Edition)

FRANK D. GRAHAM;
revised by CHARLIE BUFFINGTON

5 1/2 × 8 1/4 Hardcover 960 pp. 530 Illus.
ISBN: 0-672-23329-0 $27.50

This all-inclusive, one-volume guide is perfect for engineers, firemen, water tenders, oilers, operators of steam and diesel-power engines, and those applying for engineer's and firemen's licenses.

Mechanical Trades Pocket Manual (Third Edition)

CARL A. NELSON

4 × 6 Paperback 364 pp. 255 Illus.
ISBN: 0-02-588665-7 $14.95

A handbook for workers in the industrial and mechanical trades on methods, tools, equipment, and procedures. Pocket-sized for easy reference and fully illustrated.

PLUMBING

Plumbers and Pipe Fitters Library (Fourth Edition, 3 Vols.)

CHARLES N. McCONNELL

5 1/2 × 8 1/4 Hardcover 952 pp. 560 Illus.
ISBN: 0-02-582914-9 $68.45

This comprehensive three-volume set contains the most up-to-date information available for master plumbers, journeymen, apprentices, engineers, and those in the building trades. A detailed text and clear diagrams, photographs, and charts and tables treat all aspects of the plumbing, heating, and air conditioning trades.

Volume I: Materials, Tools, Roughing-In

CHARLES N. McCONNELL;
revised by TOM PHILBIN

5 1/2 × 8 1/4 Hardcover 304 pp. 240 Illus.
ISBN: 0-02-582911-4 $20.95

Volume II: Welding, Heating, Air Conditioning

CHARLES N. McCONNELL;
revised by TOM PHILBIN

5 1/2 × 8 1/4 Hardcover 384 pp. 220 Illus.
ISBN: 0-02-582912-2 $22.95

Volume III: Water Supply, Drainage, Calculations

CHARLES N. McCONNELL;
revised by TOM PHILBIN

5 1/2 × 8 1/4 Hardcover 264 pp. 100 Illus.
ISBN: 0-02-582913-0 $20.95

The Home Plumbing Handbook
(Fourth Edition)
CHARLES N. McCONNELL

*8 1/2 × 11   Paperback   224 pp.   210 Illus.
ISBN: 0-02-079651-X $17.00*

This handy, thorough volume, a longtime standard in the field with the professional, has been updated to appeal to the do-it-yourself plumber. Aided by the book's many illustrations and manufacturers' instructions, the home plumber is guided through most basic plumbing procedures. All techniques and products conform to the latest changes in codes and regulations.

The Plumbers Handbook
(Eighth Edition)
JOSEPH P. ALMOND, SR.;
revised by REX MILLER

*4 × 6   Paperback   368 pp.   170 Illus.
ISBN: 0-02-501570-2 $19.95*

Comprehensive and handy guide for plumbers and pipefitters—fits in the toolbox or pocket. For apprentices, journeymen, or experts.

Questions and Answers for Plumbers' Examinations
(Third Edition)
JULES ORAVETZ;
revised by REX MILLER

*5 1/2 × 8 1/4   Paperback   288 pp.   145 Illus.
ISBN: 0-02-593510-0 $14.95*

Complete guide to preparation for the plumbers' exams given by local licensing authorities. Includes requirements of the National Bureau of Standards.

HVAC

Air Conditioning: Home and Commercial (Fourth Edition)
EDWIN P. ANDERSON;
revised by REX MILLER

*5 1/2 × 8 1/4   Hardcover   528 pp.   180 Illus.
ISBN: 0-02-584885-2 $29.95*

A guide to the construction, installation, operation, maintenance, and repair of home, commercial, and industrial air conditioning systems.

Heating, Ventilating, and Air Conditioning Library
(Second Edition, 3 Vols.)
JAMES E. BRUMBAUGH

*5 1/2 × 8 1/4 Hardcover 1,840 pp. 1,275 Illus.
ISBN: 0-672-23388-6 $53.85*

An authoritative three-volume reference library for those who install, operate, maintain, and repair HVAC equipment commercially, industrially, or at home.

Volume I: Heating Fundamentals, Furnaces, Boilers, Boiler Conversions
JAMES E. BRUMBAUGH

*5 1/2 × 8 1/4   Hardcover   656 pp.   405 Illus.
ISBN: 0-672-23389-4 $17.95*

Volume II: Oil, Gas and Coal Burners, Controls, Ducts, Piping, Valves
JAMES E. BRUMBAUGH

*5 1/2 × 8 1/4   Hardcover   592 pp.   455 Illus.
ISBN: 0-672-23390-8 $17.95*

Volume III: Radiant Heating, Water Heaters, Ventilation, Air Conditioning, Heat Pumps, Air Cleaners
JAMES E. BRUMBAUGH

*5 1/2 × 8 1/4   Hardcover   592 pp.   415 Illus.
ISBN: 0-672-23391-6 $17.95*

Oil Burners (Fifth Edition)
EDWIN M. FIELD

*5 1/2 × 8 1/4   Hardcover   360 pp.   170 Illus.
ISBN: 0-02-537745-0 $29.95*

An up-to-date sourcebook on the construction, installation, operation, testing, servicing, and repair of all types of oil burners, both industrial and domestic.

Refrigeration: Home and Commercial (Fourth Edition)
EDWIN P. ANDERSON;
revised by REX MILLER

*5 1/2 × 8 1/4   Hardcover   768 pp.   285 Illus.
ISBN: 0-02-584875-5 $34.95*

A reference for technicians, plant engineers, and the homeowner on the installation, operation, servicing, and repair of everything from single refrigeration units to commercial and industrial systems.

PNEUMATICS AND HYDRAULICS

Hydraulics for Off-the-Road Equipment (Second Edition)

HARRY L. STEWART;
revised by TOM PHILBIN

5 1/2 × 8 1/4 Hardcover 256 pp. 175 Illus.
ISBN: 0-8161-1701-2 $13.95

This complete reference manual on heavy equipment covers hydraulic pumps, accumulators, and motors; force components; hydraulic control components; filters and filtration, lines and fittings, and fluids; hydrostatic transmissions; maintenance; and troubleshooting.

Pneumatics and Hydraulics
(Fourth Edition)

HARRY L. STEWART;
revised by TOM STEWART

5 1/2 × 8 1/4 Hardcover 512 pp. 315 Illus.
ISBN: 0-672-23412-2 $19.95

The principles and applications of fluid power. Covers pressure, work, and power; general features of machines; hydraulic and pneumatic symbols; pressure boosters; air compressors and accessories; and much more.

Pumps (Fifth Edition)

HARRY L. STEWART;
revised by REX MILLER

5 1/2 × 8 1/4 Hardcover 552 pp. 360 Illus.
ISBN: 0-02-614725-4 $35.00

The practical guide to operating principles of pumps, controls, and hydraulics. Covers installation and day-to-day service.

CARPENTRY AND CON-STRUCTION

Carpenters and Builders Library
(Sixth Edition, 4 Vols.)

JOHN E. BALL;
revised by JOHN LEEKE

5 1/2 × 8 1/4 Hardcover 1,300 pp. 988 Illus.
ISBN: 0-02-506455-4 $89.95

This comprehensive four-volume library has set the professional standard for decades for carpenters, joiners, and woodworkers.

Volume 1: Tools, Steel Square, Joinery

JOHN E. BALL;
revised by JOHN LEEKE

5 1/2 × 8 1/4 Hardcover 377 pp. 340 Illus.
ISBN: 0-02-506451-7 $21.95

Volume 2: Builders Math, Plans, Specifications

JOHN E. BALL;
revised by JOHN LEEKE

5 1/2 × 8 1/4 Hardcover 319 pp. 200 Illus.
ISBN: 0-02-506452-5 $21.95

Volume 3: Layouts, Foundation, Framing

JOHN E. BALL;
revised by JOHN LEEKE

5 1/2 × 8 1/4 Hardcover 269 pp. 204 Illus.
ISBN: 0-02-506453-3 $21.95

Volume 4: Millwork, Power Tools, Painting

JOHN E. BALL;
revised by JOHN LEEKE

5 1/2 × 8 1/4 Hardcover 335 pp. 244 Illus.
ISBN: 0-02-506454-1 $21.95

Complete Building Construction
(Second Edition)

JOHN PHELPS;
revised by TOM PHILBIN

5 1/2 × 8 1/4 Hardcover 744 pp. 645 Illus.
ISBN: 0-672-23377-0 $22.50

Constructing a frame or brick building from the footings to the ridge. Whether the building project is a tool shed, garage, or a complete home, this single fully illustrated volume provides all the necessary information.

Complete Roofing Handbook
(Second Edition)

JAMES E. BRUMBAUGH
revised by JOHN LEEKE

5 1/2 × 8 1/4 Hardcover 536 pp. 510 Illus.
ISBN: 0-02-517851-2 $30.00

Covers types of roofs; roofing and reroofing; roof and attic insulation and ventilation; skylights and roof openings; dormer construction; roof flashing details; and much more. Contains new information on code requirements, underlaying, and attic ventilation.

Complete Siding Handbook
(Second Edition)

JAMES E. BRUMBAUGH
revised by JOHN LEEKE

5 1/2 × 8 1/4 Hardcover 440 pp. 320 Illus.
ISBN: 0-02-517881-4 $30.00

This companion volume to the *Complete Roofing Handbook* has been updated to reflect current emphasis on compliance with building codes. Contains new sections on spunbound olefin, building papers, and insulation materials other than fiberglass.

Masons and Builders Library
(Second Edition, 2 Vols.)

LOUIS M. DEZETTEL;
revised by TOM PHILBIN

*5 1/2 × 8 1/4 Hardcover 688 pp. 500 Illus.
ISBN: 0-672-23401-7 $27.95*

This two-volume set provides practical instruction in bricklaying and masonry. Covers brick; mortar; tools; bonding; corners, openings, and arches; chimneys and fireplaces; structural clay tile and glass block; brick walls; and much more.

Volume 1: Concrete, Block, Tile, Terrazzo

LOUIS M. DEZETTEL;
revised by TOM PHILBIN

*5 1/2 × 8 1/4 Hardcover 304 pp. 190 Illus.
ISBN: 0-672-23402-5 $14.95*

Volume 2: Bricklaying, Plastering, Rock Masonry, Clay Tile

LOUIS M. DEZETTEL;
revised by TOM PHILBIN

*5 1/2 × 8 1/4 Hardcover 384 pp. 310 Illus.
ISBN: 0-672-23403-3 $14.95*

WOODWORKING

Wood Furniture: Finishing, Refinishing, Repairing
(Third Edition)

JAMES E. BRUMBAUGH
revised by JOHN LEEKE

*5 1/2 × 8 1/4 Hardcover 384 pp. 190 Illus.
ISBN: 0-02-517871-7 $25.00*

A fully illustrated guide to repairing furniture and finishing and refinishing wood surfaces. Covers tools and supplies; types of wood; veneering; inlaying; repairing, restoring and stripping; wood preparation; and much more. Contains a new color insert on stains.

Woodworking and Cabinetmaking

F. RICHARD BOLLER

*5 1/2 × 8 1/4 Hardcover 360 pp. 455 Illus.
ISBN: 0-02-512800-0 $18.95*

Essential information on all aspects of working with wood. Step-by-step procedures for woodworking projects are accompanied by detailed drawings and photographs.

MAINTENANCE AND REPAIR

Building Maintenance
(Second Edition)

JULES ORAVETZ

*5 1/2 × 8 1/4 Paperback 384 pp. 210 Illus.
ISBN: 0-672-23278-2 $11.95*

Professional maintenance procedures used in office, educational, and commercial buildings. Covers painting and decorating; plumbing and pipe fitting; concrete and masonry; and much more.

Gardening, Landscaping and Grounds Maintenance
(Third Edition)

JULES ORAVETZ

*5 1/2 × 8 1/4 Hardcover 424 pp. 340 Illus.
ISBN: 0-672-23417-3 $15.95*

Maintaining lawns and gardens as well as industrial, municipal, and estate grounds.

Home Maintenance and Repair: Walls, Ceilings and Floors

GARY D. BRANSON

*8 1/2 × 11 Paperback 80 pp. 80 Illus.
ISBN: 0-672-23281-2 $6.95*

The do-it-yourselfer's guide to interior remodeling with professional results.

Painting and Decorating

REX MILLER and GLEN E. BAKER

*5 1/2 × 8 1/4 Hardcover 464 pp. 325 Illus.
ISBN: 0-672-23405-x $18.95*

A practical guide for painters, decorators, and homeowners to the most up-to-date materials and techniques in the field.

Tree Care (Second Edition)

JOHN M. HALLER

*8 1/2 × 11 Paperback 224 pp. 305 Illus.
ISBN: 0-02-062870-6 $16.95*

The standard in the field. A comprehensive guide for growers, nursery owners, foresters, landscapers, and homeowners to planting, nurturing, and protecting trees.

Upholstering
(Third Edition)
JAMES E. BRUMBAUGH

5 1/2 × 8 1/4 Hardcover 416 pp. 318 Illus.
ISBN: 0-02-517862-8 $25.00

The esentials of upholstering are fully explained and illustrated for the professional, the apprentice, and the hobbyist. Features a new color insert illustrating fabrics, a new chapter on embroidery, and an expanded cleaning section.

AUTOMOTIVE AND ENGINES

Diesel Engine Manual
(Fourth Edition)
PERRY O. BLACK;
revised by WILLIAM E. SCAHILL

5 1/2 × 8 1/4 Hardcover 512 pp. 255 Illus.
ISBN: 0-672-23371-1 $15.95

The principles, design, operation, and maintenance of today's diesel engines. All aspects of typical two- and four-cycle engines are thoroughly explained and illustrated by photographs, line drawings, and charts and tables.

Gas Engine Manual
(Third Edition)
EDWIN P. ANDERSON;
revised by CHARLES G. FACKLAM

5 1/2 × 8 1/4 Hardcover 424 pp. 225 Illus.
ISBN: 0-8161-1707-1 $12.95

How to operate, maintain, and repair gas engines of all types and sizes. All engine parts and step-by-step procedures are illustrated by photographs, diagrams, and trouble-shooting charts.

Small Gasoline Engines
REX MILLER and
MARK RICHARD MILLER

5 1/2 × 8 1/4 Hardcover 640
ISBN: 0-672-23414-9 $1

Practical inform
maintain
eng   -cycle
                    ers, edgers,
              owers, emergency
e   rs, outboard motors, and
ot   ment with engines of up to ten
hor power.

NEW EDITION FOR 1993

Truck Guide Library (3 Vols.)
JAMES E. BRUMBAUGH

5 1/2 × 8 1/4 Hardcover 2,144 pp. 1,715 Illus.
ISBN: 0-672-23392-4 $50.95

This three-volume set provides the most comprehensive, profusely illustrated collection of information available on truck operation and maintenance.

Volume 1: Engines
JAMES E. BRUMBAUGH

5 1/2 × 8 1/4 Hardcover 416 pp. 290 Illus.
ISBN: 0-672-23356-8 $16.95

Volume 2: Engine Auxiliary Systems
JAMES E. BRUMBAUGH

5 1/2 × 8 1/4 Hardcover 704 pp. 520 Illus.
ISBN: 0-672-23357-6 $16.95

Volume 3: Transmissions, Steering, and Brakes
JAMES E. BRUMBAUGH

5 1/2 × 8 1/4 Hardcover 1,024 pp. 905 Illus.
ISBN: 0-672-23406-8 $16.95

DRAFTING

Industrial Drafting
JOHN D. BIES

5 1/2 × 8 1/4 Hardcover 544 pp. Illus.
ISBN: 0-02-510610-4 $24.95

Professional-level introductory guide for practicing drafters, engineers, managers, and technical workers in all industries who use or prepare working drawings.

Answers on Blueprint Reading
(Fourth Edition)
ROLAND PALMQUIST;
revised by THOMAS J. MORRISEY

5 1/2 × 8 1/4 Hardcover 320 pp. 275 Illus.
ISBN: 0-8161-1704-7 $12.95

Understanding blueprints of machines and tools, electrical systems, and architecture. Question and answer format.

HOBBIES

Complete Course in Stained Glass
PEPE MENDEZ

8 1/2 × 11 Paperback 80 pp. 50 Illus.
ISBN: 0-672-23287-1 $8.95

The tools, materials, and techniques of the art of working with stained glass.

Prices are subject to change without notice.